THE POST-TRUTH ERA

LITERATURE AND MEDIA

THE POST-TRUTH ERA

LITERATURE AND MEDIA

Edited by

PRAVEEN ABRAHAM & RAISUN MATHEW

AUTHORSPRESS

Worldwide Circulation through Authorspress Global Network
First Published in 2021
by
Authorspress
Q-2A Hauz Khas Enclave, New Delhi-110 016 (India)
Phone: (0) 9818049852
E-mail: authorspressgroup@gmail.com
Website: www.authorspressbooks.com

The Post-Truth Era: Literature and Media
ISBN 978-93-91314-09-5

Printed at Manipal Technologies Limited, Manipal

Foreword

Amidst the onslaught of murky post-truths, alternative facts, and fake news, there has been a growing concern over the dismantling of truth in today's political discourse. Despite the fact of post-truth and disinformation existing across the world, the absence of a singular public discourse stands common to all such narratives. In the tug-of-war between falsification and falsehood; ignorance and manipulation, the very existence of truth stands on shaky grounds. The normativeness of disinformation spills over to antagonism, geo-political conflicts and power struggles that tear into the fabric of ethics and peaceful co-existence of human communities. The resultant distortion and attack of truth is in a way an outcome of the 24 hour 'breaking-news' culture and the ubiquitous excesses of social media and other elements of the virtual landscape. One argument draws attention to the 'truth' while another argument forcefully presents the 'other side' of the same truth with a contextual framework.

The volume titled *The Post-Truth Era: Literature and Media* edited by Praveen Abraham and Raisun Mathew walk through the landscape of post-truths from across the world. In the process, they bring together diverse domains such as conspiracy ideologies, gender politics, cultural obliteration, surveillance media, performativity, artistic production, gaming discourse to name a few. The work explores disinformation in the realms of literature and media from a multidisciplinary perspective that adds currency and relevance to the engagement. The diversity of domains and perspectives negotiate various aspects of subversion of truths and the plethora of 'interpretations'. The edited volume through a delineation of well-knit chapters reflects with clarity, the premise that satisfies personal emotions and beliefs which eventually undermine facts and truths. The editors' scholastic compilation of relevant works by various writers is a significant addition to the sphere of literature on post-truth.

Dr Beena G
Professor, Research Guide & Controller of Examinations
REVA University, Bengaluru, India

Acknowledgements

The academic interest behind this editorial project was to gather interesting intellectual perspectives on post-truth from the disciplines of literature and media studies. The journey to fixing the theme of the book arose from the conversations between us about the gradually shifting milieu around the globe that gave critical hints on the obnoxious state of factual truth midst of the perpetual continuance of the alternative, fake and pseudo truths. In the light of the uncertainties prevailing in various contemporary socio-political and economic states of affairs, we felt that focusing on the diverse quintessence of the theme would help to deliver essential and lively perspectives to the existing academia on post-truth. As an intellectual endeavour, every step to destiny was exciting, informative and contenting. We are extremely grateful to all thirty authors who have lent their scholastic perspectives to this text with an unscathed belief and confidence in us. The urge to disseminate diverse research-oriented viewpoints to the existing intellectual knowledge in the field has received immense support from the authors of the twenty-seven chapters. The journey to publishing the gathered intellectual perspectives would have not been a reality without the wholehearted and emphatic decision of the Authorspress Team to provide uninterrupted assistance to us. Furthermore, the unanimous support from our parent institutions, department authorities, research supervisors, and family members have helped to formulate the ideas vehemently. From its very inception, the strength and grace showered by the Almighty have been the backbone of hope even in the course of the precarious tones of the pandemic. Though sincere thanks and regards for the rest can be expressed here, we believe that our expression of gratitude to the Almighty can never be limited to mere words.

Praveen Abraham
Raisun Mathew

Contents

Introduction

Living in the complexly intertwined post-truth world, one would easily get misguided by the emphasis on the theory and praxis of subjectivity than objective veracity. The realities that have been projected so far even by the people of authenticity might end up in falsity. The bombardment of information from the different corners of existence often snowballs the unending perpetual quest to identify what is true and false. The constantly evolving characteristics of the world, especially in the contemporary scenario of the advanced technological developments, have magnified the significance of literature and media in influencing at various levels that are pivotal in evolving the attitude and outlook of society. While media reports the reality in a society through its various platforms such as print and online, literature reflects the diverse expressions of it blended with the fictional elements highlighted through the creative spheres of writing. Though they exist as two distinct disciplines, are bound together to produce independent and combined effects in humankind. The efforts to influence and get influenced by the public produce expressions of mutuality between literature and media. Same as no writer can break free from becoming influenced by the time which he/she lives, the age too cannot escape from the thoughtful interferences of writers that can create noteworthy changes in the world.

The permanence and universality of a literary piece of work, when considered from the perspective of a reader, appeals to the world in representing the intersectional characteristics irrespective of the spatial and temporal segregations. The gradual evolution of society has strong bonds with the inconsistency in the lifestyle, beliefs, cultures, language, ideologies etc. The stubbornness to reside in the same norms and values would curb the development and progress of societies. It is always recommended to move ahead with the newfangled notions suggested from different domains of life. Media serves a consequential role in commencing, accentuating and endorsing the changes that equally have positive and negative impacts in the society. When the involvement of media in featuring the life of people is conspicuous, both the silent and salient traits of society become prominently visible. Thus, the balance, impartiality and objective approach expected to be provided by the media is attained through access, diversity and plurality.

Discussions on the concept of post-truth have equally gained prominence in the disciplines of literature and media. Being, directly and indirectly, capable of dominating the normative structures of a society, the term has turned out to be increasingly prevalent for the past few years. Though misinformation, fake news and alternative news are components that initiate situations of post-truth scenarios in a society, the denial of factual, objective and scientific truth for embracing information, knowledge and opinions that fascinates the feelings, emotions and personal perspectives of a person or a society leads to such conditions. An imprudent attitude to misleading and confusing knowledge that circulate through various platforms, shared through different communication sources and projected as propaganda advocacy are threatening alarms to the ethical and moral consciousness of a society. The ideological supremacy intended to establish through alternative truths by the practitioners, propagators and carriers of fake news try to compel people to believe it even without any proper substantiating shreds of evidence. All these definitions of post-truth give us the idea that – personal feelings and emotions sometimes matter more than objective facts, evidences and truths. These feelings, emotions and beliefs of people are taken advantage of by the propagators of such alternative facts and drafts. When such a situation arises where people are more attached to what influences their feelings and beliefs more than the scientific and expert views; there begins the instability of society. This instability of the society becomes problematic when information controls the people rather than people control the information. Back in 1992, when the term was coined by the Serbian-American playwright Steve Tesich in an essay published in *The Nation* magazine, the usage had intended to denote a transparent meaning differing from what it means in the contemporary political and social scenario. It meant 'after the truth was known' from the direct notions of the term similar to the usages in post-war and post-colonial. This is particularly about a state in which the factual truth becomes of no value or importance to the people when they have much more relatable alternative truth before them.

A similar idea was also introduced by Ralph Keyes in 2004 when he wrote his book that had the title 'Post-Truth Era'. He connected it with the existing media-oriented world where some lies are not treated as lies, but something that is viewed as acceptable in certain conditions. He said that this particular situation where lies take the position of alternative truth leads to the beginning of a post-truth era and thus redefined the term post-truth. Though the present situations have the advantage of the modern communication technologies and information-gathering techniques compared to the previous decades, they are highly used to spread disinformation, fake news and propaganda rather than its advantageous facility to identify and sort between the authentic and the fake. The word that gained importance in its usage in the year 2016 was selected as the word of the year by the *Oxford English Dictionaries* mainly because of its high demand in the political contexts during the 58th quadrennial presidential election in the United States of America and the United Kingdom European Union membership referendum. The popularity of the term as post-truth politics tremendously continues since 2016 connected with the past and ongoing pseudo-democratic policies of authorities affiliated to governments around the world that occasionally showcase their fascist attributes.

Even before the coinage of the very word, literature around the world has addressed the consequences and disruptions that can be unfortunate outcomes of information that manifest no acquaintance with the expression of factual truth. Literature that is more inclined to develop through various perspectives tends to possess its attachment with alternative truths when it redirects its power to frame meanings from the author to the diverse readers having distinct identities and ideologies. It produces many interpretations forming identical situations of alternative truths for the same primary source. Thus, twice or more removed realities from the society appear to have more than one truth acknowledging that truth remains distant and unattainable. The realms of thought and reflection produced by literature have made invisible marks to get explored through critics and readers in the works of George Orwell's 1984 and *Animal Farm*, Sinclair Lewis' *It Can't Happen Here* (1953), Philip K. Dick's *The Man in the High Castle* (1962), Eva Rossmann's *Patriots* (2017) and so on.

With the increase in the feasibility to access different communication methods in the twenty-first century, the role of media in promoting and impeding the circuitous track of post-truth has also expanded. The print, electronic, digital and online platforms have their part in creating and spreading alternative information in the name of factual truths with high impact. Having access to social media and digital platforms, the reach and entrapments of post-truth among people in the contemporary world have become a swift process. The post-truth era thus is a wholesome contribution of the political, social, traditional, cultural, economic and much more related spheres of life.

The Post-Truth Era: Literature and Media has dedicated chapters based on the disciplines of literature and media studies that contribute to explore and discuss the applicability and presence of the concept of post-truth. Beyond the interconnection between the two disciplines with that of the major theme, this book highlights different thematic perspectives based on literature and media studies from thirty academic savants. The systemic distrust of legitimate political institutions caused by conspiracy myths is delineated by Denis Newiak. He researches on how conspiracy fanatics are staged in pandemic scenarios and addresses the issue suggesting learning from the fictional worlds of series and films that can deal with the danger posed by paranoids, crisis profiteers and their followers. Dr. Minu Susan Koshy explores post-truth as a mechanism through which those in power retain their ideological influence and how the media enables the propagation of fake news, misinformation and believability, thereby sustaining the post-truth economy and polity. Patrick Agbedejobi offers a theoretically driven discussion based on the intersection of affective meaning of post-truth with nudge theory. He aims at espousing post-truth as a strategy to focus on digital media communication and technologies of communication for highlighting the political propaganda. One can therefore understand the elements of persuasive political speeches that appeal to emotions rather than the epistemic truth. Cerin Babu examines John Boyne's *The Boy in the Striped Pyjamas* to understand the role of the speaking subject and how his/ her language attains force, effectiveness and meaning in a post-truth discourse. The chapter tries to probe into the significatory power of language and the mechanism of how meaning is made when texts and images are united to create a post-truth reality in the pretext of Derrida's concept of differance.

The fluidity of subject formulation in the cyber-textual discourses has eliminated any possibilities about their denotative structural values. Video games functioning through such hyperreal schemata have been endowed with the power to create homogenise assumptions, without being the locus of criticism. Manodip Chakraborty presents the burning issue of the contemporary gaming phenomenon, while analysing it as a cultural tool to create a global panoptical system. Indu Peter attempts to traverse across the conundrum of cyberspace, which though not immune to the oppressive totalisation, strives to give visibility to subaltern voices, suspicions and suspense which are often thwarted by the hegemonic noises in this post-truth era. Three different domains, namely - nation, gender and health are explored to expound how in times of universal deception, social media proffers us the scope for a counter-narrative that combats the socio-political hegemony and the obfuscation of facts. Roshima Uday & Dr. Abubakkar K.K discusses the plight of Indian citizens amidst Covid-19 and the role of the Media in deceiving the people through fabricated data. The chapter provides an analysis of the situation by locating India within a post-truth society. Pranjal Bhatt studies how the post-truth era has affected India at conjoining political, social and cultural terms especially by leaving behind our traditional menstrual practices and resulting in the ripple effect which traces the harm to the physical and psychological health of women across the country.

Though the notion of post-truth could be traced long back to human history, it cannot be denied that it flourished colossally in the digital age. Shemin K posits that post-truth could be perceived as an offshoot of the digimodernist culture that came into existence as a result of the digital revolution. Considering the present Pataphysical ambience of Posthumanist manoeuvre, there seems to evolve a Cyberia resulting in the sheer metamorphosis of reality and the reality-induced truth which is now manipulated and therefore termed Post Truth. Nipan Nath's survey of Borges' select visionary works confirms the anticipation of this Cyberia representing the spatio-temporal hypo-epistemological locale of contemporary post-truth vicissitudes. The popular and academic treatments of the concept of post-truth that has emerged as a hot topic of constant deliberation and public debate sometimes differ in respect to its meaning but are broadly understood under the sub-titles of fake news, rumours, hoaxes and political lying. Dr. Mallika A. Nair analyses how the polarisation of factual events are contrived through Media Constructivism to formulate a propagandist and predefined end. This can also be one of the most emphatic ramifications of the post-truth ideology.

Cults have existed for time immemorial but their relevance in the twenty-first century has demanded a need for us to inspect closely to understand how people are enticed into these dangerous groups. Josephine Mercy opines that the ideologies of cult leaders like Charles Manson and Ayn Rand help us in unravelling the techniques employed by such disingenuous minds to gain a massive following. Harry C. Joseph examines John Green's *The Fault in Our Stars* with particular reference to the possibility of a fifth dimension rather than an imaginative one. Hazel refers to it as a "third space" where she finds close to Gus and hence a 'space' wherein their love could survive the limitations of time. This 'third space' thus is more or less a distant utopia free from the constraints of the fourth dimension of 'time' as it transcends the latter.

Bhagatian fiction addresses the "post" condition of India and tries to illumine the post-truth embedded in everyday practices. Dr. Kavitha Gopalakrishnan attempts to delineate that a dialogic engagement with co-texts has the potential to draw attention to the political implication and the agentive potential of the "author". Also, it intends to analyse the "I" of Bhagat under the Derridean logic of parergon as post-truth politics and rhetoric are at the heart of its exigence. Bornali Nath Dowerah produces the view that Verhaeghe's arguments unravel the dimension of post-truth. Her chapter seeks to probe the contestations of Paul Verhaeghe, in his book titled *What About Me?*. He indoctrinates identity dynamics and the fallacy that drives the human race to choose between truth and lies. Irene Ann George and Abhishek Manikandan examine the targeted advertising relayed in the 2021 Kerala Assembly elections from the post-truth point of view. Close analysis of the same reveals an increased emphasis on emotions, veering away from fact-based advertising.

Real news and fake news are circulating at a similar frequency and often people cannot distinguish what is 'real' and what is 'fake' sometimes the fake outrages real. The digital age and culture frequently change the views and attitudes of people across the world. Sinoj Antony and Dr. Ishfaq Ahmad Tramboo discuss the notion of hyperreality and its influence upon postmodern concepts and science fiction. Namitha Nandan has her perspectives combining insightful thoughts on the post-truth politics of gender and technology. The chapter unmasks the covert sexism of Artificial Intelligent assistants that had for ages been mistaken for humourous naiveté or a motherly attitude. It is an eye-opener for the modern era that basks in the glory of technology and takes pride in the great strides made towards gender equality. Greenu Ans Thomas analyses the working of post-truth politics through means of media propaganda especially concerning the recent political biopics in India. Through the spoof movie *Kammarasambhavam* which anticipated the hypocrisy of biopics, it delves deep into the distinction between the 'real' and 'reel' representations of political personalities. Jaya Singh has the most relevant topic of the critical time. Her chapter "Where Do We Burn Our Dead" discusses viewing death in the post-truth era where bodies have emerged out of sacred rivers as anonymous, restless and unacknowledged. It discusses the indifference towards truth when accountability is refused to the dead bodies which are further reflected in a prolonged sense of mourning and constant digital viewing.

Classical Fairytales were used as a medium to impart restrictive knowledge that proclaimed its idealisations as absolute. Dr. M. Samadhanam Emimal attempts to highlight the predicaments of postmodernism in redefining the concept of truth and its contemporary significance through an interpretive approach on a retold fairytale *Briar Rose*. Her chapter aims at critiquing the stand of truth and its validity in postmodern context by accentuating the existence of complacent truths which eventually paves way for the emergence of multiple versions. The chapter by Ann Mary compares the present stance of fakeness and its influence in society and social media, with that of an individual's personal life and family. The chapter analyses and underlines solutions to the fact that post-truth and its integrals have their dangerous influence in society and individual lives alike; while the latter is going undiscussed. Through the discussion of "Fake News: The Hype and the Truth", Rahul Joshi aims to look at how the spread of false news has affected the democratic domain and what policies can be put in place to combat the issue. He seeks to examine the policy actions taken by India and the Western countries to curb the spread of fake news.

Shalabha Rachel Abraham's "Factual Criticism in Post-truth India" is an attempt to discern the status of constructive, factual criticism in India during recent years, and why has it been considered as so hostile an endeavour in the post-truth era, than ever. Marathi Dalit Cinema reflects acute casteism prevalent in Maharashtra pertaining to different facets such as the caste hierarchy, caste-discrimination, domination, oppression, humiliation, revenge, atrocity, honour killing, caste-based conflicts and its worst effects on the present generation. Dr. Rajendra Gholap seeks to study the dilemma of the post-truth era relating to the influence of dominant social hierarchy and the power politics supporting prejudiced casteism.

In an era of worldwide political, psychological and ecological upheaval, as humanity grapples with truth and fact dichotomies, the stage becomes an increasingly relevant space to engage with socio-political issues of universal significance. Within the mediated reality of scripted Realism, an audience finds succour and regains hope through these purgatorial performances. Philipp Sulim's chapter is a study of the relevance of Stanislavsky's "system" creating realism in acting and its contemporary significance in a post-truth society. The post-truth age stands on the rhetoric carried out by the authorities who plays an effective way in carving out the new norm for the society through a goal-oriented approach that conceals their falsehoods. The chapter by Anusree A. Wilson provides insight into the persuasive rhetoric employed by the authorities in Kamila Shamsie's *Home Fire* to make their schemes get fulfilled.

Each chapter in the book thus makes its unique style to explore and discuss post-truth to conclude with its findings and perspectives which make the reading of the book interesting and exciting. In short, the twenty-seven chapters would help the readers to get acquainted with the developments and discussions in the disciplines of literature and media studies from the focal point of the concept and theme of post-truth. At the same time, the academic perspectives from distinct angles have successfully encompassed the contemporary position of post-truth and also about the ongoing researches, difference in the contextual meanings and the existing and futuristic possibilities. We, therefore, hope that this book will be useful for academic reference to professors, scholars and students in the fields of literature, media studies and other disciplines that are interlinked to have connections with each other via the topic of discussion in the book. The theoretical and conceptual research shared by the book will develop a deeper understanding and advanced perception in the scholars to productively contribute knowledge and solutions to the ongoing tensions and ambiguities caused by the substantial effects of post-truth.

Praveen Abraham
praveenkattakkayam@gmail.com

Raisun Mathew
raisunmathew@gmail.com

CHAPTER 1

Fighting Conspiracy Ideologies: Learning from Pandemic Movies to Counter the Post-Factual

Denis Newiak

The Coronavirus as a staged instrument of oppression, secret vaccination deaths, or politicians drinking children's blood: even before the outbreak of the Covid 19 pandemic, conspiracy theories have been booming and their dogmatism threatens social peace and democracy. Conspiracy myths generate systematic distrust of legitimate political institutions and can contribute to social polarisation, political populism, and extremist escalation. Why are increasing numbers of people drifting into such delusional parallel worlds – and how could this be prevented?

Although psychology and sociology have developed empirically based theories on these pressing questions, they have only occasionally found answers to the growing complexity and overall societal dimension of the problem and have so far hardly been able to offer effective intervention. In motion pictures and television series, in contrast, conspiracy ideologies have always been a topic: through their cinematic means, they have always dealt with the relationship between reality and illusion, truth and fiction, objectivity and dream, sense and madness. Series and films not only serve as a discursive space for social self-understanding. Through their complex narratives, constellations of characters, and aesthetics, they also offer vivid and thus catchy attempts to explain the emergence and spread of conspiracy myths. At the same time, they make some astonishingly concrete suggestions for dealing with and combating conspiracy ideologies.

What can we learn from the fictional worlds of series and films for dealing with this very real contemporary phenomenon? In my current book, *It's All Been There Before* (Newiak, 2021), I am dealing with this question from the perspective of pandemic movies. After the outbreak of Covid-19, many were surprised how the somehow unlikely scenarios of science fictions films have turned into reality: the lack of personal protective equipment, the demoralisation of system-relevant medical staff, and a growing sense of social isolation between home office and curfew are just some of the stunning 'prophecies' in virus movies as *Contagion* (USA 2007) and television series like *Sløborn* (D 2020–).

It is no wonder that these fictional worlds also deal with the complex problem of the growing danger from conspiracy ideologies: visual popular culture speaks out about what is currently becoming relevant without being expressed concretely, thereby making collective hopes and fears visible before they have even made their way into the general linguistic discourse (Newiak, 2020). In doing so, TV and movies transfer confusing contexts into vivid, empathetic, "subjunctive narrative forms" (Kirchmann, 2006, p. 167). They can be understood as a "central place of macro-social self-conception" (Hickethier, 2008, p. 47), serving the "conducting of self-observation of the social system" (Luhmann, 1996, p. 174). Film and television provide their spectators with orientation in times of constantly changing certainties (Bonß, 1995) and diminishing securities (Beck, 2007): they produce an understanding and feeling for "what is possible and impossible here and now, tempting and repulsive, urgent or indifferent" (Keppler, 2006, p. 317), allowing us to deal with complex modern challenges that cannot be adequately addressed in political, civil society and scientific discourse due to taboos, bias or simply cognitive overload (Steinborn & Newiak, 2020). The fictional worlds of the cinema and TV "represent an explicitly fictional reality to which the observer can nevertheless orientate himself" and which lets the audience "navigate better through the real world and the complexity of its relationships" (Esposito, 2014, p. 56). By doing so, film and television do not only produce a common concept of a societal truth in times of modern confusion and disorientation (Berger & Luckmann, 1995), but also allow to productively criticize the real social living conditions and thus modernise society by rethinking social cohabitation models (Newiak, 2019). The filmic fictions then can be used as a reservoir of future knowledge, containing concepts and designs on how to deal with upcoming challenges and trends, for example how to rethink urban life in the era of megacities (Krämer et al., 2015).

Based on some examples, I want to show with help of hermeneutic-analytic tools from film and television studies, how conspiracy ideologies and ideologists are represented in pandemic filmic fictions – and how knowledge contained in popular visual culture can be used to better counter the real danger of conspiracy theories in the future. This chapter is based on a book chapter *Unheard prophets, unheard profiteers: Self-reflective premonitions* from my current book on pandemic films (Newiak 2021, p. 41-53). In my chapter, I argue that film and television help to separate productive justified criticism (which is also formulated by the filmic art forms themselves) from destructive forms of post-factual insanities (that are mostly serving egoistic individual interests). By showing different types of reaction to a global outbreak, popular culture can help to understand how to use the chances provided by the "prophets" as well as how to cope with the risks produced by the selfish "profiteers", spreading their mad thought-constructs for their personal advantage.

Pandemic Movies and their 'Prophets': Unwanted 'Bringers of Bad News'

In the classic pandemic film *12 Monkeys* (USA 1995), psychiatrist Dr. Railly deals with a phenomenon that she at first believes to be nothing more than an exotic mental illness, namely the so-called 'Cassandra complex'. She explains: "Cassandra, in Greek legend, was condemned to know the future but to be disbelieved when she foretold it. Hence, the agony of foreknowledge combined with the impotence to do anything about it" (minute 46). But then Railly is kidnapped by such an apparent 'madman' who insists on exactly this ability: James Cole (Bruce Willis) was sent from a post-apocalyptic year 2035 to her present to gather information about what was yet to come for mankind in the past. A virus pandemic would claim 99 percent of humanity. Cole finds himself in a role that, in a self-reflexive way, also alludes to the pandemic genre itself: as a 'madman' from the future – as science fiction films themselves tend to be perceived – his warnings ultimately remain ineffective: "You won't think I'm crazy when people start dying next month. First, they'll think it's just some weird fever. Then they'll find out. They'll catch on" (minute 58). Cole almost succeeds in stopping the actual terrorist at the airport before a genocidal plan is executed, but the security does not believe in the story of the deadly virus any more than the rest of mankind (overwhelmed by the prophecy) does. Since Cole knows that the pandemic is already past in his present, he cannot stop it, just as science fiction movies have not been able to sensitize political leaders to the real threat of a pandemic. Cynically, the effort of serious preparation for pandemics in Cole's world, like in our own reality, would be minimal compared to the total damage that the film characters, as well as people in social reality, now have to deal with.

James Cole's uncompromising truth overloads the imagination of defensively reacting humanity: as an apparently deranged man who believes he is from the future but actually only speaks unpleasant truths, he is taken to a psychiatric institution where he initially fails to fulfil his important prophetic task. The film, on the other hand, portrays the apparently mentally ill man, not as a madman, but as a lonely misunderstood person, who childishly dreams of a trip to the beach, nostalgically listens to the sounds of a past "Wonderful World" and then even doubts his own sanity due to his obvious deviations from the norm. As in the original from 1995, in the television series of the same name (USA 2015-2018), Cole is basically shown as a sympathetic figure who sacrifices his life for the good of humanity. But as in reality (where warning epidemiologists and politicians sometimes get harassed), as a 'bearer of bad news' who questions the sustainability of the accustomed comfort of life, he becomes a lunatic with 'crude visions' that overwhelm the collective imagination. Democratically, the film thus explicitly warns against leaving unwelcome isolated counter-opinions unheard or even suppressing them as pathological, since they can point to important real dangers in an otherwise homogenized and self-reinforcing uniform discourse. However, Cole is largely denied communication with the outside world, so that the alleged nonsense does not 'spread around' as an "epidemic of insanity", as another inmate (Brad Pitt) nervously describes it.

The "unheard prophet" almost belongs to the standard repertoire of the apocalypse film, but these prophets are not always able to concretize their foreboding, which is fed by a mixture of neurosis, special powers of observation, and fear. Their incapacity to formulate their predictions understandably only worsens their social position and increases their isolation. Thus, in the German end-time drama *The Coming Days* (D 2010), Western societies are at a crossroads: in 2012, the hunger for oil has plunged humanity into a fourth Gulf War, and domestic and foreign political tensions threaten to escalate through poverty, violence, and terrorism. Hans, an up-and-coming energy consultant who is on the brink of blindness, decides to retire to a remote mountain hut together with his pregnant girlfriend: "The world as we know it, Laura, will soon no longer exist. The world in which we grew up, it will end. This war will not be limited to the Gulf. There will be other resource wars in Africa, in Asia.... The world economy will soon collapse, there will be ecological collapse. There will be pandemics again, the Spanish flu. There is a prophecy that the Russians are coming..." (minute 43). For Hans, it is relatively irrelevant which of these diverse horror scenarios will actually occur: he is just convinced that modernity has failed, and that the only way out is the retreat into a 'pre-modern' way of life in a mountain hut – close to nature, far away from the dysfunctionalities of civilisation.

Mad But Harmless: Hoarders and Their Longing for an Anti-Modern World

This close-to-nature type of the nostalgically dreamy self-sufficient person is contrasted in the films by the seemingly over-anxious "hamster" who stores up supplies in the apartment in case Western civilisation collapses. In the trashy pandemic satire *Phase 7* from Argentina (2010), the majority of the quarantined residents of an apartment complex in Buenos Aires face a looming wave of disease with astonishing disinterest – with the exception of Horazio, armed to the teeth with food, breathing masks, and guns, who has everything ready in his apartment to sit out the apparent 'end of the world' he foresees: "All my life I've been told I was paranoid – at school, in the family, in therapy..." (minute 40), but now his hour has come as a 'self-fulfilling' prophecy. On the one hand, he is prepared to defend his supplies against intruders by all means – in case of doubt using force –, but on the other hand, he longs for a friend with whom he can share his plans and supplies and who will keep him company during the apocalypse. Certainly, Horazio is entangled in a web of crude conspiracy theories ("Do you really think this is a flu epidemic? This is about a controlled decimation of the population, ordered by the top! But I'm prepared...!", minute 40), but these rather incoherent speculations remain just ramblings of thoughts that do not want to fit into a consistent 'political program' and serve as a mere occasion for the stockpiling that turns out to be quite useful after all, instead of fighting the 'powerful' ones.

As it befits a misunderstood prophet who can anticipate the future, the clairvoyants in the pandemic films remain lonely lunatics who try to assert themselves with their individual opinions against a horde of unbelievers. But regardless of whether these self-proclaimed prophets get to the heart of the matter in their preparation for the crisis triggered by a pandemic, whether their preparations are proportionate or not: as long as they do not pose a danger to others and adhere to law and order, especially to the rules of conduct such as quarantine, there is no reason

– as film and television quite unanimously plead – to be too suspicious or even to fight them. Rather, the ability of individuals to anticipate certain imminent dangers that could threaten the general public can be seen as an opportunity – just as the future prospects of science fiction films should not be dismissed as entertainment but can be understood as a warning against unlikely risks.

Crisis Profiteers in Pandemic Cinema: The Critical Voice as 'Wolf in Sheep's Clothing'

The situation is completely different when such a supposed 'Messiah,' with his prophecies, does more harm than good, or even wants to bring about the anarchic state himself – and profits from it. Such a scenario is the core theme of the comparatively realistic feature film *Contagion* (USA 2011). While the scientific community is quick to conclude that the virus must have originated from a cross between wild and farm animals (as well as, most likely, the Coronavirus, WHO 2021), the established conspiracy theorist Krumwiede (Jude Law) – disguised as a blogging journalist – considers the disease to be quite arbitrary first the result of heavy metals in food, then a biological military weapon, and finally "a bad day to be a rhesus monkey" (minute 37). With his crude theories, the shady character draws millions of naïve frightened people to his website, which is supposedly "in search of the truth." The film initially portrays the figure of Krumwiede as a supposed maverick who, with his crazy assumptions, may be off the track, but in his socially important role as an investigative reporter, he needs to be tolerated because his findings may actually reveal hidden power relations and conflicts of interest.

But his seemingly investigative 'reports' are not in fact intended to enlighten a highly unsettled population, but solely to satisfy his narcissism and urge for financial enrichment: while researchers are working on a vaccine, the seemingly 'investigative reporter' maintains lucrative contacts with generous hedge fund managers and suggests on his mass-visited blog that a tincture of forsythia – a plant used in homoeopathy – would have cured him of the disease. With no certainty about the effectiveness of the plant extract, panicked people storm the pharmacies to get their hands on a vial of the apparent miracle cure – while the real conspirator Krumwiede (with little confidence in his own "cure" hidden in a completely sealed infection protection suit) roams the streets littered with garbage and sick people, handing out leaflets about the alleged lies of the CDC – and earning millions of dollars from his murderous lie.

After people take irresponsible risks and pay speculators enormous sums of money to get the promising tincture, he then strikes again and wants to warn people of the invented dangers of the now available vaccination: "Maybe it causes autism or narcolepsy or cancer ten years from now. Who knows?... We're all guinea pigs, starting from today" (minute 82). Referring to the alleged accumulation of vaccination damage during the swine flu of 1976, which is often brought up by opponents of the vaccination, the fake news producer tries to talk up his own money-grabbing machinations and continues his profitable 'education' campaign. "I can't even imagine all the civil suits people are gonna file against you... and now you wanna tell people not to get vaccinated when that's the best chance they've got. If I could throw your computer in jail, I would," summarises the investigator, who reluctantly has to let Krumwiede go on bail – collected by his 'apostles' (minute 91). The real danger here, as the film tells us, is not only from infection with the virus itself, but especially from the insecurity of the population. As Dr. Cheever, the epidemiologist responsible at the CDC, says:

> In order to become sick, you have to first come in contact with a sick person or something that they touched. In order to get scared, all you have to do is come in contact with a rumor, or the television or the internet. I think what Mr. Krumwiede is spreading is far more dangerous than the disease.
>
> (minute 67)

Here the apparent prophet becomes a sneaky profiteer, who as a wolf in sheep's clothes initially remains unrecognised. Even if it seems problematic and unbalanced that in *Contagion* the only critical reporting in the film appears in the form of the criminal egoist who deliberately spreads disinformation, the film points to an important potential danger: charismatic persons with a wide reach on the Internet, nowadays especially in the 'social media' networks, could take calculated advantage of the fear of a medically less educated population group, especially against the background of a scientific knowledge deficit, in order to profit from this information gap in a deliberate way. They could even accept the death of many people by spreading their misbelief – if they could benefit from it. It is almost irrelevant whether the self-proclaimed prophets believe in their miracle cures themselves or not: the damage they cause by spreading panic and doubt into scientifically based knowledge and medical research could beat the consequences of the virus itself. At the same time, as the film shows, such conspiracy theorists obviously take advantage of existing structural weaknesses in orthodox medical care – the market and pricing power of legally well-protected pharmaceutical companies, the uncertainties and potential side effects of new drugs that always remain despite all testing and effectiveness, insufficient transparency in the development of patents and the awarding of industrial contracts, and individual wrongdoing – to spread fundamental scepticism against science and state sovereignty.

Reacting Appropriately to Conspiracy Ideologies

In the world of *Contagion,* the state tries to dispel the doubts by randomly drawing lots by lottery machine for the order in which the scarce vaccine is administered, by gradually making it available free of charge to each individual and, despite all-time constraints, by testing it extensively before mass production, which creates trust and defuses critical voices about vaccination. But the film also points out the danger of an unequal distribution of the vaccine between countries, as the industrial nations, which can produce the vaccine in large quantities quickly, probably want to be self-sufficient first. In *Contagion,* some desperate people are therefore resorting to drastic measures and are taking the WHO staff hostage to extort rapid vaccine deliveries.

Even if democracy, as the film shows, must and should tolerate individual opinions that deviate from the scientific consensus, the specially protected pluralism of opinion ends when this freedom is used as a weapon specifically against the dignity, freedom, and health of others. The film suggests not only that strict proof of efficacy should be demanded of every medicine available on the market, whether homoeopathic or not, but also that the population should be protected from disinformation campaigns employing a proactive information policy that integrates nongovernmental and independent experts. At the same time, films such as *Outbreak* (USA 1995), in which a virus epidemic really does get out of control due to military power-strategic interests, show how important a free press is, especially in times of crisis, which must not be prevented from doing its work under any circumstances. The film argues for actively supporting journalists in their work especially in dangerous situations, so that they can contribute to the supply of information and the formation of opinion.

Film and television do not always play a showcase role. For example, the first season of the series *Sløborn* (D 2020–), released shortly after the start of the Covid 19 pandemic, surely does impressively address the dangers of political division and right-wing radicalism: under the pretext of curfews and military presence, supposedly 'freedom-loving' citizens revolt against the alleged virus' 'true' source (needless to say: the foreigners) and plan an uprising. In disturbingly realistic images set against an idyllic German island backdrop, the series shows how the collapse of the state's monopoly on the use of force and the collapse of the health system give the heavily armed neo-Nazis an easy ride. However, in the way the series stages the Bundeswehr soldiers as bloodthirsty thugs and gives the impression that the systematically misinforming authorities are cramming together the healthy and the sick, it fuels conspiracy theories rather than educating them about their dangers and aberrations. At the very least, the series points to the unsettling effect of images of collective loss of power and the risk of manipulating official information, causing the characters to gradually lose track of what is still true and what is untrue in their world.

Learning from Science Fiction: A Conclusion

Fictional scenarios from film and television provide the opportunity to deal creatively and productively with complex social phenomena, such as conspiracy ideologies. Popular filmic art does not only allow communication about the impending dangers of a post-truth society, but also implicitly and explicitly suggests possible countermeasures: a professional free press, consistent criminal law action against disinformation campaigns, protection of democratically legitimised parliamentarians and executive power, transparent and proactive public relations even in times of crisis, containment of the danger of manipulating videos ('deep-fakes') and official information, protection of the health care system and vulnerable population groups – all of these measures can take the wind out of the sails of conspiracy theorists, as they make use of growing insecurity in times of emergencies with, at the same time, increasingly complex social conditions and discourses. Politics and society can learn from film and television how to counter these dangers without making the mistake to think that pop-cultural entertainment has patent remedies for every late-modern problem, and to assume that it is immune to dramatisation and stereotyping. Despite these shortcomings, with the help of critical reading, film and television can help find answers to highly topical questions such as the beginning of the 'Post-truth Era'.

References

Beck, W. (2007). *Weltrisikogesellschaft. Auf der Suche nach der verlorenen Sicherheit.* Suhrkamp.

Berger, P., & Luckmann, T. (1995). *Modernität, Pluralismus und Sinnkrise. Die Orientierung des modernen Menschen.* Bertelsmann-Stiftung.

Bonß, W. (1995). *Vom Risiko. Unsicherheit und Ungewissheit in der Moderne.* Hamburger Edition.

Esposito, E. (2014). *Die Fiktion der wahrscheinlichen Realität.* Suhrkamp.

Hickethier, K. (2008). Fernsehen, Rituale und Subjektkonstitutionen. Ein Kapitel Fernsehtheorie. In K. Fahlenbrach, K., I. Brück, & A. Bartsch (Eds.): *Medienrituale.* Rituelle Performanz in Film, Fernsehen und Neuen Medien (pp. 47-58). VS Verlag für Sozialwissenschaften.

Keppler, A. (2006). *Mediale Gegenwart. Eine Theorie des Fernsehens am Beispiel der Darstellung von Gewalt.* Suhrkamp.

Kirchmann, K. (2006). Philosophie der Möglichkeiten. Das Fernsehen als konjunktivisches Erzählmedium. In O. Fahle, & L. Engell (Eds.*): Philosophie des Fernsehens* (pp. 157-172). Fink.

Krämer, S., Maikämper, M., Pätsch, C., Petersen, C., Rott, B., Rukschcio, B., & Weidner S. (2015). *Von Science-Fiction-Städten lernen. Szenarien für die Stadtplanung.* Bundesinstitut für Bau-, Stadt- und Raumforschung. BBSR.

Luhmann, N. (1996). *Die Realität der Massenmedien.* VS Verlag für Sozialwissenschaften.

Newiak, D. (2019). Serial Horrors of Loneliness: The Impossibility of Communitisation in The Walking Dead. Zer – *Journal of Communication Studies,* 47(25), 51-64. https://doi.org/10.1387/ zer.20728

Newiak, D. (2020). Das Ende der Stadtgemeinschaft? Urbane Einsamkeiten und städtebauliche Antworten am Beispiel von Her. In A. Steinborn & D. Newiak (Eds.): *Urbane Zukünfte im Science-Fiction-Film: Was wir vom Kino für die Stadt von morgen lernen können* (pp. 127-148). Springer Spektrum. https://doi.org/10.1007/ 978-3-662-61037-4_8

Newiak, D. (2021). *It's All Been There Before: What We Can Learn About the Coronavirus Crisis from Pandemic Movies.* Ibidem.

Steinborn, A., & Newiak, D. (2020). Wahrscheinliche' Zukünfte: Urbanes Leben mit Science-Fiction neu gedacht. In A. Steinborn, & D. Newiak (Eds.): *Urbane Zukünfte im Science-Fiction-Film. Was wir vom Kino für die Stadt von morgen lernen können* (pp. 1–10). Springer Spektrum. https://doi.org/10.1007/978-3-662-61037-4_1

World Health Organisation (2021). WHO-convened Global Study of Origins of SARS-CoV-2: China Part. Joint WHO-China Study. February 2021. *Joint Report.* who.int/publications/i/item/who-convened-global-study-of-origins-of-sars-cov-2-china-part

Discussed Films and TV Series

12 Monkeys (USA 1995, © Universal City Studios, Inc. / Twelve Monkeys Productions, Inc.)

12 Monkeys (USA 2015–2018, © Universal Network Television, LLC)

The Coming Days ("Die kommenden Tage," D 2010, © Badlands Film)

Outbreak (USA 1995, © Warner Bros.)

Phase 7 (ARG 2010, © Aeroplano S.A.)

Sløborn (D 2020–, © *Syrreal Entertainment*, ZDF, ZDF Enterprise, TOBIS Filmproduktion, Nordisk Film)

CHAPTER 2

"*Quid Est (Post) Veritas*": Decoding Post-Truth and (Un) Believability in the 21st Century

Dr. Minu Susan Koshy

"*Quid est veritas?*" (*King James Bible*, 1769/2017, John 18:38) – Pilate asks this question to Jesus right before his crucifixion when Jesus says "I am witness to the truth" (*King James Bible*, 1769/2017, John 18:37) and without waiting for an answer, Pilate tells the people assembled that he sees no fault in Jesus. Jesting Pilate – "Quid est veritas?" – still remains one of the most debated parts in the Bible as Pilate's intention or even what exactly he meant by it, is not evident. What, after all, is Truth? Pilate's question points fundamentally to the concept of truth as relative or even to the postmodern possibility that 'truth' in itself does not exist. Truth as a philosophical concept has been at the centre of philosophical discourses for centuries, beginning with Plato and Aristotle. Today, in an era of increased democratisation of knowledge, easy access to data generation through online media and the possibility of easy transfer of information and news, often fake, across the globe, the question is not about 'Truth' but about 'Post-Truth': "Quid est *post-veritas?*" First used by Steve Tesich in 1992, 'post-truth' refers to situations wherein invoking emotions and appealing to personal sentiments shape public opinion, with objective facts being partially or totally disregarded. Post-truth has a definitive impact on public opinion, predominantly in the political context where populist governments have come to power in several countries including the US and India, by the power of *post-veritas*, pointing to the emergence and reinforcement of "post-truth politics – a political culture in which politics (public opinion and media narratives) have become almost entirely disconnected from policy (the substance of legislation)" (Roberts, 2010, para.8).

As Steve Fuller (2018) comments on Thomas Kuhn's account of science," 'truth' is no longer the arbiter of legitimate power but rather the mask of legitimacy that is worn by everyone in pursuit of power" (p. 4). In order to obtain power, the machinations of post-truth are utilised to their fullest possible extent by endowing events, objects and people with 'believability', irrespective of factual evidence to the contrary. Facts that discredit one's ideological/political positions are completely disregarded and often veiled from public view, while opinions and emotionally charged propaganda which support fallacious claims are given wide publicity. Media, especially social media, function as potent means of accomplishing this task by propagating fake news and misinformation, which are the most conspicuous sources of strength for the post-truth situation. Post-truth is unique in that there is "clear intent to influence others" and the enunciator believes that "the crowd's reaction actually *does* change the facts about a lie" (McIntyre, 2018, p. 6). My chapter attempts to explore post-truth as a mechanism through which those in power retain their ideological influence and how the media enables the propagation of fake news, misinformation and believability, thereby sustaining the post-truth economy and polity.

Media, Fake News and Misinformation in the Post-Truth Era

One of the keywords in any discussion of the post-truth situation is 'media'. How does the media promote post-truth and create a world of alt-facts? While it is easy to place the blame squarely on social media, it is irrefutable that even traditional media plays a prominent role in creating a post-truth reality by disseminating fake news and more significantly, biased information. That TV channels and newspapers are often funded by corporates and political parties is a well-known fact; as such the news and information broadcasted by these media outlets would naturally tilt in favour of the groups funding them. This would be clear even from a preliminary observation of news channels, newspapers and magazines. The case of *Republic T V* is an instance. A background check of the investors in the channel reveals that most of them have affiliations to the ruling party, directly or indirectly. This explains the adamant stance taken by its owner and journalist Arnab Goswami on issues such as the JNU Sedition Row of 2016 (*Times Now*, 2016). Panellists with alternate viewpoints were silenced and a biased view of events, which most often ('coincidentally') coincide with the state's narrative, was presented, thereby influencing public opinion. In the US, *Fox News*, which broadcasts explicitly partisan news, is hugely popular despite or maybe, because of the personal opinions that are often aired as 'news'.

Fake news is frequently broadcasted by such media in order to promote their agenda. Although fake news existed from time immemorial in the form of lies and slandering of public figures in all cultures, it has assumed gargantuan proportions in recent years with the booming of the social media culture. Facebook, Twitter and Watsapp often become 'news channels' propagating information that may or may not be true. Social media is particularly dangerous in the post-truth era owing to its potential to misinform large masses of people in a matter of seconds. A post or video on Facebook or Watsapp can be forwarded any number of times to unlimited recipients, thereby influencing their perceptions even before the news can be detected as fake. The spiralling number of cases in India where fake news circulated via Watsapp and Facebook has led to lynching, riots and other forms of violence stands as testimony to the immense potential of social media to wreak havoc in the social and political systems in a country.

The Muzaffarnagar Riots of 2013, which resulted in the death and displacement of more than 50,000 people, was triggered off by fake news circulated on Watsapp, leading to clashes between the Hindu Jats and Muslims. The impossibility of ascertaining the veracity of events is evident from the existence of multiple theories regarding the reason for the original clashes. While some attribute it to theft, others claim that an instance of eve-teasing led to the sparking off of hostility. The people acted on a video circulated via Watsapp showing two men being lynched. However, later the video was identified as a two-year-old one from Pakistan or Afghanistan or from the Gulf. The conflicting accounts regarding the origin of this video itself point to the unreliability of online media and the lack of adequate mechanisms to detect the exact sources from which data originates. The comments made by the police regarding the role social media played in sparking off the riots is significant:

- "The video surfaced on August 29 and a day later we had blocked it on the Internet. However, it was passed on from phone to phone through WhatsApp and within a few days, thousands of people had viewed it. This only served to inflame sentiments" (Inspector General, I.G Vishwakarma).

> "We did not imagine so many people would have access to the net on their mobile phones and WhatsApp. Moreover, it is impossible to intercept messages and videos transmitted through this application" (Unnamed official).
>
> (Anujeet, 2013)

These two comments reveal several things regarding the potential of social media to sustain the post-truth society: first, through its instant messaging facility and the existence of groups with hundreds or thousands of members, a piece of news can reach innumerable recipients within minutes; second, it is not easy or sometimes even possible to detect whether the information is true or not and even if it is detected to be false, nothing can be done to prevent it from circulating in the first few minutes and by the time the app is blocked, it would already have reached the intended recipients; thirdly, as even the most powerful law enforcement agencies acknowledge, authorities are helpless in the face of social media 'news' which wreak havoc through informal channels, sometimes even threatening national security; in already charged environments, people tend to believe inflammatory news and act upon them, even when they are unsure of the veracity of the information.

The Muzaffarnagar Riots are not an isolated incident where social media triggered violence through misinformation. The Dadri lynching incident, which occurred in "an atmosphere already vitiated by social media" (Manmohan, 2015), was followed by inflammatory Watsapp and Facebook posts which served to heighten tension. *The Quint* ("Hunted", 2018) reports that in two months (May-July 2018), 19 people lost their lives in India due to lynching caused by rumours circulated via Watsapp messages. The news website lists several such incidents which occurred due to rumours of child-lifting in Maharashtra, Gujarat, Assam, Karnataka and Telangana. 113 murders due to lynching took place in India from 2015-19, according to the report titled "Hunted: India's Lynch Files", published by *The Quint*, with a substantial number being from the Cow Belt, owing to real or presumed cattle slaughter or theft, the news of which sometimes circulates via social media. 40 of the 118 victims are Muslims, pointing to how the community is targeted by fringe groups, thereby portraying the inextricable link between post-truth and right-wing politics, the professed agenda of the latter being the suppression and/or elimination of minorities who are threats to the religious homogeneity they envisage for the nation. The role social media plays in inciting violence, often leading to lynching and murder, mainly of vulnerable groups, cannot thus be ignored. The specific act of violence is often followed by a spate of vicious incidents propelled by 'manufactured' news of retaliation by the community to which the victim belonged, thus further poisoning the atmosphere. That the communities of the persecutors as well as the victim are more than willing to believe such stories that portray them as the victims is natural considering the fear psychosis that grips people in the aftermath of violent incidents. The post-truth society flourishes on such insecurities and fears, further encouraging extremist ideologies and violence in order to achieve explicit or veiled political agendas.

Here the question as to why fake news is produced and why it receives a massive audience becomes significant. One reason for its proliferation is what Nicole Cooke (2018) terms "the political economy... of information" (p. 11), whereby media, especially online media, publishes news and propagates information intending to make money. Blogs and YouTube videos with high viewership obtain money and popularity; as such, the brains behind such media, find unverified and slanderous pieces of news the best sources for generating an audience and maintaining traffic. Facebook and Twitter function on similar principles, with "Likes" and "Shares" being major incentives for the users, the majority of whom desire popularity, likeability and attention. As such, the veracity of content often goes unchecked in the rush to produce and circulate 'viral' videos or news in order to obtain instant popularity. Besides, the internet generation constantly checks Facebook, Watsapp, Twitter and other media to see what is new, what is happening in others' lives, what trend is the 'in-thing', and to read some 'light-hearted' gossip and more importantly, to assuage FOMO or the Fear of Missing Out. Such tendencies are of benefit to media, especially to those circulating fake news, which then caters to the interests of such users by 'manufacturing' information, thereby leading to misinformation.

"Iterative journalism... [in which] media personalities report what they've heard, not what they have discovered or sought out directly" (Cooke, 2018, p. 14) adds to the post-truth scenario, articulating second-hand information with very little or zero authenticity. This is especially conspicuous in the case of FM broadcasting and talk shows where personal ideologies are blended with 'heard' content and articulated in an unrestrained fashion. Social media has also given a platform for citizen journalists – "average individuals [who] have so much access to technology that it is all too easy to capture pictures, audio and video and upload them to Twitter, Facebook, YouTube, and any other online sites"

(Cooke, 2018, p. 15). Thus, we have all become 'journalists' capable of creating, circulating and commenting on issues ranging from celebrity lifestyles to nuclear warfare, with the potential to 'twist' and 'photoshop' news, videos and pictures to suit our ideologies and interests. Martin De Saulles (2012), in *Information 2.0* speaks of "the disintermediation of traditional gatekeepers, including information professionals" (p. 57) in the context of citizen journalism. Since it is difficult to regulate content posted online, the 'news' circulated by people with no knowledge of journalism escapes screening and verification and reaches viewers directly, leading to the propagation of fake news.

There were numerous instances where fake news managed to gather immense popularity before it could be detected as fake. In 2018, *Times Now* published an article that claimed that Abu Dhabi's Sheikh Sultan began his speech with 'Jai Siya Ram'. It was actually from a speech given during a Ram Katha (Safoora, 2018, n.p). Other instances include the Pizzagate conspiracy theory in the USA, the news of unrest in Kashmir which is circulated every few days and the news of Mullaperiyar dam leaking (which went viral during 2018 Kerala floods), among others. The easy availability of photographs and the ease with which images can be edited have also contributed to the propagation of fake news and misinformation through visual icons.

Majoritarian Nationalism and the 'Politics' of Misinformation

Misinformation and fake news have been used extensively to promote various ideologies across the world. But nowhere is it more conspicuous than in the case of states advocating majoritarian nationalism, as in the case of India. News and photographs are often manipulated to suit the agenda of self-declared 'nationalists. Instances include the photoshopped pictures and use of images such as that of the crowd gathered to see Sunny Leone in Kerala being passed off as the photo of a national party's Janaraksha Yatra in 2017, pictures posted by a politician showing slaughtered cows lying on the roads in Kerala, which was actually a picture from Bengal or Bangladesh as the language on the signboards attest to, and the Pulitzer-winning photo titled "Raising the Flag at Iwo Jima", being passed off as "Indian jawans, Indian soldiers dying, but holding up the tricolour, at the border" (Sengupta, 2016, n.p.).

There are several interesting observations about post-truth that emerge from these instances:

1. There is an inextricable link between right-wing politics and post-truth, since both rely on narrow sentiments and populism

for asserting the legitimacy of their arguments and agenda. Trump's promise to keep immigrants outside the USA and the right-wing agenda of turning India into a Hindu-Rashtra, which is hardly a secret anymore, thanks to their propagation over the media, are proof of how narrow parochial sentiments are exploited to obtain votes.

2. The link between religion and post-truth is also conspicuous. This is a natural corollary of the intricate connection between right-wing politics and religiosity. Indeed, the fact that one of India's states is ruled by a religious leader who, shortly after the incident of children suffocating to death is a hospital in the state due to lack of piped oxygen supply had the audacity to eulogise the health sector of the state during a political campaign, is proof of how religiosity is no bar to and in fact, encourages blatant lies to promote political agendas.
3. Religion and nationalism are utilised as means of achieving political goals as these are two factors that evoke the maximum amount of emotional response from the common people as is evident during election campaigns.
4. Post-truth also thrives on creating paranoia among the people irrespective of whether they are minorities or the majority. By posting pictures of slaughtered cows and circulating Watsapp messages showing certain majority communities and their belief systems being attacked, politicians seem to create insecurity among the majority who feel threatened. At the same time, the minorities are pushed into a fear psychosis where they become acutely aware of their vulnerability and react irrationally.
5. Right-wing post-truth politics specifically targets Muslims by creating and promoting Islamophobia as we observed in the videos. Post 9/11, the world in general and America in particular, have been suspicious of Muslims. In the Indian scenario, Hindutvavadis have always openly professed their dislike for the community. As such, growing Islamophobia is another effect of post-truth politics.
6. As Ignas Kalpokas remarks in his 2019 work *A Political Theory of Post-Truth*, "mediatisation directly enables the post-truth era" (p. 57). The term indicates a process "whereby the media increasingly influence and penetrate various social spheres (such as politics), exerting a strong influence over them not just as

mediators, but also through their very existence, omnipresence and internal logic" (p. 53). Now news channels, newspapers and social media are not just sources whereby citizens obtain information regarding political issues, but platforms where the average citizen or politician can turn into an amateur journalist and/or propagandist, issuing misinformed comments which become influential in the political arena as the case of Pizzagate, Brexit etc.

Apart from these, the post-truth scenario also relies on the suppression of facts in order to achieve the desired effects and to avoid unpleasant ones. For instance, during demonetisation, the government hid the fact that it had only 32% of the value of the demonetised currency at the time and used 'rationing' of notes and the promotion of digital payments (seemingly to make India a cashless economy) to buy time and avoid trouble. Fudging with data has become commonplace with even non-negotiable 'facts' such as GDP rates and fiscal deficit being tweaked to bolster up its claims of ushering in development. That the government upped the previous years' GDP rates right before the presentation of the budget in February 2019 and suppressed the fact of the double-digit growth during the previous regime stands testimony to the extent to which post-truth has come to rule our country. Data pertaining to unemployment rates and farmer suicide rates are suppressed with ministers even going as far as to say that no data is available or that new surveys will be conducted, when unpleasant statistics were revealed, thereby pointing to the openness with which the state tweaks even statistical data to its advantage.

The post-truth world is predominantly one in which the past is questioned to suit specific political agendas. History becomes a tool in the hands of propagandists who utilise it to create 'alt history' that articulates their versions of events. As Foucault remarks, "power and knowledge are inextricably intertwined. We have narratives, we don't have the truth" (qtd. by Tharoor at the JLF 2017). This is perhaps the most conspicuous in the case of India where there are frantic attempts by the state to rewrite history by modifying school textbooks and to pass off *puranas* as historical accounts. Nationalism, which is one of the elements exploited by the politicians across the world, assumes a significance of gargantuan proportions in India considering the diversity in the country and the resultant suspicions of the majority regarding the patriotism of the minority and indeed the patriotism of individuals and groups opposing the extreme right narratives. The suspicion is not a natural one – it is created in the minds of the common people by propagandists through such measures as rewriting history in order to designate certain communities as historically being dangerous – another post-truth strategy. The failure of the right-wing to distinguish between myth and history is often not a result of the Dunning-Kruger effect – 'the too stupid to know you are stupid' effect. Rather, despite knowing the facts, 'alternate facts' are injected as truth into the minds of the masses with the clear intent of manipulating them for political gain.

The speech by a cabinet-rank minister at the inauguration of a seminar on Guptvanshak-Veer: Skandgupta Vikramadithya' at Banaras Hindu University deserves attention:

> ... there is a need to rewrite history from India's point of view but without blaming anyone. It is our responsibility to write our history. How long are we going to blame the British? Who is stopping us from amending history, researching and creating reference texts by rewriting history in popular languages? We don't have to dispute the facts, only write what the truth is... what our point of view is, and it will stand the test of time.
>
> (*The Hindu*, 2019, n.p.)

The comment is interesting on several counts.

- First, it sums up in part the right-wing perception of history as 'truth' with a singular face – one which happens to be in conformity with their ideology, one which is 'our point of view'. While history can and should be rewritten and reinterpreted in the face of new evidence, rewriting it in order to create an alternate 'truth' suiting one's political agendas is dangerous. This is particularly so when the said ideology is religion-centric and harks back to a sometimes imagined 'glorious' past. The article titled "Rewriting History" which appeared in *The Hindu* on 18 October 2019 sums up this position:

> His call to "rewrite history" is predicated on specific, predetermined outcomes and cannot be seen in isolation from his regime's and his political organisation's overall world view. The Hindutva-oriented right-wing glorifies India's ancient past, largely through a literal reading of epics and religious texts... This blinkered view of the past actually flows from a reductionist approach to the world in terms of religion-centric identities based more on faith than on facts. (n.p.)

- Secondly, there is an equation of truth with opinion even while facts are acknowledged as significant. That facts have always been twisted by various groups and articulated as alternate history is common knowledge, considering the revision of school textbooks in various parts of the country and the projection of Muslim rulers in India as plunderers and violent rulers who harassed Hindus, with the attack even targeting rulers like Akbar who explicitly favoured secularism and during whose periods songs in praise of Hindu gods and goddesses were composed. The equation of "truth" and "our point of view" reminds one of Shashi Tharoor's remark at the Jaipur Literary Festival 2017: "You are entitled to your own opinions, but you are not entitled to your own facts". Extreme nationalists seem not to know the difference between the two even though they seemingly adhere to 'not disputing facts'.

- Thirdly, there is an emotional appeal to the nationalist sentiments of the audience when he drags the British into the picture and talks of "our responsibility to write our history". By reminding the people of past injustices, a desire for justice through a 'rewriting' of history is created, thereby subtly justifying the state's consistent attempts at erasing secular leaders from history and the eulogisation of early right-wing leaders like Veer Savarkar.
- Fourthly, the authoritarian tone in the rhetorical question "who is stopping us from amending history... ?" cannot be ignored. This reflects not just the attitude behind the political events unfolding in our country but also the gradual movement towards fascism that the post-truth era inevitably brings.
- Finally, the choice of the venue where the statement was issued raises questions. Central universities have traditionally been secular spaces, or at least expected to be secular spaces irrespective of the religious tags in their nomenclature. That such a space becomes the venue for a seminar about a single Hindu ruler and not a particular historical period or specific group of rulers, and especially a ruler who stands for a specific type of nationalism, is in itself suspect. Besides, when the supposedly open space of a university becomes the loci of enunciation of narrow sentiments and authoritarian questions pointing to the rapid emergence of a fascist mentality among representatives of the state, we need to wonder where post-truth India is headed.

Attempts to fit Indian history within the Hindu mythological framework, creating a post-truth Indian history are on at a frenzied pace, with historians, even those heading committees of repute such as the ICHR, claiming that the *Ramayana* and *Mahabharata* are historical sources. In fact, during an interview with *The Economic Times*, the ICHR chief, Y. Sudershan Rao went so far as to say: "If Rama's story is not true, how has he survived in the collective memory for so long? People do not care whether Rama is historical or not. He is the truth for them. India's need is a special study of its past and the truth of its past cannot be denied. Rama's existence need not be proved by historical procedure" (*The Economic Times*, 2014, n.p.). Truth is redefined to suit politico-religious ideologies and the people's belief systems are used as screens to hide the lack of authenticity to fake claims. The need for the historical procedure itself is dismissed – another symptom of a post-truth society transforming itself into a fascist state with a single narrative.

Twisting history to create an alternate truth is evident from the appointment of a committee of scholars in 2017 to "use evidence such as archaeological finds and DNA to prove that today's Hindus are directly descended from the land's first inhabitants [and] that ancient Hindu scriptures are fact not myth" (Rupam & Lasseter, 2018, n.p.). The members were appointed not to conduct an objective historical study, but to 'find' archaeological evidence that can 'fit' the aforementioned arguments. This is part of a larger plan to revise Indian history and the leader in charge explicitly stated that the committee's findings will be included in school textbooks. The construction and propagation of alternate truths become complete, misinforming the masses and propelling them to accept myth as history, thereby creating a post-truth society rooted in 'alt-historical facts'. The renaming of places named after Muslim rulers, the erasure of secular democrats like Gandhi and Nehru from historical narratives and textbooks and the creation of doubt in the minds of the common people by including questions such as "How did Gandhiji commit suicide?" in school examinations are symptoms of a post-truth society standing at the threshold of fascism.

Such instances of what Hannah Arendt terms "organised lying" whereby "deliberate falsehood is used as a weapon against truth" (qtd. in Finchelstein, 2019, n.p.), especially with regard to history, are not limited to India. Another glaring case in point is Poland where the Gdansk Museum of the Second World War became a site of conflict, with the populist Law and Justice Party attempting to modify the museum and the exhibits to portray a glorified image of the nation. The museum director, Pawel Machcewicz, was dismissed and a crony of the party, Karol Nawrocki, was appointed as the new director. He made quite a lot of modifications, one of the most striking ones being the insertion of a picture of a Polish family murdered for hiding Jews at the entrance to a hall featuring photographs of Jews massacred in the Holocaust. The intention, obviously, was to convey the message of the nobility of Poland and to project Polish citizens as victims. While the museum was intended as a symbol of the destruction wrought by war and as a warning for future generations to refrain from violent means of achieving ends, the government attempted to transform it into a symbol of the martyrdom of Poland. The replacement of the video featuring images of the war and refugee crisis in Syria and Ukraine with one of the Polish soldiers, portrays how a cultural artefact is forced to deviate from its purpose and serve as a site for proclaiming cheap patriotism. The victimisation of Jews, the role Poland played in the war and other proven historical facts were replaced with a twisted historical narrative of Poland's past glory, appealing to people's emotions, reinforcing the post-truth scenario. Another instance is that of the Brazilian President Jair Bolsonaro arguing that the Nazis were leftists (Finchelstein, 2019, n.p.), that Brazil never had a dictatorship (thereby denying the authoritarian nature of the Fifth Brazilian Republic) and eulogising dictators like Pinochet and Alfredo Stroessner. Such instances of history being manipulated to promote the interests of populist parties, enabling fascism through post-truth politics abound in the global scenario today.

Satire in the Post-Truth World

An arena that merits special attention is the close link between satire and post-truth, especially satire as manifested in trolls, memes and pseudo media sites such as *The Onion*, *Faking News*, *Duffelpost*, *Fauxy* etc., which create fake news reports for entertainment. While some of these sources declare that the news/trolls and reports are for the purpose of entertainment alone and are not to be construed of as real, others such as *NewsWatch33* and *NewsBuzz Daily* mix real news with fake news to escape detection, often misleading the viewers by creating confusion. At a time when we frequently hear people saying "Just read the trolls on XYZ website to know what is happening", "Just listen to the ABC satirical commentary and you will actually get to know what happened", the power of such sites and programmes to mislead and confuse the common people is massive. Often, we are unable to detect the irony or the satirical nature of a 'news' article unless we are aware that the website or channel is designed specifically for satirising real news.

Trolls on a specific issue posted by two opposing political parties will definitely be at variance with each other; satirical news channels could publish biased news and pass it off as comedy; and sometimes, such pieces of news are taken up by mainstream media outlets and published as real news as happened in the case of an article titled "IRCTC website running slow due to fog: committee report" which appeared in the satirical news site *Faking News* on December 20, 2013 (it was published as a real news report by the leading media outlet *India Today* in its December 2013 issue). Satire often becomes a political weapon which, even while serving to challenge authoritarian regimes and policies, also contributes to malicious propaganda against rivals and gives rise to speculation and confusion, elements on which the post-truth society thrives.

Concluding Thoughts

The post-truth era is one fraught with dangers. With the unlimited potential of the media to spread misinformation masking it as 'believable' truths, with the number of citizen journalists with zero credentials on the rise, with the rise of fascist regimes drawing support and zeal from emotional outbursts and concocted stories, it is imperative that we remain alert and verify the credibility of people, events as well as so-called truths. 'Alt-facts' masquerade as truth today. If the post-truth regime is to be reined in, we first need to first strip off the masks of believability that 'alt-facts' assume. For this, we need to understand that alt-facts arising from and thriving on emotional manipulation are not facts and they can never ever be facts or the truth. *Post-veritas* is the adjective qualifying an unhealthy, unethical society; we cannot turn our faces away from the flow of innocent blood in the deluge of post-truth insinuations, for, unlike Pilate, we need to stop for answers and cannot wash our hands of the guilt incurred by omission or commission.

References

Bhadrakumar, M.K. (2019, April 13). Modi's post-truth politics. *The Week*. https://www.theweek.in/ columns/mk-bhadrakumar/2019/04/12/modis-post-truth-politics.html

Chopra, R. (2014, November 17). Ramayan, Mahabharat historical sources, West dubs them myth: Y Sudershan Rao. *The Economic Times*. https://economictimes.indiatimes.com/opinion/interviews/ramayan-mahabharat-historical-sources-west-dubs-them-myth-y-sudershan-rao/articleshow/45171587.cms

Cooke, N. A. (2018). *Fake news and alternative facts: Information literacy in a post-truth era*. ALA Editions.

Edelman, M. (2001). *The politics of misinformation*. Cambridge University Press.

Finchelstein, F. (2019, April 23). Why far-right populists are at war with history. *The Washington Post.* https://www.washingtonpost.com/outlook/2019/04/23/why-far-right-populists-are-war-with-history

Fuller, S. (2018). *Post-truth: Knowledge as a power game.* Anthem Press.

Hunted: India's lynch files. (2018). *The Quint.* https://www.thequint.com/ quintlab/ lynching-in-india

Jain, R. and T. Lasseter. (2018, March 6). By rewriting History, Indian Nationalists Aim to Assert their Dominance over India. *Reuters Investigates.* https://www.reuters. com / investigates/ special-report/india-modi-culture/

Kalpokas,I. (2019). *A political theory of post-truth.* Palgrave Pivot.

Keyes, R. (2004). *The post-truth era: Dishonesty and deception in contemporary life.* St.Martin's Press.

King James Bible. (2017). King James Bible Online. https://www. kingjamesbibleonline. org/(Original work published 1769)

Levitin, D. J. (2017). *Weaponized lies: How to think critically in the post-truth era.* Dutton.

Majumdar, A. (2013, September 12). Video circulated on Watsapp reportedly to blame for Muzaffarnagar riots, say officials. *First Post.* https://www.firstpost.com/ tech/news-analysis/video-circulated-on-whatsapp-reportedly-to-blame-for-muzaffarnagar-riots-say-officials-3636349.html

Mcintyre, L. (2018). *Post-Truth.* MIT Press.

Need to rewrite history from India's point of view. (2019, Oct.17). *The Hindu.* https://www.thehindu.com/news/national/need-to-rewrite-history-from-indias-point-of-view-amit-shah/article29724706.ece#comments_29724706

Rai, M.(2015, October 06). Like in Muzaffarnagar, social media misused in Dadri. *The Economic Times.* https://economictimes.indiatimes.com/news/politics-and-nation/like-in-muzaffarnagar-social-media-misused-in-dadri/articleshow/ 49235908.cms

Roberts, D. (2010, April 01). *Post-truth politics.* Grist. https://grist.org/article/2010-03-30-post-truth-politics

Safoora (2018, February 15). Times Now wrongly attributes a speech beginning with 'Jai Siya Ram' to Abu Dhabi crown prince. *The Siasat Daily.* https://archive. siasat.com/ news/times-now-wrongly-attributes-speech-starting-jai-siya-ram-abu-dhabi-crown-prince-1318582/

Saulles, M. D. (2012). *Information 2.0.* Facet Publishing.

Sengupta, S. (2016, February 21). The tricolor over Iwo Jima: The BJP confuses Photoshop for history yet again. *Scroll.* https://scroll.in/article/803920/the-tricolour-over-iwo-jima-the-bjp-confuses-photoshop-for-history-yet-again

Singh, R. (2013, December 20). IRCTC website running slow due to fog: committee report. *Faking News.* http://onlinefakingnews.blogspot.com/2013/12/irctc-website-running-slow-due-to-fog.html

The Quint. (2019, August 6). *Here's a round-up of all the fake news about unrest in Kashmir* [Video]. YouTube. https://www.youtube.com/watch?v=RtXS8jy7P-c

Times Now. (2016, February 11). *Tribute to Afzal Guru at JNU – Students crossed all lines?– The Newshour Debate* [Video]. YouTube. https://www.youtube.com/watch?v=oGN2KOJMaeM

TRT World. (2018, February 13). *Fake news propagated by Indian media goes viral* [Video]. YouTube. https://www.youtube.com/watch?v=AKrQ8fjRFb8

WatchMojo. (2018, January 31). *Top ten biggest fake news stories* [Video]. YouTube. https://www.youtube.com/watch?v=TmlI4581g-o

Weatherall, J. O, C. Connor, & C. Stephens. (2019). *The misinformation age: How false beliefs spread.* Yale University Press.

CHAPTER 3

Beyond Misinformation: Post-truth and Nudge Theory

Patrick Agbedejobi

This chapter seeks to analyse the relationship between post-truth and nudge theory. Thus, the pertinent question of this chapter is - what role does nudge theory play in the post-truth era?

Nudge theory as postulated by Richard Thaler and Cass Sunstein (2009) posits that when people are faced with choices related to public policies, nudging is actualised when people follow their automatic system (gut feelings, emotional response or reaction) rather than the reflective system (conscious thought or logical reasoning). Despite the limited view of Thaler and Sunstein definition (2009) restraining nudging to public choices, several other scholarly works have expanded the field in which nudge theory can be utilised, namely: politics – voting, electoral speeches, educational policies, behavioural and choice architecture, marketing strategies, populism research to mention but a few (Weijers et al., 2020; Ewert 2020; Schubert 2017; Chriss 2015; Desai 2011; Oklopcic 2019).

The similarity between nudge theory and post-truth communication is intensified by the preference of subjective feelings and perspective as against logical thinking, epistemic truth or objective preference. One can, therefore, associate such submission to the utilisation of post-truth rhetoric by politicians to amass support for public choice(s) posed by policies, manifestoes or political speech. In the same vein, some elements of politicians' persuasive speech act appeal rather to the emotion in the post-truth era than epistemic truth. This symbolises a form of direct or indirect persuasion which reiterates the core principles of nudge theory. The foregoing explains Mongin and Cozic's (2018) assertion that nudge is: "any aspect of the choice architecture that predictably alters people's behaviour without forbidding any option or significantly changing their economic incentives" (p.109).

In a nutshell, Mongin and Cozic (2018) understanding of nudge is represented in three phases: firstly, nudge as an intervention that interferes with choice conditions minimally, secondly, an intervention that utilises rationality failures instrumentally, and thirdly, an intervention that seeks to reduce negative effects of rationality failure. As such, the distinction between the automatic system and the reflective system resounds the inevitability of making emotional, unconscious thinking, fast and effortless decisions. To buttress this point, Thaler and Sunstein (2008), Stanovich (1999) categorised nudging into System 1 and System 2; where system 1 represents the automatic way of processing information and system 2 embraces reflective and deductive reasoning which informs decision making or choice.

This chapter perceives nudge theory intersection with post-truth as an intervention through speech act by politicians which exploits rationality failures of its audience instrumentally. Thus, when a politician employs rhetoric that says, 'Make America Great Again' (MAGA) in combination with other speech act and messages, such politician is actively or indirectly nudging the audience towards a specific policy choice or political horizon. In other words, the affective choices made by the electorates on election day represents a response to post-truth intervention. This intervention could be depicted as a combination of post-truth elements, fear, uncertainty and challenge of individual or group status quo.

However, despite the theoretical submission of nudge theory and its intersection with affective meaning and post-truth politics, critics have debunked the normative and political perspective that nudging only works when indirectly exploited. Some other critics also stated that manipulating people's choices is incompatible with public policy-making in modern-day democracy (Stanovich, 1999; Weijers et al., 2020; Hansen and Jespersen, 2013). This is fostered by the perspective that state manipulation in terms of choices of citizens is contradicted by the democratic ethos of free will, deliberation and public dialogue.

Despite the foregoing claims disapproving the role of nudge theory and its affective side in modern society, the author argues that the intersection of nudge theory and post-truth politics is dependent on several enabling or underlying factors. For instance, the defining traits of postmodernity generate a democratic disconnect between the political class or representatives and the electorate. This disconnect according to

Corduwener (2019, p. 40-44) and Waisbord (2018, p. 17-18) is substantiated by the evidence of party-state entanglement and its consolidation in contemporary societies. The party-state entanglement thesis assumes that parties have moved ever closer to the state. This closeness to the state sees political parties as semi-state agents with a lost connection to society. This assumption of a disconnect between political parties due to party-state entanglement and the loss of support at the societal or grassroots level partly explains the emergence of post-truth politicians pre/post-2016. Post-truth politics and communication, therefore, post-2016 is motivated by the democratically adverse aftermaths and leftovers of such schism between those who rule and those who command.

Another crucial enabling factor is the exploitation of social media amidst the poor regulation of social media use both by the government and social media firms. The main argument proposed here is that nudging is frequently exploited in conjunction with other structural shifts and imbalances in contemporary society, like digitalisation, algorithmic personalisation, big data which contributed to the prevalence of the post-truth era. We have learned that representatives and citizens alike are often unaware of digital surveillance, privacy hacks, information gathering on social media exposed by Cambridge Analytica and the financial flows in a digital global network (the Panama and Paradise leaks). However, the forces of digitalisation, big data, bots and algorithm economy represent an infinite reservoir of opportunities for malicious forces to debilitate democratic institutions or subvert epistemic truth. Unlike in the era where people could only get information or news through local and international newspapers, the freedom to write, publish without any constraint or delay and reach a global audience is possible today. Combining the ease, speed and freedom at which information can be accessed or disseminated today, the article lends theoretical and analytical weight to the argument that post-truth is a combination of both endogenous and exogenous factors in global politics.

Political Communication in the Post-truth Era and Nudge Theory

Iyengar and Massey (2018) depiction of the post-truth era and enabling conditions provides a useful starting point for unravelling political communication. It is argued that information overload is no longer the core problem. Instead, distrust in epistemic truth and scientific facts are influenced by misperceptions of scientific knowledge and biased information disseminated by post-truth.

Consequently, the helplessness and lack of preparation of the scientific community for the post-truth tsunami justifies the relative victory of post-truth peddlers.

By extension, Salgado (2018, p. 318) reminds us that post-truth political communication is nothing new. The newness about it is amplified by digitalisation, the speed and global audience reach, ubiquity and instructiveness of the internet alongside social media platforms which are exploited to disseminate false information or fake news. The exploitation of digitalisation by post-truth peddlers through algorithmic personalisation and bots is magnified by developers and programmers who design and programme artificial intelligence, open and closed software alongside scripts that promote innovation and new boundaries where legality or illegality of such innovations are untested.

However, it is crucial to note that the core arguments of the post-truth era are not exactly new in politics and media. The production and dissemination of false information to achieve political goals is also nothing new. Arendt extensively wrote about deception and defactualisation in politics. Arendt (1972) depicted defactualisation, as the 'deliberate denial of factual truth' 'and the capacity to alter facts', (p. 4). Arendt opined that truthfulness has never been existent in politics and lies have always been a justifiable tool in political dealings. The post-2016 era is an amplification of that fact which was further ignited by nudging and the underlying issues earlier discussed.

Therefore, the new media environment with its interactivity and global audience reach does not directly or indirectly equate to novelty. Instead, it should be settled here that the features of political communication witnessed in contemporary societies is just a replication of old propaganda magnified and intensified by a better media in terms of its uniqueness and ability to reach a wider global audience (Lippmann, 1997). Political communication in the pre and post-truth era is confronted by the conscious and intelligent manipulation of facts and emotions in a democratic society. This buttresses the nudge theory position that the masses can be manipulated by appealing to their rationality and exploiting their automatic system i.e exploitation of the basic gut feeling to promote an agenda or policy in contemporary society.

This is purely evinced by the era of the post-2016 politics where Trump and the Brexit referendum welcomed a 'new epoch of post-truth' and a democratic crisis. Similarly, Lippmann (1997) reiterated that the media is highly susceptible to manipulation and that facts were usually utilised to represent specific interpretations that benefit the partisan interest or a politician's goal. Thus, considering the aims of post-truth today, we have a rich amount of scholarship that had predicted post-truth although not in a viral or dynamically incremental manner as demonstrated by the internet and social media platforms.

Consequently, Habermas (1992) perception of the public sphere and his campaign for an active rather than passive public is quite critical to comprehending the political communication in contemporary societies. Stemming from Habermas (1992) assertion, that: 'the quality of society depends much on its capacity to communicate, debate and discuss'. Retrospectively, an active deliberative democratic society demands that each area of policy and political life is under debate and intense consensual approval to avoid division in the society. For Habermas, the reason is pivotal to communication as well as the relations between social order, social action, and discourse in the public sphere- here depicted as deliberative politics-*sich auseinandersetzen.*

Thus, if the reason is substituted for emotions or partisan interests, it is highly probable that its antithesis results in post-truth, where facts, reason or rationality are exchanged for symbolic buffoonery and fake news. The position of Habermas questions how active our present global public sphere is and the existing structures dependent on neoliberalism and capitalism. Some scholars have exploited the effects of digitalisation and information overload as the consequence of the present docile and gut feeling choices made by the masses in the public sphere. But rather than blaming digitalisation as the sole or enabling wheel of post-truth. I argue that digitalisation and its numerous aftermaths is not totally responsible for the emergence of post-truth. Instead, the arrival of post-truth political communication is dependent on contingent and underlying social issues in most polities.

In summary, the endogenous causation of the post-truth era is a function of structural and institutional neglect of the masses. These endogenous issues are deeply integrated with contemporary societies. For instance, the global financial crisis from 2007-2012 had its fair share of the polarisation currently witnessed on a global scale. It is further worsened by democratic disconnect-i.e. a lack of faith and trust in democratic institutions leading to electorates seeking alternatives. Most importantly, the rise of populism is a direct aftermath of the issues faced by contemporary societies. Hence, political communication post-2016 did not occur without a trigger nor did it solely benefit from digitalisation. Rather, the birth of post-truth is regrettably a consequence of the failure of liberal parties in European and American polities to heed the cries of neglect, marginalised communities and schism in their polities over the years. Inevitably, we now have a polarised political landscape that is ripe for the consolidation and the reign of post-truth politicians.

Conclusion

Despite the brevity of this chapter, the arguments and submission disclose a relationship between post-truth communication and nudge theory. Political communication in the post-truth era is characterised by a distinctive use of technology alongside underlying multifaceted societal issues which provoke automatic responses of the electorates. As such, nudging takes a central stage through the use of speech act, symbolic buffoonery among other strategies to engage the public through affective and persuasive tropes. The recipient of such speech is nudged towards making an automatic political choice. This chapter also disclosed that post-truth communication relies mostly on automatic as against reflexive decision making or choices.

References

Arendt, H. (1967, February 17). 'Truth and politics'. *The New Yorker*, https://www.newyorker.com/magazine/1967/02/25/truth-and-politics

Arendt, H. (1972). *'Lying in politics', Crisis of the Republic: Lying in politics. Civil disobedience. On violence, Thoughts on Politics and Revolution.* Harcourt Brace & Company.

Corduwener, P. (2020). Democracy and the entanglement of political parties and the state: party-state relations in 20th Century France, Italy, and Germany. *Comparative Political Studies,* 53(1), 40-70.

Chriss, J.J. (2015). Nudging and Social Marketing. *Society*, 52, 54-61. doi:10.1007/s12115-014-9858-y

Desai, A. (2011). Libertarian Paternalism, Externalities, and the "Spirit of Liberty": How Thaler and Sunstein Are Nudging Us toward an "Overlapping Consensus". *Law & Social Inquiry*, 36(1), 263-295. doi:10.1111/j.1747-4469.2010.01231.x

Ewert, B. (2020). Moving beyond the obsession with nudging individual behaviour: Towards a broader understanding of Behavioural Public Policy. *Public Policy and Administration*, 35(3), 337-360. https://doi.org/10.1177/0952076719889090

Habermas, J. (1992). *The Structural transformation of the public sphere: An inquiry into a category of Bourgeois Society.* Polity Press.

Hansen, P., & Jespersen, A. (2013). Nudge and the Manipulation of Choice: A Framework for the Responsible Use of the Nudge Approach to Behaviour Change in Public Policy. *European Journal of Risk Regulation,* 4(1), 3-28. doi:10.1017/S1867299X00002762

Iyengar, S & Massey D. (2018). Scientific communication in a post- truth society. *Proceedings of the National Academy of Sciences of the United States of America*, 116(16), 7656-7661.

Lippmann, W. (1997). *Public opinion.* Free Press paperbacks.

Mongin, P., & Cozic, M. (2018). Rethinking nudge: Not one but three concepts. *Behavioural Public Policy,* 2(1), 107-124. doi:10.1017/bpp.2016.16

Oklopcic, Z. (2019). Imagined ideologies: Populist figures, liberalist projections, and the horizons of constitutionalism. *German Law Journal,* 20(2), 201-224. doi:10.1017/glj.2019.13

Salgado, S. (2018). Online media impact on politics. Views on post-truth politics and post-postmodernism. *International Journal of Media & Culture,* 14(3), 317-331.

Schubert, C. (2017). Exploring the (behavioural) political economy of nudging. *Journal of Institutional Economics,* 13(3), 499 - 522. doi.org/10.1017/S1744137416000448.

Stanovich, K. E. (1999). *Who is rational? studies of individual differences in reasoning.* Psychology Press.

Thaler, R.H., & Sunstein, C.R. (2009). *Nudge: Improving decisions about health, wealth, and happiness.* Yale University Press.

Waisbord, S. (2018). The elective affinity between post-truth communication and populist politics. *Communication Research and Practice*, 4(1), 17-34.

Weijers, R.J., Koning, B.B., & Paas, F. (2020). Nudging in education: from theory towards guidelines for successful implementation. *European Journal of Psychology of Education,* https://link.springer.com/article/10.1007%2Fs10212-020-00495-0

CHAPTER 4

Signs and the Science of Truth: Language, Power and Performance in the Post-truth Era

Cerin Babu

The postmodern age is characterised by permissiveness and narcissism which drives people to cocoon themselves in comforting lies and employ forms of casual deception to achieve their goals. In short, people subvert truth in such a way that it will not affect, threaten or sabotage their personal ideologies. These features make post-truth applicable to both political and personal discourse dictated by social norms or as they say, social contract intended to gain social acceptance. This chapter in fact tries to probe into the significatory power of language in a post-truth scenario, the mechanism of how meaning is made when texts and images are united to create a post-truth reality in the pretext of Derrida's concept of *différance*. The chapter attempts to examine Irish novelist John Boyne's *The Boy in the Striped Pyjamas* to understand the role of the speaking subject and how his/ her language attains force, effectiveness and meaning in a post-truth setting.

As Lee Mc Intyre (2018) points out, there are myriad ways in which people subvert the truth. He cites falsehood, willful ignorance, and lying as different forms in which post-truth is manifested. Despite all these forms, he says, the most virulent form of post-truth is self-deception and delusion whereby someone actually believes a lie that virtually all credible sources will dispute (p. 17). Thus, the distortion of what is accepted as truth is seen on all levels-personal and social. This chapter attempts to examine the phenomenon of post-truth on a personal level, taking out instances from the novel *The Boy in the Striped Pyjamas* for the same. The novel narrates the story of Bruno, a German boy living in

Berlin during World War II. His Father is a commandant in the Nazi army who finds a new job in a place he calls 'Out-with' and their family had to move to their new home in Out-with. Being a boy who loves adventure, he is excited for once, despite his gloomy surroundings, when he finds Shmuel, a pale, thin boy, on the other side of the tall fence surrounding his new home. The story progresses through the narration of Bruno about his maid Maria and their help Pavel, the soldiers who roam around his new home at all times, his attempts to steer clear of his troublesome sister Gretel. It describes how he identifies with Shmuel, the Jewish boy, their secret meetings and consequent epiphanies regarding the truth of the situation. His friendship with Shmuel leads to unexpected consequences in the end. This chapter attempts to read the novel in such a way that Bruno, the German boy protagonist is seen as the recipient of the post-truth phenomenon and his Father, the commandant in the Nazi army, as the agent of post-truth. The arguments and reasons for the same will be discussed in the subsequent paragraphs.

Reflexivity and Loss of Faith

It is discerned that the advocates of post-truth attempt to invalidate truth and the rhetorical strategies adopted with this intent derive their effectiveness from two discursive strands. The first strand is the endless reflexivity, characteristic of this age, which is exemplified by continuous questioning and critiquing that never yield consensus or come to an agreement (Gibson 2018). Every statement, opinion, ritual or social norm is criticised and questioned. Bruno, for example, in the novel is seen continuously questioning his mother and their maid Maria regarding his Father's job and their sudden shifting of home. It is this curious and probing frame of mind that leads him in the end to realise actuality regarding what is otherwise portrayed by his family as natural and normal. It is evident that the truth value of anything is questioned, challenged and modified 'as time calls for it. It follows that any element of knowledge or fact will be revised at any point of time in future. Truth is not guaranteed for eternity. Any statement that is pronounced true is actually true only 'for the time being'. It will be replaced and makes room for the new 'truth' and this goes on forever. There is hence a generalised uncertainty. Here, the term, 're-embedding', as Giddens puts it, gains relevance. This term points out to how faith is held up in interactions between lay people and institutional authority. For instance, the professional demeanour of the doctor, confidence and attire of the lawyer, mannerisms and authority of the teacher showcases a certain sense of certainty. However, it is not complete. There is always uncertainty, scepticism and fear. For instance, in the novel by Boyne, it is found that even though Bruno is not entirely sure about what job his Father did, he understands that his work is important and that he is a man to watch.

> But when they asked Bruno what his Father did, he opened his mouth to tell them, then realised that he didn't know himself. All he could say was that he was a man to watch and that the Fury had big things in mind for him. Oh, and that he had a fantastic uniform too.
>
> (Boyne, 2006, p. 18)

The uniform his Father wore, its grandeur, the soldiers waiting to follow his orders and the aura his Father has, had kept Bruno in awe and complements his notion of his Father being an authority, an important man who is not to be messed with.

The second strand is a fundamental loss of faith in institutions that lend credence to some truths over others- a phenomenon that Slavoj Zizek termed as 'Demise of Symbolic efficiency.' According to Slavoj Zizek, Symbolic efficiency refers to the ability of the institutional authority to pronounce what is true and what is false and simultaneously gain public acceptance for the same. He calls the institutional authority the 'Big Other' (Gibson, 2018). However, this Big Other, we should understand, is just a set of flawed humans who is no different from any of us. These two strands- loss of faith and endless reflexivity form the basis of post-truth politics.

Construction of Reality: Role of Narratives and Power Structure

The modern age believes that truth is neither given to nor disclosed to but produced by human minds. As per the structuralist school of criticism, human beings use a system of signs-language – to create reality or a part of it, which places them very much in their comfort zone. Here, language acquires a status more than that of a system to aid communication. They are the tools in the hands of humans to create reality. Human beings are innate storytellers. Stories are the human way of making sense of things. Narrative structures are a device that humans use to slot information into a meaningful form. People liven up to social and political participation by means of fictional narratives and their emotional appeal. For instance, people vote for a particular political leader because they liked, in fact, loved the narration created and presented by the leader at that point of time. It has very little to do with truth or fact. Such narratives tap into the deeper recesses of social consciousness and connect to or relate to a deeper public want. Since the narrative presented, more or less narrates a world as envisioned by the majority public, there will be a greater consensus among the public in this matter. This becomes their story, their truth. Not unlike how people believe in myths and legends, which has no truth value but fantasy and romance attached to it, they will believe in this story too, thus showing their willingness to undermine truth even when they know that the narrative is not based on fact or reality. This becomes their truth for now. Since everybody has a story, all humans are agents of post-truth in one way or the other.

Thus, post-truth remains a phenomenon that distorts both political and personal discourse. The rest is determined by their status, their position in the power structure and other external factors. This happens within a family too as it can also be considered as a unit/ system which is not devoid of a hierarchy or a power dynamic. It is clear that post-truth is a result of man's want of comfort- where he does not want any fact/ statement threatening his position or peace of mind. Consequently, post-truth is a weapon in the hands of people who want to subvert a power structure. Needless to say, there is nothing wrong in suggesting that while the powerful in the society uses post-truth to safeguard or build up their authority and control over the weaker sections. However, the people at the far end of the hierarchy of power, the weak ones, have their options which are three-fold: they can choose to believe what is being narrated/ presented before them; or they can have their doubts regarding the facts being presented but choose not to voice out their apprehensions about the truth of the narrative; or they can choose to rebel against the one in control of the discourse to subvert the power structure. The response to the narrative being presented depends upon various factors.

On keen observation, it is discerned that a post-truth phenomenon will have an agent (the one who causes the event or the one who presents the lie/ 'alternate' truth) and a listener or recipient (who could be one person or as in political discourse, the public). As in the novel, we can identify Bruno as the listener/ recipient who accepts the authority of his commandant Father who can be regarded as the agent of post-truth considering the way he hides horrific details regarding the truth of the situation – that the other side of the fence is actually a concentration camp meant for torturing Jewish people – to his son

Bruno. Much is not revealed to Bruno who either due to his ignorance or due to the love and loyalty he has for his Father, believes his Father to be a good and virtuous man and not even for a moment doubts him. Bruno, as we discussed earlier, blindly believes the narrative that his family narrates to him regarding the life and people and life on the other side of the fence. His sister says at one instance in the novel: "it must be a rehearsal…Not the type of children I want to play with. They are filthy" (Boyne, 2006, p. 36).

The response to the narrative being presented by the agent before a person/ public depends on the status quo, their respective positions in the power structure, the relationship between them (particularly when we think about family as a structural unit) and sometimes even complete ignorance on part of the listener/ public regarding the matters being discussed. At times as mostly seen in totalitarian regimes, the power structure demands the recipient/s or the public to be loyal and unquestioning to the higher authority, otherwise, their safety and security are threatened. Sometimes people need things to go on as it is without any turbulence that revelation of truth might set off. Taking advantage of the various factors, powerful people manage to weaponise fiction and deploy it in order to gain trust, loyalty or control over the public or the individual. Just like how Bruno's Father establishes himself as the authority at home and remains 'Out of Bounds at All Times and No Exceptions' (Boyne, 2006, p. 22). He finds himself unable to question his father, for he is his loving Father at all times and everyone in his family listens to his Father and obeys him no matter what.

So, there is always a powerplay to win social acceptance (whether voluntary or involuntary) and post-truth has become part and parcel of this social contract. Social control is maintained by creating a fog of narratives. The dominant narrative is contradicted by alternative narratives, thus finding it difficult to prove the credibility of the knowledge source which accounts for the existence of multiple truths. The goal here is not to come up with an all-comprehensive narrative but rather it generates complex, multiple narratives which speaks the same language but reflects multiple dimensions which are at times contrary to the dominant narrative. This generates scepticism.

Post-Truth and Performance

It is said that, in classical oratory and rhetoric, the effectiveness of a performance or presentation depends largely on the persuasive power of the orator who strives to present an argument in such a way that it is factual at the same time rational. It is effective mostly when it can tap into your emotions. Keeping this in mind in conjunction with the idea of how humans use narratives to make sense of things or to create their own version of reality, it can be said that, everything is a performance. The agent of post-truth can be equated to an actor who performs on stage in this context. He performs in such a way that people experience the reality that appeals to their emotions. But there are other factors also which aid this process. The actor on stage makes use of his dialogues, tone, intonation, costumes. The novel witnesses Bruno's Father presenting a narration and 'performing' (hiding the facts) before his kids with all his grandeur, for several reasons. He wants to establish himself as the authority in his family. He, being a doting father, also wants to hide the gruesome details of life and people on the other side of the fence from his kids which might tarnish his image as a perfect human being.

> Father was at the centre of them and looked very smart in his freshly pressed uniform. His thick dark hair had obviously been recently lacquered and combed and as Bruno watched from above, he felt both scared and in awe of him. He didn't like the look of the other men quite as much. They certainly weren't as handsome as Father...Nor were their voices so booming or their boots so polished. They all held their caps under their arms and seemed to be fighting with each other for Father's attention.
>
> (Boyne, 2006, p. 39)

Post-Truth and Signification: How it Works?

As discussed earlier, signs do create reality and language is a tool in the hands of humans to create the reality that is best suited for them. As Ferdinand de Saussure explains in his structuralist theory, language is a system of signs which is constituted by a signifier and signified. The words used (signifier) implicates an innate meaning (signified) that makes possible communication. However, as an extension to this, Jacques Derrida argued that if the relationship between the signifier and signified is arbitrary and all language is relational, then the process of 'reading' is a movement from one signifier to another. There is no end to signification. We are not faced with a signified but rather with another signifier and this goes on. As Derrida points out, every signifier refers to other words/ signifiers in an endless postponement-deference-of meaning. Writing and language is difference – a combination of difference and deference (Nayar, 2010, p. 33-42). In this context, it is important to analyse what happens in a post-truth situation. To make it clear, what happens when a person (from hereafter referred to as an agent of post-truth) speaks a lie, or more accurately, a part of the truth? How is it understood by the listener? What are the factors that determine the listener's understanding of the situation and acceptance of the truth element, if at all there is one, in what is spoken? Who is the master of this discourse? Is it the agent who initiated the post-truth discourse or is it the recipient?

These are very relevant questions in the context of the post-truth scenario. Suppose the agent of post- truth delivers a statement to the recipient who could be an individual or the public as a group. As and when the agent speaks out the alternate truth statement and the recipient receives it, the process of signification begins in which the listener has an active role to play. If you look at it through the linguistic lens, one can infer that the statement (or the text as per linguistic terminology), offers clues to the recipient to decode. He/she deciphers the meaning of the statement through the process of difference and deference. Signification is always a negotiation between language and the listener/ recipient. According to Derrida, signification thrives primarily on difference and every signifier is made up of an absence. If that is so, it follows that, in a post-truth scenario, the recipient understands the alternate truth (or lie) statement by juxtaposing it with the truth (because a lie is ultimately indicative of the existence of truth). This juxtaposition of the truth and untruth is followed by a process of selection on part of the recipient. In fact, though it may seem paradoxical, the recipient can choose between the truth and the lie. The process of selection out of these binaries by the recipient will be coloured by various factors which include his/ her ideologies, relationship with the agent, position in the power structure etc. Given the circumstances, it can be inferred that though the powerful agent uses post-truth to control the weak recipient, the master of this discourse turns out to be the recipient because the process of signification and production of meaning is in the hands of the listener and not of the speaker (the agent in this context). The novel, for instance, portrays how Bruno despite the restrictions from his Father, he accompanies Shmuel to the other side of the fence promising that he will help Shmuel to search for his Father. If not fully, Bruno realises, despite his Father's narration, for a fact that life on other side of the fence is not as pleasant as he thought it would be. Although Bruno's Father has been portrayed right from the outset as the authority, the one in control, he turns out to be helpless in the end when he loses his son in the camp to probably death or a fate that is even worse.

> Father stayed at Out-With for another year after that... he went to sleep every night thinking about Bruno and he woke up every morning thinking about him too.... a few months after that some other soldiers came to Out-With and Father was ordered to go with them, and he went without complaint.
>
> (Boyne, 2006, p. 139)

It is seen that Bruno's epiphanies throughout the course of the novel regarding various characters transformed him so much so that he took things into his control. The novel describes the first time when he recognised that their maid Maria was in fact a person with a life and an opinion of her own. He also realises that Pavel is not just a help but was once a doctor. This led him to the epiphany that not everything was as it appeared. He did have a glimpse of the truth or at least a part of it that shocked him. He considers Shmuel as his best friend and willingly goes with him to the other side of the fence against his Father's orders. Thus, even though Bruno accepted whatever his Father told him as the truth initially (which is largely due to his ignorance), he realised the facts and chose to help Shmuel; a tiny but relevant attempt on part of Bruno to question the authority; a minor attempt at subversion of power. This is transformation.

Thus, to put things into perspective, it can be said that how the speaker/ recipient interprets truth matters more than what is being spoken. The agent or speaker might intent to mean something but it may not always be understood as exactly as he/ she wants, by the recipient. After all, as Derrida says, the meaning is inevitably postponed.

Conclusion

This chapter concludes by stating that post-truth is a personal discourse as much as a political one. What is considered applicable to the political arena also applies to our personal sphere of which each individual family is a fundamental unit with a power dynamic. Despite the attempts made by the agents of post-truth to uphold people's faith in institutional authority, it fails as there is scepticism and fear in the minds of the public. The existence of multiple truths or their dimensions makes it impossible to vouch for a single and absolute truth. Truth or reality is a human construction. Human beings use signs to construct a reality that caters to and not threaten their beliefs and ideologies. Every person is an actor narrating his/ her reality. He/ she is an agent of post-truth. His/ her conviction, beliefs and ideologies, position in the power structure, and relationship with other beings determine his/ her perception of truth. Once an agent of post-truth initiates the dialogue, the process of signification helps the recipient to perceive the statement being made by the agent. Perception however is part and parcel of the negotiation that happens between the recipient and the text (in this context, the statement made by the agent). The agent of post-truth has very little participation in this process. As Derrida says, there is no absolute signified (Nayar, 2010). In the process of signification, due to the combined mechanism of difference and deference, the recipient juxtaposes truth with untruth. Though the power and control may be within the hands of the agent as he represents authority, it is surprising to note that the choice between the binaries of truth and untruth is seemingly in the hands of the recipient. What he chooses to believe determines who is in power.

References

Arendt, H. (1967). Truth and Politics. In David Wood & Jose Medina (Eds.), *Truth: Engagements across Philosophical Traditions* (pp. 295-314). Blackwell Publishing.

Benesch, K. (2020). Is Truth to Post-Truth what Modernism Is to Postmodernism? Heidegger, the Humanities, and the Demise of Common-Sense. *European Journal of American Studies*, (pp. 15-1). https://doi.org/10.4000/ejas.15619

Boyne, J. (2006). *The Boy in the Striped Pyjamas.* Random House Books. https://www.pdfdrive.com/the-boy-in-the-striped-pajamas-e55344757.html

Buffachi, V. (2021). Truth, Lies and Tweets: A Consensus Theory of Post-Truth. *Philosophy and Social Criticism, 47*(3), 347-361. https://doi.org/10.1177%2F0191453719896382

Corby, J. (2019). The Post-Literary, Post-Truth, and Modernity. *CounterText*, 5(1), 33–69. https://doi.org/10.3366/count.2019.0150

D' Ancona, M. (2017). *Post-Truth: The New War on Truth and How to Fight Back.* Penguin.

Fridlund, P. (2020). Post-truth Politics, Performatives and the Force. Jus Cogens, 2(3), 215-235. https://doi.org/10.1007/s42439-020-00029-8

Fuller, S. (2018). *Post-truth: knowledge as a power game.* Anthem Press.

Gibson, T. A. (2018). The Post-Truth Double Helix: Reflexivity and Mistrust in Local Politics. *International Journal of Communication, 12*(19), 3167-85. https://ijoc.org/index.php/ijoc/article/view/7738

Giddens, A. (1990). *The Consequences of Modernity.* Stanford University Press. https://www.pdfdrive.com/the-consequences-of-modernity-by-anthony-giddens-e49855792.html

Hyvönen, A-E. (2018). Defining Post-truth: Structures, Agents, and Styles. *E-International Relations.* https://www.e-ir.info/2018/10/22/defining-post-truth-structures-agents-and-styles/

Keyes, R. (2004). *The post-truth era: dishonesty and deception in contemporary life.* St. Martin's Press. https://www.pdfdrive.com/the-post-truth-era-dishonesty-and-deception-in-contemporar y-life-e194608387.html

McIntyre, L. (2018). *Post-Truth.* The MIT Press. https://www.pdfdrive.com/post-truth-d184705858.html

Nayar, P. K. (2010). *Contemporary and Literary Cultural Theory.* Dorling Kindersley.

Sim, S. (2019). *Post-truth, scepticism & power.* Palgrave Macmillan. https://www.pdfdrive.com/post-truth-scepticism-power-e189934963.html

CHAPTER 5

Surveillance, Media and Memory: The Absence of Truth and the Discourse of Gaming

Manodip Chakraborty

Homo-sapiens are among the very few vertebrates, living on this planet that can potentially cause harm through violence to their own species. Any form of understanding of such violent human nature will always end in controversiality. When and why there arose a form of *restraint* on the potentially violent nature is also debatable. In the diachronic evolution, this 'restraint' has acquired its metaphoric equivalents as 'government', 'society', 'culture', 'politics', 'democracy' and such others – all are the means 'to restrain'. Such restraint elements are always in an avant-garde position "anxious and fearful about the sources of injury that they could not see" (Rosen, 2005, p. 19). To put an end to the *sources of injury,* they are continuously experimenting with their elements of manipulations and as it happened, in the 21st century social media platforms have emerged as the *acknowledged phenomenon.* The power-politics have long realised that if by providing 'them' with the illusions of choice; a particular form of the platform can be made available to the masses – it becomes easier to exercise control on their restrainment(s). The *pedagogical* way, where a child (raw material) is programmed to learn (with or without his/her will) the discourses of society by repetitive rote learning; is the exact discursive tool, used by the media to feed us. The repetition of a singular semantic act on the screen enables the individual's prefrontal cortex, to accept them as 'truth' – irrespective of validity or invalidity. The subject's own *consciousness*, even before its proper conscious manifestation has been turned into a product of circulation at the hands of media. What is truth, from what is non-truth, cannot be demarcated anymore. As it is not the 'intellectuals', who are in control of what will be counted as valid 'knowledge'; but media is – all for the sake of restraining the violent element of human nature.

Manifesting Consents: Surveillance and Discourses

Estranged individuals in contemporary society are programmable transhumans – organic on the outside, codified on the inside. The individuals' overindulgence on Facebook, Whatsapp, Twitter, YouTube, and such other media platforms as essential amenities clearly hints at being them more than just entertainments. They possess the mechanisms to tap into the inner selves of individuals. The bourgeoning status of media is a necessity for the proper functioning of democratic ideals. By digging the similes and metaphors from the past 'events' (known or unknown), social media can alter any form of established 'essences'. As Gabrielle Cosentino (2020) has observed: "We now live in a post-truth world... such world, primarily operating on social media, is taking more and more dystopian contours" (p. 11).

The natural outcome against such a 'contour' is revolt – but *revolt* too in the hands of media has become a commodified metaphor. As not only our physical face-to-face discourses are under surveillance, where a representative of the superior authority will dictate the decorum of communications; "even without a specific surveillance programme at the place we run the risk of being under surveillance when we communicate using digital media" (Taekke, 2011, p. 3). The erection of such a panoptical media atmosphere ensures the production of every act – whether human or non-human, determining their legitimacy even before their actual manifestation in the real world.

Such desperate measures at legitimisation are not primarily because they are concerned with the correction of an individual's behaviour, but because of their collective phobia of an imaginative *threatening* that could uproot their democratic ideals. This omnipresence of a threatening element, hints towards the presence of an omnipotent human drive, something that has not yet been 'legitimised'; something that could always return to threaten any erected manifestations. The invention of *authentic discourses* in this context – served as an impetus to prevent any form of backlash – all forms of 'consents' are 'authenticated', all forms of 'perversion' are 'relegated'.

As the element of *threatening* or violence is common to all animal species and for human beings, it is phylogenetic in nature; located in "the sympathetic nervous system, a part of the autonomous nervous system that controls the internal state of the body" (Archer, 2009, p. 205). Many of the peaceful individuals under its sway are "capable of physical violence" (Payne, 2015, p. 17). Therefore to maintain their status-quo, the media apparatus need to eradicate any form of 'first-person point of views' – search for 'self', 'facts'; analysis of 'meaning of facts' – which will eventually lead to a diagnosis of hidden paradoxes of society, and ultimately to violent conjecture.

Consciousness and Spectatorship: The Non-existent Domain of Video Games

What they needed is not simply a spatial domain that can control the discharge of violent apparatus, but also a place that can superimpose their discourse of truth as the univocal *truth*. Violent video games surfaced as the *paratextual* tool in this respect. Signified as the under-rated object, it possesses a space that exists in cybertextual discourses, i.e. it is equally present and absent. Being present at the level of virtual reality it can function as the discharge mechanism from the potentially violent individuals (who are fearful of a *discharge* in the real world), also being an absent space (from *real* reality) it cannot return to threaten the superficiality of governmentality. "Spectators" in this regard "have a double relationship to special effects, simultaneously being complicit – with the illusion while also being critical of how the illusion is achieved" (Ayers, 2019, p. 88). But, the gaming sphere perpetually obscures such approaches, thereby eternally restricting the individuals in discursive hypertextual schemata.

Video Games are the conscious space of absence. The gamers are potentially aware of its virtuality, yet individuals cannot restrain themselves from being immersed in it. Being immersed in the gameplay, the gamer or the subject suffers "a loss of a sense of time, place or self" (Dovey & Kennedy, 2006, p. 8). These subjects prefer the loss of spatiality and temporality of their existence for a non-existent space, not simply because it is immersive; rather the *gaming mechanism* is designed with a *reward mechanism* – the very carnal satisfaction that every human-animal hankers after. Why the obsessions for a non-existent reward mechanism? As psychoanalysis has long established the loss of *'the object'* in psychosexual development is the root cause for any form of human manifestations. The collective ontological or epistemological exuberances to date have failed to satisfy this craving for the *object*. As a natural output, the fragmented individuals are still looking for a potential 'object' (sign) that have *the potentiality* to replace their lack of *'the object'* (the signified). Such reward mechanisms based on individual achievements are largely absent from the real world scenario. The media-dominated *real-world* rewards only those subjects who have abandoned their subjectivity and have accepted the norms and mechanisms of governments as just and upright.

Configuring the Real: Immersive Non-reality

Such immersed gamers spent hours after hours without any tinge of the doubt for the real. They are tricked into believing that by conquering the gaming world, they are contributing to their real existence – that they have gained a sense of pride and leadership. What these gamers do not understand is that it is not *they* who play the game; on the other hand, it is the gaming mechanisms that play with *them* – controlling even their micro-level existence. As Jane McGonigal (2012) has realised her artificial obsession of clearing the bathroom is the most important job to do; in order to have a higher existence in gaming:

> Whenever you complete one of these chores, you log in to the game, to report the success. Every chore grants you a customised amount of experience points, virtual gold, treasure, avatar power-ups, or points that increase your virtual skills and abilities...you can customise the in game reward to make the least popular chores more attractive – hence, the battle in my apartment to clean the bathroom first.
>
> (p. 124)

During the process of immersion, to blur the distinction between reality and artificiality – the conglomerated gaming schemata and social media have counted the verbal, non-verbal cues emitted by the individuals. They do this, without coming to the surface of the gaming devices. The catchy media phrases as "Tintin and the Dead Eyed Zombies" (Tinwell, 2015, p. 20), initiates the future gamers 'consciousness', by making him/her aware of the presence of a non-existent meaningful world. Such transgression at the threshold of cybertextual discourse, pitches the individual(s) against the elements of endless possibilities. As the "complexities" of a cyber-spacial discourse "cannot be reduced to the finite structure of a specific program or machine" (Aarseth, 1997, p. 35) – the subjects are made to feel liberated from any visible constraints of real-life discourses.

This functionalism of cybertextual discourses of video games was made even more severe with the introduction of mobile gaming and Wi-Fi connectivity. The unending flow of information that could be accessed without any spatial or temporal restrictions gave the gaming subjects the key to unlock the door through which they could discharge their violent psychic energy – for the sake of being identified as 'ethical individual'. To ensure the continuous flow of technology and connectivity, the government too introduced "band plans and radio licensing schemes" (Gow & Smith, 2006, p. 124); such schemes not only provides the individuals with *access* to the online gaming world, but they also collect the codified data-sets from the gamers – to be decoded in the hands of media individuals, inorder to introduce new reforms.

Entangled in such a complex web, the gaming subject is stimulated to continuously seek the in-game reward mechanisms, that will momentarily satisfy his/her violent ego. But here too lies another problem – as "nobody knows what winning is. Not for certain anyway. We have various ideas about it, but there's no general consensus about it" (Castronova, 2021, p. 10), the individual upon entering the gaming world loses himself in an endless chain of signifiers. It is just a matter of time before the *conscious subject* will be transformed into a *raw material* – to be codified according to the modulations of the collective societal norms, without even being aware of it.

The gamer's proneness to the immersion process is largely controlled by the intertextuality of gaming elements and their attempts at generating a "pure representation of reality" (Allen, 2000, p. 177). Such pure representation is the manifested product of a media culture – where the constructed reality is nothing but a manipulation of signs. The "digital networked culture is intensely concerned with bodies and embodiment" (Kosnik, 2016, p. 227) – in order to produce *consumers*. The gamers are not passive about this mechanism either. It seems that they actively exhibit their consent towards it and thereby allowing the virtual *semiotic systems* to programme their memory. As Umberto Eco (1984) has explained:

> Semiotic systems are models which explain the world which we live, obviously, in explaining the world, they also construct it. Among all these systems, language is the *primary modelling system* and we apprehend the world by means of the model which language offers.
>
> (Lotman, p. x)

One reason for such allowance is the *pleasure apparatus* that comes with gaming as an attachment. These pleasure seeking individuals consciously blur the distinction between the real and the hyperreal and in doing so become a subject waiting to be modified under the 'absent' panoptical power. As Baudrillard has observed in a different context:

> The eye... is no longer the source of an absolute gaze, and the ideal of control is no longer that of transparency. This still presupposes an objective space and the omnipotence of the despotic gaze. It is still, if not a system of confinement, at least a system of mapping. More subtly, but always externally, playing on the opposition of seeing and being seen, even if the panoptic focal point may be blind.
>
> (Baudrillard, 1994, p. 29)

The individual's refuge in such gaming apparatus is thus marked by the decline of any form of materiality, death of concreteness and identification with metaphoric abstractions. The 'knowledge' (the accumulation of which is 'memory') gained in the course of interactions (between gamer and the game) – is not valid knowledge at all. As

> The legitimisation of knowledge (thereby the authenticity of one's memory)...is an agreement between men, defined as knowing intellects and free wills, and is obtained through dialogue...which manipulates it in order to maintain and improve its performance. It is the object of administrative procedures...its only validity is as an instrument to be used toward achieving the real goal, which is what legitimises the system – power"
>
> (Lyotard, 1984, p. 60-61)

Conclusion

The gaming apparatus is no longer restricted to the non-existent virtual space; through the process of immersion, they are actively constructing what one count as 'consciousness'. Such noetic alteration that functions on repetitive act mechanism(s) can normalise any form of unjust activity as just – be that decapitating someone in the name of 'military protection', or negating any form of avant-garde formulations as 'terrorism'. Being an instrument of media and government, violent video games have surfaced from the absent world to configure the present world – according to the preferences of the people in *power*. Video games' ability to tap into the human memory has led us into a truly post-truth temporality – stimulating every aspect of exposed individuals towards utter desolation. Through competitive and repetitious tasks of violent virtual activity, the gaming sphere is now able to flood the amygdala region of the brain, responsible for the 'hit and run' mechanism. Amygdala operates on the signals of *what is fear and what is not.* It is also responsible for storing of memory-signals at their respective locations inside the human brain. The violent video games' tapping in this region has altered its capacity of demarcating from what is *truth* to what is *false*, from what is *fear* to what is *joy*. The transformed gamers now feel more at home when presenting a scenario of mass murder as the truth of democracy. They now seek asylum in guns and in militarisms. The gaming sapiens now came to see infiltration, surgical strikes not as acts of violence, but as acts of retribution, justification of democratic sovereignty – functioning for the welfare of *them* (the whole humanity). To diagnose any form of the *authenticity* of the violent games' orientations will always lead to paradoxical pluralism – as by transforming the individuals into gami-duals, the societal apparatus has liquidified all definitions of 'sense'(truth) and 'non-sense' (non-truth).

References

Aarseth, E. (1997). *Cybertext: Perspective on Ergodic Literature.* The John Hopkins University Press.

Allen, G. (2000). *Intertextuality.* Routledge.

Archer, J. (2009). The Nature of Human Aggression. *International Journal of Law and Psychiatry,* 32, 202-208.

Ayers, D. (2019). *Spectacular Posthumanism: The Digital Vernacular of Visual Effects.* Bloomsbury Publishing.

Baudrillard, J. (1994). *Simulacra and Simulation* (Sheila Faria Glaser, trans.). The University of Michigan Press. (Original Work Published 1981).

Castronova, E. (2021). *Life is a Game: What Game Design Says About the Human Condition.* Bloomsbury Publishing.

Consentino, G. (2020). *Social Media and the Post-Truth World Order: The Global Dynamics of Disinformation.* Palgrave Macmillan. https://doi.org/10.1007/978-3-030-43005-4

Dovey, J, & Kennedy, H. (2006). *Game Cultures: Computer Games as New Media.* Open University Press.

Gow, G., & Smith, R. (2006). *Mobile and Wireless Communications: An Introduction.* Open University Press.

Konshik, A. (2016). *Rogue Archives: Digital Cultural Memory and Media Fandom.* The MIT Press.

Lotman, Y. (2001). *Universe of the Mind: A Semiotic Theory of Culture* (Ann Shukman, trans.). Indiana University Press. (Original Work Published 1990).

Lyotard, J. (1984). *The Postmodern Condition: A Report on Knowledge* (Geoff Bennington & Brian Massumi, trans.). University of Minnesota Press. (Original Work Published 1979).

McGonigal, J. (2012). *Reality is Broken: Why Games Make Us Better and How They Can Change the World.* The Penguin Press.

Payne, K. (2015). *The Psychology of Modern Conflict: Evolutionary Theory, Human Nature and a Liberal Approach to War.* Palgrave Macmillan.

Rosen, S. (2005). *War and Human Nature.* Princeton University Press.

Taekke, J. (2011). Digital Panopticism and Organisational Power. *Surveillance and Society,* 8 (4), 441-454. https://doi.org/10.24908/ss.v8i4.4181

Tinwell, A. (2015). *The Uncanny Valley in Games & Animation.* CRC Press.

CHAPTER 6

The Descent of Dissent: Displaced Public Spheres of Fifth Estate in the Post-Truth Era

Indu Peter

"In times of universal deceit, telling the truth will be a revolutionary act"

George Orwell

Postmodern Conundrum

The Postmodern condition is rendered by and large as "incredulity towards metanarratives". It is a metaphor for a deterritorialised space, which is marked by an ambiguous plurality and a process of 'constant becoming'. Deterritorialisation refers to the dissipation of arborescent and hierarchical structures which circumscribe the world within singular and monolithic meanings and urges one to turn towards the rhizomatic and liberated existence governed by multiplicities and dispersed identities.

Yet, as we ply across the contemporary times, we realise that the once destratified spaces which eschewed essentialisation and monolithic universals are yet again being territorialised and demarcated by contiguity and bifurcation. The authoritative regime narrows down the world into a single vantage point that suits their interests, thereby turning a blind eye to the actual truth and many-sidedness of a matter. Subsequently, the parologies are supplanted with homologies. The subaltern voices, suspicions and suspense are often thwarted by the hegemonic noises of the ones in power. Recently, this is effected by the use of post-truth.

Post-truth often enrobes itself in varied guises like deception, half-truth, conspiracy theory, outright lie, denial, propaganda, etc. In the present day, as truth becomes a thing of the past, reason takes a backseat and emotions and imagination occupies the forefront. Facts and fiction are often intertwined, populaces persuaded, numbers exaggerated, new history and truths invented and adversaries silenced to gain political and social supremacy over the others. Consequently, the democratic ideals are swamped and liberal human sentiments are shoved down the drain in the post-truth world.

Traditional Media vs. Social Media

Ideally, media being the fourth pillar of democracy ought to rise above the oddities of post-truth. However, as we scrutinise the modern media arena, we tend to realise that the media, which is supposed to be the watchdog that unravels the flaws in society, has ended up being flawed thus impairing the very framework of democracy. Mass media and traditional media in particular have become pawns in the hands of the ones in power and to our dismay purvey the narratives of the official propaganda.

Even as traditional media grapples under the siege of post-truth, we find that the disembodied space of social media becomes performative and acts as an alternate public sphere in contemporary times. This is especially true in the case of trolls and memes which elicit laughter upon the follies of society. It offers a space to articulate our protest and contest the dominant discourses which reign control with the free play of lies and half-truths. Whilst the authoritative regimes thwart dissent and attempt to homogenise the heterogeneity of language games, the fifth estate refuses to be fixed owing to its fluidity as well as subversive nature and thereby gives rise to an anti-regime that proffer an alternate public sphere.

The *public sphere* as posited by Habermas consists of private people gathered together as a public articulating the needs of society with the state. It is a social space that generates, challenges and combats the state dynamics and affects policymaking. Thus in a world awash with deceit and false claims, the fifth estate rises above the doctrines of prejudice and hate-mongering, and strives to fashion a public sphere to question the odds and subvert the fascist discourses. Accordingly, while the entire world rallies after homogenising meta-narratives of power, social media becomes a tapestry of little narratives resisting the same.

Fifth Estate – An Avatar of Power or an Arbiter of Truth

Yet, whether the Fifth estate is an Avatar of Power or an Arbiter of Truth is a very slippery ground to dwell on. It would be mere wishful thinking if we assume that in the post-truth era when the truth is eclipsed and lies are spread in wanton, social media remains completely impervious to these changing climes. Whereas it has in itself the ability to espouse, counteract and re-appropriate the significations entrenched in popular culture and media, it is also true that lately, a rather bleak side of social media has emerged which alter intellectual uprightness, whet polarisations and bombard one with fake news.

The lack of accountability in the online space has resulted in the creation of many an alternate reality, which cater to different propagandas and reeks of misinformation. The unverified and free transmission of fake news, filter bubbles, half-truths, the proliferation of seemingly authentic accounts and political extremism tend to threaten the liberal democratic order of the times.

The emblematic expression of the online users delineated in the forms of hashtags, memes, likes, dislikes, shares, comments etc. propounds a sense of visual activism and political engagement. Though on one side it garners a political subordination of reality as a means of asserting dominance, on the other hand, it also offers the users an inclusive platform to counter, dissent and defies these disinformation campaigns. Levitin (2017) voices:

> The Internet promises that it is a great democratising force, allowing everyone to express their opinions, and everyone to have immediate access to all the world's information...you have a virtual world of information and misinformation cohabiting side by side, staring back at you like identical twins, one who will help you and the other who will hurt you.
>
> (p. 202)

In other words, the alternate discursive arena in social media thus subsumes not just a unified singular entity rather a multitude of variegated publics both dominant as well as subordinate, true as well as false. Hence, one has to employ his critical faculty to reap its true benefits. It seems like a double-edged sword which though on one hand endangers the facts and truths and jeopardises the liberal order, however also provides one with the tool to resist the befuddlement of facts. Thus though slightly displaced, there is a Counter-Narrative on the move which makes it possible to put the displaced public sphere of the fifth estate in place.

Counter Narrative on the Move

In the post-truth era of "the obfuscation of facts, abandonment of evidential standards in reasoning, and outright lying" (McIntyre, 2018, p. 19), we shall peruse three domains namely – nation, gender and health as it finds expression in cyberspace, wherein we find ourselves whipsawed between dominant public discourses and egalitarian counter publics. Although on one hand, the dominant discourses mar these domains with charades of lies, we shall see social media mercilessly deconstructing these fraudulent claims on the other, to keep alive the democratised equitable space

Narrativising Nation

In a world of nation-states, where national security and interest transpire as pivotal tropes, we see the onslaught of dissent and the onset of blatant attempts to silence any disaccord. As the democratisation of space often becomes a myth, the various forms of representation attempt to totalise rather than provide fluid and fractured multiplicities. The xenophobic, pseudo nationalist politicians rebuff facts and repudiate truth to devise their propaganda and aver their political supremacy. In any authoritarian state, truth thus becomes the first casualty. They colour, choose and characterise everything in a political milieu such that their version of truth gets paraded as the one absolute truth.

Of late, the Centrists in India uphold a pseudo-religious nationalism that is rooted in Hinduism and the Hindi language. Amidst the Centre's attempts to endorse saffronisation, endeavours were made to make Hindi the national language of India. It was argued that there should be one language for the entire nation and that language had to be Hindi. Consequently, Twitter and Facebook abounded with *#StopHindiImposition* hashtags. Diverse Indians rallied together for the cause of the promotion of linguistic equality across social media. The celebrated journalist Faye Dsouza tweeted, "Mother tongue: Konkani, State Language: Kannada, Mother-in-law's tongue: Marathi, Learnt from friends in B'lore: Tamil, Malayalam and some Telugu, Learnt from Doordarshan: Hindi. We Don't have one language", thereby upholding India's unity in diversity. Eventually Centre had to call off this propagandist move owing to the ubiquitous protests against Hindi imperialism that raged in the social media. The counter-narrative questions the actions of state machinery such that social media becomes a more democratic space.

Another instance of Bharatiya Janata Party-led Central Government kicking fake news into gear happened when Prime Minister Narendra Modi made fraudulent claims of India defeating Coronavirus, as the first wave of COVID-19 slanted in the middle of January, even though the scientists had cautioned of a dire second wave. He gave a false sense of hope and security to Indians, opened the country to market. Medical practitioners and scientists across the country had turned on to social media during that time trying to forewarn the people of the impending second wave. Subsequently, it became clear that the State's unbridled optimism was heavily misplaced as the number of COVID-19 positive cases started skyrocketing. Despite exporting millions of free doses of COVID-19 vaccines to other countries as part of Vaccine diplomacy, when India faced a shortage of COVID-19 vaccines the State claimed that free vaccinations to Indians are an impossibility due to the economic liability it posed. Social media was once again bombarded with memes and tweets, one troll created a montage of the news article of State's claims that it requires a hefty 3000 crores to increase the COVID -19 vaccine production with the news of the purchase of the VVIP Air India 1 Jet for the Prime Minister which costs a gargantuan 8458 Crore Rupees thus revealing the hypocrisy of the State. Such memes save the masses from being kept in the dark.

There are numerous instances wherein we see the masses resisting the State's tyrannical narratives in many a creative way with the aid of the fifth estate. One such instance from recent times is how 'Mallubroiders', a Malayali Embroidery Artists Collective started *#SaveLakshadweep*, an embroidery campaign against the fascist policies which were forcefully implemented on the archipelago by the new Administration. Around 35 Embroidery hoops featuring the beauty of Lakshadweep were made and the campaign was very well received all over the globe. The netizens swore their solidarity with the people of Lakshadweep, who were in turmoil following the authoritarian and saffronised promulgations put in place to disrupt the culture and tradition of the Union Territory.

As Sim (2019) rightly points out: "When post-truth is backed up by totalitarian political power, then it can become a very formidable opponent, a very real threat to the democratic ideal" (p. 36). Social media offers one the scope to counter such a fearsome foe and uphold the liberal humanist ideals of the society.

Reimagining Gender

Patriarchy has always distorted the idea of gender from time immemorial. Even in the postmodern era, it strives to silence the feminine and ostracise those who dare to voice against the inequalities of life. Popular media has played a significant role in normalising violence against women and asserting gender roles in society. The misogyny at work tends to celebrate feminine frailties, exhort womanly beauty and chastise a woman. The politics of caste and creed creep into the fold. Many male chauvinists also take to social media to contend their dominance over woman, but the beauty of social media lies in its potential to counteract such fascist discourses in its way.

Conversely, women have fashioned a discourse of protest against the inadvertent advances of misogyny and patriarchy thereby subverting the very essence of sexism on social media. Although on one hand, patriarchy tries to normalise the violence on women and silencing of women, on the other hand, men and women join hands and become the voice of the voiceless. The *#MeToo* campaigns which ran across the globe gained their momentum solely because of the reach social media provided to it. In the form of comments, likes and shares these stories spread like a wildfire and it kindled the hearts of many women who were sexually abused at one point or the other to muster the courage to speak out. When some misogynistic men try to point fingers at the victims, social media combats them effectively. The *#MeToo* movement led to the persecution of many perpetrators who were walking scot-free till then, as in the case of the Hollywood producer Harvey Weinstein who is facing criminal charges for sexual harassment.

Women are also constantly objectified, idealised and idolised by society to chop their wings off. She is either dehumanised as a mere thing of beauty or is presented as a goddess to impede her import and voice. The patriarchal society deifies the mother as someone who wilfully sacrifices her whole life for the sake of her family. But Department of Women and Child Development, Government of Kerala posted an online flyer on 09 May 2021(Mother's Day) in the guise of a dictionary entry redefining a Mother. It went like this, "Mother (Noun): An embodiment of unconditional love, an ever-patient superwoman; An ordinary person with love, sadness, anger and tiredness just like anybody else". This poster which was celebrated far and wide on social media urged one to accept a mother for what she truly is instead of weighing her down with over expectations. The mass outrage against the image of a mother in oxygen support cooking food with the caption "Unconditional Love= *Mother* She is Never Off Duty" is another example of how social media resists the assertion of gender roles and toxic glorification of motherhood. Social media thus enables one to bid goodbye to regressive ideological machineries and helps women embrace a liberated existence. Social media serves as a welcome space not only for women, but also for queer, lesbian, gay and bisexual individuals too. It empathises with their problems, gives them a voice and questions the homophobia which is wantonly spread in society.

In addition to repudiating toxic masculinity, moral policing, misogyny, body shaming and social evils like dowry, the fifth estate throws light on varied progressive narratives of gender and also subverts the cloud of lies which surround them. It also puts equal parenting, menstruation hygiene, masturbation, post-partum depression, etc. on a normal footing. The alternate subaltern discourse acts as a counter-public in itself which subverts the populist notions of patriarchy.

Health through a Looking Glass

In the arena of health too, a lot of misinformation is spread in the guise of truth in the post-truth era. Social media over and again finds itself filled with anti-vaccination campaigns, cons of organ donation, a profusion of pseudo-scientific facts and internet hoaxes on health along with the testimonials of quack doctors like Mohanan Vaidyar and Jacob Vadakkancherry. However, social media platforms like Infoclinic and Treat by Alter Doctor contest these dominant narratives, inculcates a scientific temper among people and shatters unscientific superstitions and misconceptions associated with health care.

Most recently Facebook was plagued with a post that claimed that Luc Montagnier, a world-famous virologist and Nobel Prize winner had forewarned that all the people who were vaccinated with COVID -19 vaccines will die within two years. This dire warning terrified people and on fact-checking, it was revealed that this was nothing but fake news and that Montagnier had never said the same. In this information age, fact-checking helps in distinguishing the true from false.

Fraudsters use social media to dupe patients with fake news and alternate medicines. In his book *Post-Truth, Scepticism & Power,* Stuart Sim maintains that:

> Alternative medicine is another area that can be accused of making use of post-truth techniques, offering scientifically dubious treatments to a clientele who are, for a variety of reasons, susceptible to the post-truth approach to

> health matters. The claims made for the vast majority of the products sold under the heading of alternative medicine are decidedly spurious, rarely standing up to any properly rigorous testing regime.
>
> (p. 28)

This reflection sheds light on people's tendency to readily suspend their disbelief and run after the miracle cures in the market. Yoga guru Baba Ramdev falsely claimed that Patanjali's 'Coronil' was approved by the World Health Organisation as medicine for COVID-19, when WHO had not certified any traditional medicine for COVID-19 treatments. After being debunked, Patanjali was forced to clarify that the drug was approved not by WHO but by DCGI, the Government of India. In this post-truth era, it is very important to verify the credibility of the medicines promoted in social media before use.

"The danger of post-truth is not just that we allow our opinions and feelings to play a role in shaping what we think of as facts and truth, but that by doing so we take the risk of being estranged from reality itself." (McIntyre, 2018, p.190) Today when we are standing in a crossroad where belief becomes a symbol of truth, the world tends to in fact take a detour back to the regressive times of the past. Though science is advancing frantically, there seems to be an antipathy towards progressive feats like vaccination, organ donation etc. However, in social media you find this regressive machinery being deterritorialised. The singular denouements of quack doctors are challenged using memes and trolls and other rhizomatic offshoots of polyphonic voices which find celebration owing to the democratic nature of cyberspace. Humour is used as a trope to deconstruct the idea and throw light on the hollowness of their arguments and pseudo-facts. The participatory nature is yet another tool that aids the process.

Conclusion

In the postmodern world where the digital experiences closely assimilate itself with everyday life, unlike the traditional media which has deteriorated into public relations, the fifth estate emerges itself as a public sphere that offers us a space to articulate multiple truths as well as fight the fascistic forces and their discourses of post-truth. Further, a more inclusive discourse that challenges and counterposes itself is in the making in the fifth estate, which attempts to neutralise or repress these hegemonic overtures.

Therefore, in the post-truth era of political subordination of reality when truths are concealed, the fifth estate emerges itself as a public sphere, though at times it falls victim to the metanarratives of state, patriarchy and power. In times of universal deceit, even though the voices of dissent at times do meet its descent, having been drowned in the programmed noises of the social media and various fetishisations which pervade there, social media offers us the scope for a counter-narrative that combats the distortion of facts and thereby helps to uphold itself as a public sphere, which though might be displaced is never misplaced.

References

Ball, J. (2018). *Post-Truth: How Bullshit conquered the world.* Biteback Publishing.

Barnes, R. (2018). *Uncovering online commenting culture- Trolls, fan boys, lurkers.* Palgrave Macmillan.

Chaturvedi, A. (20201, April 8). 'We defeated Covid without vaccines': PM Modi tells CMs on way forward. *Hindustan Times.* https://www.hindustantimes.com/india-news/covid-situation-challeng ing-focus-on-micro-containment-zones-pm-modi-to-cms-101617893287824.html

Dsouza, F.[@fayedsouza]. (2019, September 14). *Mother tongue: Konkani, state language: Kannada, mother-in-law's tongue: Marathi, learnt from friends in B'lore: Tamil, Malayalam and some Telugu* [Tweet]. Twitter. https://twitter.com/fayedsouza

Kumar, A. (2016, July 25). Role of media in democracy. *Legaldesire.* https://legaldesire.com/role-of-media-in-democracy

Levitin, D, J. (2017). *Weaponized Lies: How to think critically in the post- truth era.* Dutton.

Mallick, A. (2021, May 25). Govt Looks Away as Ramdev Keeps Spreading COVID Misinformation. *The Quint.* https://www.thequint.com/news/webqoof/baba-ramdev-covid-misinformation-vaccine -coronavirus#read-more

Mallubroiders [@mallubroiders]. (2021, May 30). *Save Lakshadweep Embroidery campaign conducted by Mallubroiders.* [Photograph]. Instagram.https://www.instagram.com /p/ CPe3sgfAobr

McIntyre, L. (2018). *Post-truth.* The MIT Press.

O'Rourke, C. (2021, May 28). No, French virologist Luc Montagnier didn't say COVID-19 vaccine recipients were going to die soon. *Politifact.* https://www.politifact.com/factchecks/2021/ may/28/viral-image/no-french-virologist-luc-montagnier-didnt-say-covi

Phillips, W. (2016). *This is why we can't have nice things: mapping the relationship between online trolling and mainstream culture.* The MIT Press.

Rabin-Havt, A. (2016). *Lies, incorporated: The truth of post-truth politics.* Anchor Books.

Sim, S. (2019). *Post-truth, scepticism & power.* Palgrave Macmillian. https://doi.org/10.1007/ 978-3-030-15876-7

Varadarajan, S. (2020, February 24). India's media is failing in its democratic duty. *Al Jazeera.* https://www.aljazeera.com/opinions/2020/2/24/indias-media-is-failing-in-its-democratic-duty

CHAPTER 7

Oxygen on Wheels and People in Quandary: A Study on Media Re-appropriation of Crisis and Cacophony of State Apparatus

Roshima Uday and Dr. Abubakkar K.K.

When the perilous spike of the second Covid-19 wave hits India, vaccines have become India's new legal tender on the morbid Global market. The country pleads for hospital beds and Oxygen, diverting more people towards the black market. This deplorable situation is the result of callousness displayed by the Indian Government in holding rallies unmasked, and decisions such as letting the Kumbh Mela proceed. However, the common people cannot get access to the real situation prevailing here as the government, which cannot tolerate criticism and wants to control the public narrative, regulates the media. This marks the irony of the powerlessness of people in the greatest democracy very conspicuous. The present chapter tries to analyse different propaganda techniques like name-calling, glittering generalities, bandwagon etc employed by the government to subvert the democratic potential of new technologies. Taking up India as a case study, the chapter explores and evaluates the strategies employed in the re-scripting of the national narrative, potentially leading to new "national memory" as defined by Lorraine Ryan. The study also extrapolates the substantiality of campaigns like "Chai pe Charcha with NaMo" through the theoretical framework of Jurgen Habermas's concept of "public sphere". The chapter also incorporates Marshall McLuhan's description of media's influence in creating "re-tribalisation" in a "global village" and the writings of Arundhati Roy and David Roberts's "Post-Truth politics" in order to widen the horizon of study.

Fake News Impact

"Our inherent cognitive biases make us ripe for manipulation and exploitation by those who have an agenda to push, especially if they can discredit all other sources of information" (Lee McIntyre, 2018, p. 61-62). The truth today faces political subordination and people in power manipulate truth as a strategy to gain a despotic reign over others. This is due to the decline of traditional media and the proliferation of social media beyond proper regulations. People get trapped in the internet filter bubbles and thereby develop adherence towards any particular viewpoint that is circulated the most. In this way they decisive their own cognitive biases unknowingly. Fake news and propaganda circulate a politics of hate, affecting every sphere of society where the minority groups, journalists, and the poor are victimised the most. However, media plays the role of victimised and that of a victimiser; victimised as it faces threat from the political parties to deliver information, which favours them; and as a victimiser, they sell information infused within the seeds of nationalism and create a communal backlash. The situation is no less in India, from education to health care and in the economy obsessed with GDP, the impacts of post-truth is very explicit.

India amidst Covid-19

The second wave of Covid-19 devastates India leaving hospitals flooded with people letting no space for those who require intensive care beyond endurance. There are still many persons around who saw Partition, but the horror of the collective insanity of the time can hardly compete with the devastation inflicted by COVID-19 (Khurshid, 2021). Streets are filled with pictures of people running for arranging Oxygen cylinders and cries of those who plead to the hospital authorities for space inside. As the country grapples with the pandemic, the bureaucratic hurdles are delaying delivery of the critical resource to those in need. Experts say that India has failed to stockpile enough vaccines or invest early enough to increase its production and that the present mishap is due to the lack of centralised coordination of Oxygen supply and distribution. In addition, red tape has irretrievably mired timely delivery of the supplies. However, the media excellently exaggerates governments' successes and creates a belief among people that they have conquered the lethal malady. Superstitions and quackery supplements this media sensationalism. The authorities and media are clever enough to make people adhered to their voices by presenting statistics showing: higher rate of recovered patients, availability of hospital beds and vaccines;

and a lower rate of death and TPR (Test Positivity Rate). These tactical statistical data sound relieving to the common people who are not familiar with huge figures and facts. The result is that people developed a liberal attitude towards the virus and went after chanting slogans like "go Corona go", lit candles, clapped hands, rang bells, beat on utensils and flashed mobile torchlights to honour the health workers. The crowded participation in Kumbh Mela also gets suggested as a holy dip to become symbolic. It is no doubt that, the medical team is doing an outstanding job and such symbolic acts may provide comfort. However, considering the extremity of the situation, rather than asking the citizens to cooperate with the health workers as an honour towards them, to put in a request for such symbolic gestures may create a misconception among people that these gestures alone are the adequate measures for the needs of the hour. The absurdity is at its peak in situations where politicians ask people to use cow dung for treating and preventing a pandemic. It is regrettable to watch rational and progressive human beings shun logic and science in favour of stupidity.

Theorising Post-Truth

The Post-truth phenomena thus is a product of the symbiotic relationship between media sensationalism and political hate and lying. George Orwell uses his concept of "doublethink" to define nonstop lying as a phenomenon that reverses truth out of influence from extreme repressive leadership. As the officials in *1984* repeat 'war is peace' and 'freedom is slavery', the present condition of citizens in each country points out that the 21st century in which we inhabit today is nothing less than the dystopian world which Orwell imagined in the 20th century (Orwell, 2019). In India too, the Ministry of Truth spreads lies and the Ministry of Love tortures lovers (Orwell, 2019). Social media and other information discovery platforms create eco chambers where opinions are magnified and reinforced by repetition inside a closed system, shielded from rebuttal. This invigorates the users to adopt more extreme ideological positions. The Indian state apparatus has also used a similar strategy and declared the victory over Covid-19 by glossing over the virulence of the pandemic. Jürgen Habermas describes his concept of the "public sphere" as, "made up of private people gathered together as a public and articulating the needs of society with the state" (Habermas et. al., 2020). He considers the media system and politicians as the two inevitable elements (actors) without which a public sphere cannot function. He explains how the State colonises reason and public deliberation and illustrates them in the news media. He also alerted of professional political communication and polling that the capitalists used to validate their hold on power through the production of public opinion. Habermas (2006) classifies the actors into five as: Lobbyists, representing special interest groups; advocates, representing general interest groups or the marginalised section; expert professionals; moral entrepreneurs who generate public attention for supposedly neglected issues; and intellectuals (p. 411-426). This shows that the new media platforms give more opportunities for social interaction, political communication and enhance democratic capacities. However, media being the mouthpieces of people in power, rather than focusing on national integration and security, they share contents of more entertainment and consumerism. In today's busy world, people are not patient enough to sit in front of the TV for long hours and watch News from different channels to get unbiased information. Utilising this situation, most News channels offer a short capsule section called "1 minute news" comprising all the important headlines. However, since their main agenda is to prompt people to watch their other news programs on seeing the '1-minute news', they make that session very attractive by amplifying the contents. As part of the game of Post-truth politics, media in cases of misfortunes, weave webs to trap the opponents of their party towards which they are inclined. Therefore, it is the opposition, liberals, Muslims, activists, protesters, NGO's and the other asserted "anti-nationals", that fall victim to media's discontent. This can be termed as a phenomenon where, "a political culture in which politics (public opinion and media narratives) has become almost entirely disconnected from policy (the substance of legislation)" (Roberts, 2021).

The main tenet of Post- Truth rises from the idea where every citizen perceives reality in a form where it is mixed with the ideologies and false games of the "real" people in power (Harsin, 2018). Studies reveal that Gandhi has early recognised that societies with diverse populations inhibit a Post-Truth age. The Canadian philosopher Marshall McLuhan in his books *The Gutenberg galaxy: the making of typographic man* (1968) and *Understanding media* (1964) introduced the concept of "global village", which he described as a phenomenon where the entire world is more interconnected due to the advancement in media technologies. The concept resembles the philosophy of "vasudhaiva kutumbakam (the world is one family)" as described in the

Hindu Maha Upanishads. However, the whole idea in both contexts was to transcend national boundaries and bring people around the world close together. Even so, the media advancements took a different path. McLuhan compares the present plight of the media addicted people with the ancient system of tribalisation and declares that there is a re-trabilisation process taking place in the Post-Truth society (Norden, 2009). During the primitive ages, the tribes had a leader who would make important decisions in their group and the other people would obediently wait in front of their leader to hear his decisions and will act accordingly, without giving a chance for their rationality to function. According to McLuhan, the present society also acts in a similar fashion, waiting in front of the social media to grasp the information which the power-driven Media wish to deliver; it is their biased thoughts that govern their intellect. Political campaigns aim at 'image making' rather than focusing on issues relating to national policy and governance. Despite that, some claims that Post-Truth politics and society are the product of postmodern theory (McIntyre, 2018). The critical comment made by Arundhati Roy on the present scenario is noteworthy. She has remarked that the system has not collapsed, whereas, it is the government that has failed and what we witness today is an unreserved crime against humanity (Roy, 2021). Lorraine Ryan (2016), a lecturer in Employment Relations & Human Resource Management in the Department of Work & Employment Studies, explains the concept of National memory as based on the public's reception of national historic narratives and the ability of people to affirm the legitimacy of these narratives:

> National memory making is significant in the present times in the context of two developments: the ways in which communication technologies have shaped political communication and the divisive politics of the times. Digital technologies and online spaces have emerged as the most significant of public spaces of both discursive and performative politics. This has been facilitated by a combination of factors unique to neo liberalism viz., the enmeshing of politics, corporate sector and media. Fundamental to these developments have been the ways in which new communication technologies have altered.
>
> (Ranganathan, 2019, p. 1)

Conclusion

Thus to wrap up, the chapter has brought into the light, how the democratic potential of new technologies is subverted in a Post-Truth society. The media and online spaces re-appropriate the past and co-opt in the nation-building project. Today this re-creation and re-construction of History form part of discursive nationalism and results in the "fire-hosing of falsehood" (Paul & Matthews, 2016). With the importance of media and its political vulnerability stated clear, it proves that the Indian media has played a pivotal role in taking the country towards the Covid surge. However, the COVID-19 pandemic exposed some crucial and innate traits in us – anxiety, ignorance and bravado, but most importantly, our stupidity. A new and apt word was thus coined – "Covidiot" (Pugalia, 2021). The chapter while concluding suggests some measures to overcome the evils of media re-appropriation, resulting in a Post-Truth condition (Harsin, 2018). The first step is to overcome the colonialism of the social media world and to get them to contribute to the public service and commons-based media. The users should be warned of the risks involved in accessing unreliable sources. Children and the youngsters, who are the future citizens of India, must be taught that these are not the Utopian platforms, which many critics have claimed at the beginning of the IT revolution. As there are many state authorities that make the citizens blind with their statistical data, providing statistical literacy can help to eliminate faulty conclusions due to the non-demographic nature of human intuitions. Regarding India's present pathetic exigency due to the Covid virus, the regulation and administration of the pandemic have to be handed over to an unbiased body consisting of members from the ruling party and public administers from the oppositional party along with experts of the health department. Enhancing the transparency of online news, implementation of IT regulation acts with 100% accuracy and creating awareness about media and information literacy can also help people to access the right information and restrain from click-bait headlines; and thereby liberate the world from Post- Truth condition.

References

Appadurai, A. (2020). The Revolt of the Elites. *Graduate Institute Geneva.* https://www.graduateinstitute.ch/communications/news/revolt-elites

Habermas, J., Burger, T., & Lawrence, F. (2020). *The structural transformation of the public sphere: an inquiry into a category of bourgeois society.* Polity.

Habermas, J. (2006). Political Communication in Media Society: Does Democracy Still Enjoy an Epistemic Dimension? *The Impact of Normative Theory on Empirical Research. Communication Theory,* 16(4), 411-426. https://doi.org/10.1111/j.1468-2885.2006. 00280.x

Harsin, J. (2018). Post-Truth and Critical Communication Studies. *Oxford Research Encyclopedia of Communication.* https://doi.org/10.1093/acrefore/97801902 28613. 013.757

Jennings, W., Stoker, G., Willis, H., Valgardsson, V., Gaskell, J., Devine, D., McKay, L., & Mills, M. C. (2021). *Lack of trust and social media echo chambers predict COVID-19 vaccine hesitancy.* https://doi.org/10.1101/2021.01.26.21250246

Khurshid, S. (2021, May 12). India's COVID Mishandling: Govt is Testing Courts' Self-Esteem. *The Quint.* https://www.thequint.com/voices/opinion/salman-khurshid-on-covid-crisis-modi-govt-supreme-court-high-courts-oxygen-medical-essentials-short-supply-kumbh-super-spreader

Kitchens, B., Johnson, S. L., & Gray, P. (2020). Understanding Echo Chambers and Filter Bubbles: The Impact of Social Media on Diversification and Partisan Shifts in News Consumption. *MIS Quarterly,* 44(4), 1619–1649. https://doi.org/ 10. 25300/misq/ 2020/16371

McIntyre, L. (2018). The Roots of Cognitive Bias. In *Post-Truth* (pp. 61–62). MIT press.

McLuhan, M. (1968). *The Gutenberg galaxy: the making of typographic man.* University of Toronto.

McLuhan, M. (1964). *Understanding media.* McGraw-Hill.

Norden, E. (2009, December 24). The Playboy Interview: Marshall McLuhan. *Next Nature Network.* https:// www.nextnature.net/story/2009/the-playboy-interview-marshall-mcluhan.

Orwell, G. (2019). *1984.* Maple Press.

Paul, C., & Matthews, M. (2016). The Russian "Firehose of Falsehood" Propaganda Model: Why It Might Work and Options to Counter It. *Perspective.* https://doi.org/10.7249 /pe198

Pugalia, S. (2021, April 2). What Covid Pandemic 'Revealed': Every Day Is April Fools' Day. *Bloomberg Quint.* https://www.bloombergquint.com/quint/covid-pandemic-stupidity-misinformation-fake-news-trump-boris-johnson-bolsonaro-governments-india-vaccine-response

Ranganathan, M. (2019). Re-scripting the nation in 'post truth' era: the Indian story. *Asian Ethnicity,* 1-15. https://doi.org/10.1080/14631369.2019.1698942

Roberts, D. (2021, April 5). Post-truth politics. *Grist.* https://grist.org/article/2010-03-30-post-truth-politics

Roy, A. (2021, April 28). Arundhati Roy on India's Covid catastrophe: 'We are witnessing a crime against humanity'. *The Guardian.* https://www.theguardian.com/news/2021/apr/28/crime-against-humanity-arundhati-roy-india-covid-catastrophe

Ryan, L. (2012). Cosmopolitan memory and national memory conflicts: On the dynamics of their interaction. *Journal of Sociology,* 50(4), 501–514. https://doi.org/10.1177/14407833124 67097

Ryan, L. (2016). *Memory and spatiality in post-millennial Spanish narrative.* Routledge. Taylor & Francis Group.

CHAPTER 8

Cultural Obliteration of Menstrual Practices and Ripple Effects of the Post-Truth Era

Pranjal Bhatt

Uncanny Impact of Post-Truth Waves upon India

The fact that the world is emerging to challenge, question and revolutionise everything, to be then amplified by giving it emotions without doing a fact check; is indeed turning itself to be more uncanny. Since the onset of the Post-Truth Era, various turmoils were created by placing emotions above sensibility and reasoning. Symptoms of the post-truth world have not only been traced into political affinities of America, India and many more countries; but it has been successful in engulfing the social and cultural movements in the last five years. With the evolution of human society and moving to the Post-truth Era, it has been a new custom to nullify the old cultural practices by charging them with the labels of being discriminatory, sexist, patriarchal myths and more.

India being one of the countries holding the second largest population in the world is hugely under the influence of the post-truth wave. This groping of Post-Truth effect in India can partly be blamed due to lack of literacy and partly because of the huge diversity of culture and no single affinity to maintain synchrony of sensibility across the country. For a long period of more than 200 years, Indians were forced to believe that they are all backward and orthodox by British Raj. After this conditioning of the crowd, most of the people have crippled their ability to think objectively while the rest are blindly infatuated by the western philosophy and policies of life, making them a new hashtag trend. Politically, the government-today-is highly criticised by scholarly academicians like Arundhati Roy and media personnel such as Shobha De and Ranna Ayub. But the social and cultural issues which have been impacted due to the waves of the post-truth world now call for our attention after being long ignored.

Social Insurrection in Post-Truth Age

During this Post-Truth Age, the charges of sabotaging ancient practices rose even more concern and demand attention towards the most shunned topic i.e. menstrual practices to be viewed under a microscope. The much-silenced topic of the ongoing menstrual practices across various cultures was taken into vogue by various feminist and social workers in India. While menstruation i.e. the cycle of ovulation which a female body goes through every month is not an alien topic, it surely is taboo to be talked about openly even in contemporary times. Ironically the very name of the bestselling sanitary napkin brands such as *Whisper* propagates the idea to be quiet and not talk loud on the subject matter. Various underlying ideologies are set about the only blood that is witnessed without violence.

Divergent Menstrual Practices in India & Attitude of the Post-Truth World

In certain culture, the first menstruation is celebrated with all the members of the house, whereas in some, it is the onset of bordering out the woman away during these days of relentless blood loss. In few South Asian cultures mostly women are not allowed any human touch during the time of menstruating. If anyone fails to follow the regulated norms, then the person in contact with women is asked to immediately take a bath. In a few culture women are not allowed to sleep on the bed and were asked to move to the outskirts of the house and sleep on bamboo mattresses or the ground. Women are kept in total isolation during these days where they are neither supposed to touch anything holy nor allowed inside the premises of any pious area such as temples or mosques. If some of the religions such as Christianity and Sikhism would allow the women inside their praying halls than they are restricted to part-take into reciting any bhajans (hymns) and are thus excluded to be part of holy communication.

Countering the ideas such as associating menstrual blood with purity and impurity was necessary and much needed to be demolished, but few practices opposed in the process were actually suppressed by relegating facts. Compromising on the rich cultural tradition and rituals most of the women chose to commit to alternate called "modernity" by ditching the practices which were convinced to be discriminatory to their gender.

Discourse on Menstrual Practices in Post-Truth World

Book named *Rtu Vidya: Ancient Science behind menstrual practices* written by a Vedic scholar, Sinu Joseph highlights multiple practices followed in different parts of India by variant religions such as Hindu, Christianity and Islam and exhibits astonishing parallel similarities of menstrual practices from one culture to the other. Sinu Joseph with her profound research in the subject matter tries to debunk the circumference myth around menstrual practices. Her research underlines the hidden sciences amongst the vogue to post-truth narratives. The decoding of such science behind the much malpractice of founding menstrual practices could be the task difficult even for Derrida to undertake. There is no single answer and simplification of the questions such as:

1. Who is the one to impose these cultural norms/practices?
2. Why have been women following them for more than a century long?
3. How are these menstrual practices common among various cultures?
4. What if we do not follow these set patterns of the old century?

Deconstruction of such labelled "sardonic", "stereotypical" and "discriminatory" practices based on scientific facts is an onerous task. However, various scholars and researchers have shared their opinions emphasising them to be logical, thematic and non-orthodox. The scientific reason behind why one should avoid the human touch with menstruating women is highly explained by Sinu Joseph through the following words,

> In the case of menstruating girls/women, they tend to attract electrons from those who touch them. As a result, the person who has touched a menstruating girl experiences a loss of electrons, putting their body at risk of oxidative stress. This is why those who attend to the menstruating girl are required to take a bath before they interact with others. Water in motion (e.g. shower or waterfalls) is said to produce negative ions.
>
> (Joseph, 2020)

The explanation provided by the author continues where she introduces the use of flannel that acts as an insulator that would prevent the transfer of electrons.

> Hence, bathing is a good way to regain the loss of electrons by those who are impacted by coming in contact with a menstruating girl/woman. One of the common local practices to prevent menstruating women from affecting young children is to dress the child in flannel. Flannel is an insulator and would thereby prevent the transfer of electrons from the child's body to that of the menstruating woman.
>
> (Joseph, 2020)

Ripple Effect of Prost-Truth Era on Menstrual Health

Due to the impact of the post-truth wave upon the social and cultural entity, one did not consider the substantiate facts as mentioned above. Science also provides a different reason for not exerting and exhausting oneself while menstrual bleeding which gives quite a possible explanation on not allowing the women to cook or isolating them from the rest. The restriction against entering holy places & offer one's rendering to god sounds discriminatory but studying Yoga mudra such as *Anjali mudra* (joining of hands), *Vajra asana* (julus pose), *paschima asana* (ruku pose) and *shashank asana* (sujud pose) etc. explain how performing such yoga poses could be harmful and increases the blood loss during menstruation than usual. The old Vedic scriptures and Upanishads also discuss the human body, the philosophy and aspects of spirituality wherein it mentions the five controlling chakras of a human body. *Rtu Vidya* also discusses how praying in a certain manner activates higher chakras of the body which produces *apana vayu*, which the author asserts –

> The pull of apāna in the opposite direction (upward) would most likely cause a perceptible pain in the lower abdomen. If continued over a period of time, such temples can cause irreparable damage by changing the direction of apāna vāyu or blocking it. This could be one of the reasons for the painful menstrual disorder called endometriosis.
>
> (Joseph, 2020)

However with all the arguments and much less discussion on whether or not to follow the practices, the Post Modern and Post-Truth world moved speedily towards believing how following few of them transcends negative memories of menstruation. Women going through the feeling of alienation due to strict isolation affect their health and are now scientifically identified as one of the psychosomatic disorders wherein studies are attempted to check the effect on mind affects the body.

The discourse that rose with due intention to mark a difference for the betterment of society, has eventually lost its motive in the debates of post-truth Age by overtaking the feelings above substantial scientific evidences. In an article titled *Defining Post-truth: Structures, Agents, and Style* it is very briefly articulated that

> factual truth has a limited but indispensable role to play in pluralistic politics, comparable to material environment that both enables and limits democratic debate in important ways. I put forward an understanding of post-truth as a two-pronged process in which structures and agents mutually depend on and amplify each other.
>
> (Hyvönen, 2018)

In this amplification, there is a serious compromise of objective truth. This compromise and sheer negligence have led to showing the ripple effect of post-truth waves. Most NIH research journals reports rising cases in Polycystic Ovary Syndrome (PCOS) and Polycystic Ovary Disease (PCOD) in women. In the article *Assessment of the prevalence of polycystic ovary syndrome among the college students: A case-control study from Kolkata* jointly authored by Madhumati Chatterjee and Soma Aditya Bandhyopadhyay they have clearly specified the statistics to be –

> Approximately 4%-10% of the world population experiences PCOS although the incidence rate is higher for India, rounding off to 20%-26%. Although it has an alarming incidence globally, the syndrome is enigmatic with unclear etiology and its diagnosis is difficult as it manifests as a spectrum of symptoms than a specific one.
>
> (Bandyopadhyay & Chatterjee, 2020)

This is a ratio of the single state of Kerala. In the megacity of pro-population like Delhi, Mumbai, Bangalore, Hyderabad, Ahmedabad and more where people have rapid lifestyle changes, the ratio of PCOS victims is assumed to be much higher than this. Then the more shocking fact is the cause of the disease is still sceptical while the symptoms are very prominent and clear.

Recognising all the social parameters are entangles with the political ones and it is impossible to separate the two, The Ashoka University's Student Newspaper, *The Edict* shared their views on awaking people on one such ripple effect examined under political scene by stating,

> The side-effects of the post-truth era are not limited to policy decision. Nationalism and Patriotism are being used today as an excuse to criminalise dissent leading to the spread of belligerent public jingoism which is blurring the distinction between activism and radicalism in the minds of the masses.
>
> (Staff, 2018)

Towards the Comprehensive Conclusion

Midst this alarming situation and throbbing of the effects of post-truth Age upon India, let us not forget what Fedrich Max Muller, one of the founding members of installing Western Academic discipline of India, once said, "If I were asked under what sky the human mind has most fully developed some of its choicest gifts, has most deeply pondered on the greatest problems of our life, and has found solutions, I should point to India." It is time to revive the same faith as Muller and build self-confidence believing in the valuable traditions. This is high time to take notice of many such future ripple effects of the Post Truth Era and save ourselves from the unintentional performance of Self Harm. It is now time to bridge the gap between the "Truth" (Objective in nature that can be proven with substantial facts) and "truth" (Subjective in nature); it is time to questions old customary beliefs again by comparing and analysing new trends and peeling off each layer of palimpsest facts suppressed beneath various Indian cultures. It is time to grow from the post-truth age. It is the time to understand that we grow by comprehending the ostensible and not by relegating it.

References

Bandyopadhyay, S. A., & Chatterjee, M. (2020). Assessment of the prevalence of polycystic ovary syndrome among the college students: A case-control study from Kolkata. *Journal of Mahatma Gandhi Institute of Medical Sciences*, *25*(1), 28. https://doi.org/10.4103/jmgims.jmgims_62_19

Hyvönen, A. E. (2018, November 1). *Defining Post-truth: Structures, Agents, and Styles*. E-International Relations. https://www.e-ir.info/2018/10/22/defining-post-truth-structures-agents-and-styles

Joseph, S. (2020). *Ṛtu vidyā: ancient science behind Menstrual Practices*. Notion Press.

Staff, T. E. (2018, September 11). The Predicaments of a Post-Truth Era. *Medium*. https://medium.com/the-edict/the-predicaments-of-a-post-truth-era-f1c939b3435b.

CHAPTER 9

Post-Truth: Notion of the Real in the Digimodern Age

Shemin K.

Post-truth is a political and philosophical notion that remains at the centre of attraction of many of the academic discussions since the term was selected as the word of the year by the *Oxford Dictionary* in 2016. The term was selected as the word of the year considering the substantial upsurge of its usage in that year related to the American Presidential election and the Brexit Referendum. Inquiring into the root of the word, it could be seen that, indeed, it is a new word that was first used by Steve Tesich, a Serbian-American playwright, in one of his essays in 1992. Anyhow, researches show that the concept of post-truth existed long before the coinage of the term and it flourished colossally in the twenty-first century.

Post-Truth & Postmodernism

One of the prevalent arguments regarding post-truth is that it is a result of post-modernism. Examining the notion of post-truth, many scholars, including Lee McIntyre, held the view that it is a new phenomenon that originated towards the end of the twentieth century as a result of post-modernism. Postmodernism had challenged the existence of a single ultimate truth and advocated that there is no single truth but versions of it. Conversely, such an assertion later turned out to be an aid to post-truth. However, certain other critics like Yuval Noah Harari refute this argument and postulate that the notion of post-truth is not a new phenomenon since its traits existed long before. Harari (2019) states that "The truth is that truth was never high on the agenda of *Homo sapiens*" (p.210). Harari argues that religions, which have their origins in the forgone past, are the best examples to show that post-truth is not a new phenomenon for the cornerstone of every religion is believability, not rationality as it is for post-truth. Believability enjoyed primary preference over rationality in most of the communities around the world. Propagation of false news and lies is not new to the human race and many of the politicians and rulers of the world have been using propaganda narratives for ages. Thus, post-truth could not be considered as a result of postmodernism and it did not originate recently. Post-truth, nevertheless, has made use of post-modernism in its favour by highlighting the possibility of the existence of multiple truths. By advocating multiplicity of truth post-modernism does not propagate falsehood or absurdity. Post-truth makes use of alter-narratives for political propaganda and maintains that anything can be true if people are ready to believe in it. In the post-truth age, facts get buried and bullshit flourishes.

Post-Truth: An Offshoot of Digimodernism

The rapid boom of the post-truth traits is linked to digimodernism in a great deal. With digitalisation, the nature of communication got revolutionised and the internet became the information superhighway. In a way, today's post-truth condition could be perceived as an offshoot of the digimodernist culture that came into existence as a result of the digital revolution. With the development of the internet, existing notions of fundamental ideas like that of truth, reality, and communication got through a drastic change which eventually resulted in the birth of a new cultural paradigm. Post-truth, which is often regarded as a result of postmodernism could be analysed differently in the light of digimodernism. Digimodernism, just like post-truth, is a contemporary concept that has gained popularity in a manner even to define the century itself. Alan Kirby, the British cultural critic and blogger, came up with the notion of digimodernism in his 2006 paper "The Death of Postmodernism and Beyond". Kirby postulates that the age of postmodernism is over and a new age of digimodernism has started at the end of the twentieth century. He identifies the impact of "computerisation on all forms of arts, culture, and textuality" as 'digimodernism' (Kirby, 2009, p.1).

According to Kirby (2009), "digimodernism has decisively displaced postmodernism to establish itself as the twenty-first century's new cultural paradigm" (p.1). Towards the end of the twentieth century, many critics began to discuss the question, 'what follows post-modernism?' or 'what lies beyond postmodernism?' Alan Kirby (2009)

identifies digimodernity as "another stage in modernity" (p.2) that followed postmodernism. According to him, digimodernism and postmodernism are connected to each other at various levels. First, digimodernism could be considered as a successor to postmodernism; second, it could be regarded as a phase of hybridity where both postmodernism and digimodernism shared their features together; third, it could be argued that digimodernism inherits many flaws from its predecessor; fourth, it could be recognised as a reaction against postmodernism; and finally it could be understood as "the logical effect of postmodernism". Whatever could be the relationship, digimodernism stands itself as the new cultural order of the new era. Both the concepts of post-truth and digimodernism have much in common and they owe a lot to their predecessor, which is post-modernism. As the world moved to digimodernism, the concept of multiple truths gave way to that of post-truth since the boundary between the real and the unreal became stupefied in the digital era. In the age of post-truth, what is highlighted is not just the existence of multiple truths but the disregard of facts and logic.

Post-truth gained momentum in the current century owing much to the presence of digitally aided society and culture. The digitalised world accelerated the pace of fake news, bullshit, propaganda narratives, and half-truths. The nature of text or narrative has gone through a radical change with the advent of digital technology. Alan Kirby proposes,

> [Digimodernism] owes its emergence and preeminence to the computerisation of text, which yields a new form of textuality characterised in its purest instances by onwardness, haphazardness, evanescence, and anonymous, social and multiple authorship.
>
> (Kirby, 2009, p.1)

In effect, digimodernism is a revolution of the nature of the text and production of meaning that takes place in Web 2.0 platforms such as blogs, Facebook, chat rooms, Wikipedia, and Twitter. In the digital era, the nature of text and meaning production get altered drastically in a way that the meaning of a particular text goes through continuous changes just after the moment it gets published. In a Web 2.0 platform, the published text is directly given to the reader, and thereafter the reader becomes the co-author in the sense that every response to the text contributes meaning to it. Readers intervene and alter the content of the text and thereby reduce the role of the traditional single-author and advocate social and multiple authorship. The text elaborates itself every second and alters its form through the process; thus the text assumes a fluid nature that flows continuously and one cannot reproduce it in its original form for the meaning gets altered every moment. Digimodernism hypothesises that computerisation has reorganised or will reorganise every form of textuality and it will not be narrowed down to online platforms.

Social Media and Agnotology

Narrative or text plays a vital role in the post-truth politics for it is the foremost force that creates and manipulates truth and reality in a society. Believability in the post-truth world is dependent on the strength of the narrative. People tend to believe in something if the narrative fits into their existing belief system. If one manages to come up with a believable narrative, then that narrative becomes the truth for many in the post-truth scenario. Web 2.0 platforms opened up numerous possibilities to create and disseminate one's ideas and opinions through various kinds of narratives. In effect, it is not possible to talk about the post-truth without mentioning social media. Social media or the Web 2.0 platforms altogether made the transmission of narratives instantaneous and easy. Since there are no traditional publication processes and scrutiny, one can come up with any narrative on digital platforms regardless of its truth value: furthermore, one can publish a narrative anonymously without risking his or her identity and reputation. Since post-truth politics is all about creating believable narratives, often by undermining facts and truth, these digital narratives work as an effective tool. Thus, in the post-truth age, social media, indeed, weaponises narratives: when people encounter a narrative in their social feed they are inclined to promote it for it comes from one of their friends or family. That is, the believability of such narratives is higher than any information passed through the traditional media.

Though the digimodern period can be identified as an age of revolution of knowledge, it also becomes an age of agnotology – the culturally induced ignorance or distrust, predominantly the publication of imprecise or deceptive information in the disguise of science. The internet came up with indefinite ways to acquire knowledge and information; as a result, people find themselves surrounded by an ocean of data. But the problem is it is not easy to find which piece of information is real and which one is fabricated. It is argued that, in the post-truth world, there are, "counter-intelligence movements which aim to promote ignorance via the combination of secrecy, censorship and withholding information and concerted efforts to deceive, manufacture and manipulate understandings of particular matters" (Block, 2019, p.44). Creating doubt is one of the primary strategies of the post-truth politics. Post-truth narratives intensify their influence on the people by providing propaganda narratives that are, habitually, misleading and without a factual basis. The abundance of misleading narratives confuses the people and makes it a heavy task to reach the correct information.

Social media platforms work as an effective tool to promote agnotology. As a matter of fact, every individual in the present society lives in an 'echo chamber' provided by social media, where they live with like-minded friends, family, and acquaintances. They share information with each other and tend to believe in it blindly without looking at whether it is true or not. They get exposed to information that suits their existing beliefs and nothing more. This kind of a 'filter bubble effect' facilitates post-truth conditions.

Altered Reality

Virtual reality is another concept that emerged in the cyber cultural space. According to the *Cambridge Dictionary*, it is "a set of images and sounds, produced by a computer, that seem to represent a place or a situation that a person can take part in" (virtual reality, n.d.). Virtual reality provides an artificial environment that can be accepted as real by the user. In other words, it can be considered as a simulated experience that is different from the real world but provides apparently real experience. With the emergence of virtual reality, the already blurred borders of reality and fantasy got murkier in nature. Cyberspace provides the feeling of real experience even though the users are well aware that it is not real. However, people enjoy this alter reality and went for it further and further. Reality got so distorted in the new world that now it is impossible to distinguish the real or the original from the copy. In effect, we have entered into a world of "hyperreality" along with digimodernism.

In due course, existing notions of fundamental ideas like that of truth, reality, and communication got through a radical transformation. Now the question is not about whether a piece of information or narrative is true or not, but whether it is believable or not. In fact, both post-truth, and virtual reality work on the principle of believability. As people become ready to believe in some text or narrative, without owing much to its authenticity and factuality, then it becomes their reality.

Alan Kirby counts apparent reality as one of the major traits of digimodernism along with infantilism, earnestness, and endlessness. The digital culture recounts the notion of reality and provides the feeling of the real to the people without 'the real' in existence. People who immerse themselves in the cyberculture begin to believe the apparent real as the real itself for they can experience it as their reality. The particular concept of apparent reality in digimodernism has much in common with post-truth for it speaks about how people accept the apparent real or believable narratives over truth or reality. Examining how post-truth played a significant role in the American Presidential election, James Ball puts forth an incident. During the election campaign, Donald Trump had claimed that the unemployment rate in the nation has raised to 42 percent, whereas the actual rate was nearly 5 percent. Ball assets, Trump's claim had some basis in reality even though it "seem ridiculous" and "not a helpful way to count unemployment".

> Trump's figure includes retirees, stay-at-home parents, long-term sick and disabled people and others not looking for work, as well as those actually wanting a job and unable to find one. This isn't to say this number isn't misleading – very few voters would want to force retirees or parents into work, and the headline unemployment rate fell dramatically under Obama – but the figure has a basis in reality.
>
> (Ball, 2017, p.18)

People readily believed Trump's narrative about unemployment even though it was not factually accurate but apparently true. Along with this kind of partly true narratives, people willingly believe in utter nonsense too. What matters here is whether the narrative appeals to their emotion and is presented as believable.

Web 2.0 platforms, especially social media, often come up with fabricated evidence to intensify the believability of narratives. Habitually photos are being used out of context or photoshopped images are being used as proof for post-truth narratives. In May 2017, one of the political leaders in Kerala shared a Facebook post condemning cow slaughter in the state and used an image of corpses of cows lying on the side of the road. The social media post and the disturbing image lead to havoc in the society for it created the impression that the incident really happened in Kerala. In reality, the original image was from some parts of West Bengal or Bangladesh and it was cropped to use for the particular Facebook post in order to create misperception. Though the post was proven to be misleading, thousands of people still believe it to be true or rather they find it believable than the truth.

Conclusion

In a nutshell, it could be asserted that digimodernism, rather than postmodernism, paved the way to today's post-truth condition. Though it could not be argued that the notion of post-truth is a result of digimodernism, the emergence of "the post-truth era" could be conceived as an offshoot of digimodernism. A shift to the digital world and the digitalisation of text was an unavoidable phase in the human transition and it contributed a lot to the world. However, it also fuelled the growth of the post-truth culture where fact and truth get subordinated to believability. The Post-truth condition reflects the altered notion of reality in the digimodern age where fact-checking becomes a heavy and uninterested task.

References

Ball, J. (2017). *Post-Truth: How Bullshit Conquered the World.* Biteback Publishing.

Cyberculture. (n.d.). *In The American Heritage Dictionary.* https://www.ahdictionary.com/word/search.html?q= cyberculture

Dennett, D. (2017, February). Daniel Dennett: I begrudge every hour I have to spend worrying about politics. *The Guardian.* https://www.theguardian.com/science/2017/feb/12/daniel-dennett-politics-bacteria-bach-back-dawkins-trump-interview

Block, D. (2019). *Post-Truth and Political Discourse.* Palgrave Pivot.

Harari, Y. N. (2019). *21 Lessons for the 21st Century.* Random House Publishing Group.

Kalpokas, I. (2019). *A Political Theory of Post-Truth.* Palgrave Macmillan.

Keyes, R. (2004). *The Post-Truth Era: Dishonesty and Deception in Contemporary Life.* St. Martin's Press.

Kirby, A. (2009). *Digimodernism: How New Technologies Dismantle the Postmodern and Reconfigure Our Culture.* Continuum.

McComiskey, B. (2017). *Post-Truth: Rhetoric and Composition.* The University Press of Colorado.

McIntyre, L. (2018). *Post-Truth.* MIT Press.

Post-truth. (n.d.). *In Oxford Dictionaries.* www.enoxforddicctionaries.com/definition/post-truth

Pariser, E. (2011). *The Filter Bubble: What the Internet is Hiding from You.* Penguin.

Tesich, S. (1992). A Government of Lies. *The Nation,* 6(13), 12-14. https://drive.google.com/file/d/0BynDrdYrCLNtdmt0SFZFeGMtZUFsT1NmTGVTQmc1dEpmUC1z/view

Virtual reality. (n.d.). *In Cambridge Dictionary.* https://dictionary.cambridge.org/dictionary/english/virtual-reality

CHAPTER 10

Was 'Cyberia' Anticipated? An Ontological Survey of Borges' Select Visionary Works vis-a-vis Post (humanist+truth) Pataphysics

Nipan Nath

Much before the lexical recognition of Post Truth in November 2016, different literary genres belonging to different centuries invoked lie or falsehood in different ways: in 1798 Coleridge exemplified willing "suspension of disbelief" to create "semblance of truth" in his *The Rime of the Ancient Mariner*, in 1884 play *The Wild Duck* Ibsen through doctor Relling advocated "life-lie", in 1926 the protagonist Klamm, the Czech etymology of whose name is "delusion", in Kafka's *The Castle* stepped into a lie-guided strategy and all the three instances, quite engagingly carried their respective seeds of anticipation: killing of the Albatross merely for man-made mythological justification helps Timothy Morton to inculcate eco-critical perspective, Relling's life-lie combined with Hialmer's 'lensed' outlook while perceiving less-than-real of everything paves the way for the invention of the first camera in 1885 and Kafka's narrative of omnipresent surveillance pre-meditates the socio-political mechanism in post-Stalin Russia.

To analyse the style and relevance of this anticipated manoeuvre is to discover that Eco-criticism by replacing anthropomorphic ('worldly') concerns with ecological ('earthly') consideration, visual representation of camera by always capturing less-than-real of everything (=diminution and distortion of the real) and the 'cybernation' by allowing omnipresent surveillance of CCTV and webcam together in the last four decades have brought about a catastrophic transformation, even reversal of reality and reality-induced truth. What once was identified by Alfred Jarry as a spoof of austere scientific method Pataphysics, coming to terms with Neo-ethical parameters after the after-theory session and 9/11 attack, has evidently debunked the formal, monistic (Spinoza's) and monadological (Leibnitz's) speculations of classical Metaphysics; what earlier was pure consciousness combined with human dignity and reasoned order under Humanism can now almost be downloaded in a supercomputer that through Post-humanist blurring of the boundaries between the human body and techno-electronic prostheses may actually put morphed Gautam Buddha and virtual porn star Lulu, cyborged Mona Lisa and animated Lord Ganesha on the same pedestal of "cyberia" to be explicated later. This peregrination has necessarily resulted in the inevitably burlesquing and invariably belligerent vicissitudes of TRUTH, weft and warp of truth being para-truth, anti-truth, sub-truth, semi-truth eventuated in forgeries, fabrication, fibbery, falsehood, briefly Post Truth. The condition is philosophically apocalyptic, perhaps more a concoction than Baudrillard's identification of media as one offering "dizzying whirl of reality" (Lane, 2007, p.72), more a fiasco than Lyotard's conceptualisation of knowledge which "cannot survive unchanged" (Lyotard, 1984, p.4). Taken together, the prognosis is not good.

In the event of such essential metamorphosis of the ontology (of truth) this survey, following interpretive analysis, attempts to examine the nature and implications of the conscious and unconscious anticipation found scattered in select short fictions written by the bibliophilic visionary Borges. While Borges' *The Circular Ruins*, *The Lottery in Babylon*, *The Library of Babel*, *The Book of Sand*, *Blue Tigers* and the like will remain the primary texts, certain concepts from Postmodernist terminology as well as from Post- postmodernist worldview, shall secondarily provide for the broader theoretical framework to deal with Post Truth zeitgeist, (un)equipped with meme, not "me", with i-phone, not "I".

Understanding the Post of Truth and Human

The last part of the first section "Post Truth zeitgeist, (un)equipped with meme, not 'me', with i-phone, not 'I'" involves two paradoxes: first, in order to have a zeitgeist, there must be certain forms of defining spirit or mood based on some degree of truth which is categorically absent in case of Post Truth. It follows that in terms of philosophical foundation Post Truth is a mise-en-abyme where facts are so selected, so tactfully shaded and thus presented that it will offer the zeitgeist only when the absence of foundation itself is considered a philosophy. In the context of deconstruction Barbara Johnson once pointed out the need of discovering the other of philosophy, but instead of supplying that "otherness", the Post Truth zeitgeist through the manipulated facts merely renders a vacuum of nothingness. The facts here are not conceived or received as they are in reality, rather they are conceived, even created according to one's perception to fit into now-transformed reality. To quote McIntyre, "..... many see post-truth as part of a growing international trend where some feel emboldened to try to bend reality to fit their opinions, rather than the other way round" (Mcintyre, 2018, p. 5-6).

Secondly, under such so-formed zeitgeist if there is any ontological and existential truth, as suggested by the terms "me" and "I" above, those will be so intra-chimerical, so tactfully self-deceptive and thus hypo-representative that they seem to (equipped), but do not (unequipped) contain selfhood. Derrida once undertook a deconstructive genealogy of the concept of lie and therefore of veracity thereby maintaining the distinction, but instead of any deconstructive genealogy, Post Truth flanked with cybernetic ramifications of news media and social networking sites simply offers a mirage. The representation and the re-representation of facts in the form of news and the happy-go-lucky faces of Facebook and always the best WhatsApp status now are not foregrounding reality of any kind, rather they are certain politically convenient and intellectually prejudiced cave of opportunistic bats and narcissistic darkness. Neither memes created by one nor the one (me) who creates are the replicas of truth, because that "me" (I) too is no more the ontologically proven "I", rather Post-humanist "I" energised by i-charge, glued to i-pad, going round (pun intended) with i-phone etc..

Clubbed with Post Truth is Posthumanism which having been based on the concepts of biotic component and genetic engineering engenders replication and computer simulation with no real referent to fall back upon. There had been numerous examples of pre-human like Jambavanta and Hanuman, trans-human like zombies and revenants, Humanimal like vampire and batman, but in the late 20th and early 21st century world of cyborg incarnation one is destined to meet part-human and part-machine in *Robocop* (1987), to encounter those pigs of 1995 movie *Babe* who are genetically rendered with all possible humanoid characteristics and also to be threatened by the cyberpunks of Gibson's

Neuromancer where the difference between human being and computer, nature and technology, real and simulation are totally imploded and finally collapsed. Under this contemporary post-humanist milieu it is, therefore, almost impossible to attach human attributes onto the culturally schizophrenic "prosumers" – the single person being both the producer and consumer at the same time. For every single need of daily life, a prosumer depends upon the internet and in every single interaction, there is the possibility of deception. Ralph Keyes maintains that cyber-hood is "essentially an ethics-free zone, a perfect hothouse for the germination of the seeds of post-truthfulness" (2019, p.146).

Borges in Post (humanist) Body & Post (truth) Mind

Part I

Offering the readers the "minimum of visible world" the initial part of the narrative in *The Circular Ruins* is based firstly on a plethora of negations – no one witnessing anything, no one knowing anything about the person's homeland, even God too went unhonoured and secondly on the absence of (proper) noun – neither the sorcerer nor the sallow-skinned pupil has any specific identity, even whether the eventful night of discovering the students' passivity was ninth or tenth, whether or not the two unnamed rowers really woke the protagonist remain unanswered. All these amounts to make the story such a parody of realism that most of the narrative detour moves forward (or moves round) with dreams; that the denouement of the story reveals the essential replication of the same reality weaved through dreams or dreamt reality; that the details on the 'formation' of the dreamt persona are nothing short of posthumanist robotics. Unlike a human body born of sex, the man was to be 'produced' through dreams in painstaking details and accordingly a beating heart and pulmonary artery was dreamt, eyelids and skeleton were also dreamt and designed. It is through the sorcerer's dream that the son exists, as if a software programme simulating a stripling figure; it is due to the 'engineer's' whimsicality that no memory of the formative years was left behind in the phantasm. A parody of realism attempted via dream vision to install a non-human, faceless, sexless figure to reiterate the identical circularity for the creator as well is potentially reflective of how posthumanism, both technically and ontologically, (un)furnish the foundation for far-from-real (=dream), non-linear (=circular), semi-human (="mere simulacrum") condition conducive to Post Truth in later years.

In contrast to the deletion of the memory of education from the son's mind in *The Circular Ruins*, in *Shakespeare's Memory,* there is the addition of the Elizabethan prodigy's memory to that of Sorgel, a pedantic Shakespeare scholar. Though Sorgel first thought that he "had been offered the ocean" in the form of the bard's memory, he gradually discovered several nebulous facts Shakespeare himself desired to forget and at that discovery he could not but be terrified and oppressed already hinted at in the epigrammatic statement thus: "A man's memory is not a summation, it is a chaos of vague possibilities". Apparently fantastical this weird conglomeration of memories seems to allegorise the postmodernist art of collage and montage where layers of representation merge rendering it impossible to decipher the ontological base of human memory. If memory can be shifted, the reality upheld by that memory will also be transferred and in that case translocation of a computerised programme from one software system to another to control a humanoid entity tends to be envisaged.

To Borges, realities lie in infinity and to write a story or a poem is to invoke the mind to configure a tentative reality, summarised in the conclusion of 1939 essay *The Total Library* thus:

> One of the habits of the mind is the invention of horrible imaginings. The mind has invented Hell,....... it has imagined the Platonic ideas,....... , masks, mirrors,..... I have tried to rescue from oblivion a subaltern horror: the vast contradictory library.
>
> (Borges, 1999, p.216)

Five years later in 1944, Borges in *The Library of Babel* elaborated upon the commodious details of a library where everything is indefinite, infinite yet endlessly the same inviting more than one similarity with what a reader today encounters while reading hyperfiction. S/he will be as disoriented as a visitor in Borgesian library gets muddled while traversing the hexagonal galleries; secondly, just the way the second axiom relates "the leagues of senseless cacophony, verbal nonsense, and incoherency" s/he cannot settle down with only one part of the text like every other word as a hyperlink will lead the reader onto a new reading zone. Again, the library just like cyberspace is both liberating and restrictive: on one hand, the library will hopefully put forward a solution to the mysteries of the universe, on the other hand, such books containing the solutions can never be found. The inquisitor has to face the mirror which symbolises how the cyber world works – "a mirror, which faithfully duplicates appearances" culminating in the ontological paradox: "Men often infer from this mirror that the library is not infinite

– if it were, what need would there be for that illusory replication?" The sardonic answer to this paradox, however, is within the storyline which incorporates "All – the faithful catalog of the Library, thousands and thousands of false catalogs, the proof of the falsity of those false catalogs, a proof of the falsity of the true catalog......", all the allusions surprisingly alluding to the stages of the ontological peregrination viz. from Truth to falsity, from falsity to lie, from lie to lied facts as truths, from lied facts to Post Truth.

Part II

From the library, the issue has almost been ideally relegated to the book of sand in the story by the same name, though the course of change from joy to horror still reverberates, this time through the narration of a book collector who possesses the book, but cannot dispose it off. Compiled with random pagination the book contains an infinite number of pages, but once a page is turned over, it can never be retrieved; besides, "neither sand nor this book has a beginning or an end" as put by a man from Bikaner, who is said to be its real owner, but cannot be. As indicated by the Indian's talismanic statement, various things including the bills paid to the seller, the tentative areas for hiding the book, are either uncertain or patternless. Even "I" who suffers from insomnia is an ontologically displaced "I" who himself/herself looked upon "with my (his) eyes". In the Borgesian world, this has to happen invariably because the narrator, like Borges himself, suffers from nearsightedness and the result is "a reality defiled and corrupted" by the monstrous book. In fact, "I" along with the book of sand is metaphorically the hyperreal online personas caught in the virtual cornucopia of options culminated in hypostatisation of choice – a sort of reification that refers to the construal of a conceptual entity as a real existent: choice here is not about whether one enters the cyber world or not, but about where to get lost in the cybernation.

All the proconsuls of Babylon too had no choice whatsoever – as a major element of reality, a lottery determines the lives of the citizens, ludicrously enough, with their own consent. They are resorting to lottery even at the cost of getting right index finger amputated, suggesting an inability of writing, tongue burned to suggest a curtailment of free speech, declared invisible suggesting total capitulation of life including chance-dictated death, in the clutches of a lottery so much so similar with post-postmodernist domination of informatics with "truth being displaced by believability" (Boorstein). Be it installation of an app registering oneself for cybersex games, be it virtual pornography or security of one's bank account, everything cybernetic goes hand in hand with the unknown, unknowable authority under which what is practised is "indirect falsehood" anticipated to be termed as Post Truth.

The fetishism enforced through a multifaceted coin in *The Zahir* and the fugitive number of tigers defying mathematical accuracy in *Blue Tigers* brings adequate parallelism between Borgesian labyrinths and contemporary world affairs. The way zahir compelled people to perceive less and less of reality is similar to the present-day obsession with social networking sites, the blue tigers followed the same emotive approach the followers in *Instagram* and *Twitter* adopt while handling trolls, memes, fake news; when the narrator's "idee fixi" and "fundamental error" were singled out, the fictionalised reality started dwindling, almost as fast as clickbaiters on finding someone's comment detrimental to his/her interest un-friend or hide him/her either to carry on 'personal reality' uninterrupted or to carry out 'personalised ethics' bereft of truth on another e-platform.

Materialising 'Cyeria', Dematerialising Truth

A more detailed survey of Borgesian fictions seems to open up newer dimensions of anticipation in terms of numerous tools recently found operative: *Pierre Menard, Author of the Quixote* exemplifies straw-man argument of misrepresentation, *The Garden of Forking Paths* epitomises the possibility of alternative facts; *Borges and I* touch upon the trickery of distraction created by the logical fallacy of Red Herring – all these buttressing the plinth of fundamentalism and jingoism. If Borges' fantasy in *Dreamtigers* depicted misinformation prevalent in today's world, disinformation aimed at wilful dissemination of damaging facts, is its upgraded version available under Post Truth praxis; if cherry-picking was simply a narrative style in *Et cetera*, the same notion of selective attitude is too common a device of populism aided equally by the present mechanism of the slippery slope, ripple effect and lieholism.

As there is duping delight in nullifying truth, Post Truth triumphs, more so in anticipated 'cyberia' – a coinage chosen deliberately first to delimit the spatio-temporal parameters of Post Truth and secondly to attempt a lingo-philosophical statement wrapped in a piquant word-play. As for the first reason, Cyberia is a space created by post-humanist and cybernetic manifestations; secondly, on hearing "Cyberia" one will immediately relate it with the Russian province while reading it s/he will take it to be a spelling error, but in both the cases the reality of the word will be obtained only when the reality of real "Siberia" is suspended; proportionately the ontology of truth can be materialised only when truth in the form of Post Truth is swindled.

In 1981 for illustrating simulacrum Baudrillard took the help of a Borgesian map which was as expansive as to camouflage the entire territory the map represents. In 2021 Borges' vision of cyberia vis-a-vis post(humanist+truth) pataphysics is as anticipatory as to accommodate the entirety of 'irreal' hypo-epistemological zeitgeist. Who knows, human and truth are going to be the first single-word oxymorons!!

References

Barry, P. (2018). Theory after Theory. In *Beginning Theory.* Viva Books Private Limited.

Borges, L. J. (1998). *Collected Fictions.* Andrew Hurley (Trans.), Penguin Classics.

Dellamora, R. (Ed). (1995). *Postmodern Apocalypse.* University of Pennsylvania Press.

Keyes, R. (2019). *The Post-Truth Era.* St. Martin's Press.

Lane, R. J. (2007). *Jean Baudrillard.* Routledge.

MCintyre, L. (2018). *Post-Truth.* The MIT Press.

Nayar, P. K. (2014). *Posthumanism.* Polity Press.

Parui A. (2018). Postmodernism, Literature and Technology. In *Postmodern Literatures.* Orient Blackswan Private Limited.

Powell, J. (1998). *Postmodernism for Beginners.* Orient BlackSwan.

Rathee, D. (2019). Andh Bhakt Banerjee Debates with Dhruv Rathee. *Youtube.* https://youtu.be/ZZOeyLiBKtc

Russell, B. (2004). *The History of Western Philosophy.* Routledge.

Russell, M. J. (2015). *A Brief Guide to Philosophical Classics.* Robinson.

Sasson-Henry, P. (2006). Borges' "The Library of Babel" and "Moulthrop's Cybertext "Reagan Library" Revisited. *Rocky Mountain Modern Language Association Journal.* 60(2), 11-12 https://www.jstor.org/stable/4143854

Weinberger, E. (Ed). (1999). *Jorge Luis Borges Selected Non-Fictions.* Penguin Classics.

Williamson, E. (Ed). (2013). *The Cambridge Companion to Jorge Luis Borges.* Cambridge University Press.

CHAPTER 11

Post-truth and the COVID 19 Truce: Reflections on the Pandemic and Media Constructivism

Dr. Mallika A. Nair

> We can no longer think of ourselves as the centre of the world, we can no longer believe that we are invincible, and we can no longer underestimate the destructive power of even the smallest things-like a virus.
>
> (Fang, 2020)

The concept of post-truth has in the recent past been an object of constant deliberation and public debate. Its popular and academic treatments sometimes differ in respect to its meaning, but most associate it with communication forms such as fake or false news, rumours, hoaxes, and political lying. Polarisation of factual events to formulate a propagandist and predefined social construct happens to be one of the most emphatic ramifications of the Post-truth ideology. The intimidating effects of an outrageous pandemic and the resultant chaos indeed call for a deeper analysis that would in many ways assist in a proper understanding of human life and its socio-economic vagaries. The unprecedented effects of the lockdown enhanced the power of the media and journalism industry. Mass media has in no time become the norm of the day.

The Pandemic and Post-truth

Pandemic is a moment of epiphany; to judge, to choose and to decide. Beyond its biological and virological existence, every pandemic with its brutal honesty assumes the stature of a prophet to bring into light the calamitous effects of a long and most dominating human intervention on earth. The epidemiological catastrophe unfolds the voids of human ontology and moves the less-than-human others- sexualised others (women, LGBTQ+), racialised others (non-European, indigenous) and naturalised others (plants, animals, the Earth) to the centre stage, pushing old Anthropos off- centre. A pandemic brings home to this anthropogenic world, an ancient truth that

It is in these trying times that the human race operates as a whole. There simply cannot exist a 'you' and a 'me'; there can only be a 'we'. The classic mantra of 'person, place and time' is of paramount importance in times of a pandemic. And regulating proper communication is as important as monitoring the disease. Disease surveillance during a pandemic is in many ways directly linked to smooth, efficient and faultless dissemination of proper mass communication system. It is here that one engages with the concept of post-truth and the vagaries of fake news that circulate in society making possible solutions at roping-in the convulsive effects of a pandemic. Obviously, COVID-19 is not the first pandemic to deal with the burden of false information, fake news and lies. A lie repeated multiple times gains momentum as a wave and gathers strength so powerful that even the most salient and subtle truths are often blown up in the resultant cacophony.

Analysis of Fake in Post-truth

Post-truth identifies the proliferation of lies in two ways- one that flows from the top of a social ladder, slowly seeping down to the nether worlds of societal hierarchy. That is, the top-down phenomenon where false information is generated by politicians to manipulate the medical emergency of a pandemic into possible vote banks. Such a propagandist post-truth phenomenon often creates a dark void within which the truth lies hidden for as long as the proliferators intend it to be hidden. The situation is further worsened as the media takes up the fake news and dissipates it to the common public. The resultant scenario creates a hyper-real situation herein information is crudely designed to fit the expanse of a panic-stricken public. Many such misconceived notions were found to float around various countries of the world during the COVID-19 pandemic. The mob that got out onto the streets with lighted torches and candles to ward off the virus, or the mass assemblies where people collectively banged plates and utensils to frighten away the SARS COVID virus are only some of them. Post-truth emphatically demands these external manifestations of the fear factors within a mob as instruments of wielding the false as factual.

Now, there also exists a second way of deciphering the post-truth phenomenon. It is the bottom-up process wherein the general public's reactions to the COVID-19 Pandemic may be evaluated. There has been quite a number of parallel practices to curb the pandemic. People found relying on parallel medical practices more comforting. The YouTube shared the 'secret recipes' of infinite magical potions and drinks that would miraculously cure the Pandemic. Homoeopathy, Yunani, Ayurveda and Chinese medicine claimed a better cure than the modern scientific and medical advice for the COVID 19 Pandemic. And the laity's leanings to household remedies, without proper medical diagnosis added on to the ambiguous sarcasm with which safety measures such as the use of masks, sanitisers and measures of hygiene are looked down upon. These were but a few of the social media endeavours that add up to this second post-truth phenomenon. The Oxford University Journal on Media Communication states how the layman pounces upon all possible rumours that chance throws in front of his narrow perception only to make him/her act most ludicrously. One such impaling instance would be the alleged fallacy that a hairdryer could mitigate one of the COVID-19 symptoms when blown up the nostrils. And to make matters worse, the fear psychosis triggers an untoward need to garner whatever is offered in terms of a possible solace from the pandemic, without the slightest heed to proper scientific explanation.

> Even worse is the perception that there is no objective 'truth' and so no need to search for it or to test claims against it. Rather, truth feels fleeting claims are more or less persuasive based not on the accumulation of rigorous science or the credibility and expertise of the speaker but on the celebrity, political party, or intuition of speaker and listener.
>
> (OUP 2018, p. 4)

Mass Media communications networks like Facebook, Twitter, television news and Youtube manipulate the already misinformed news into more complex modes of disseminating false information. According to the Oxford Research Encyclopaedia, Communication, the three modes of constructing falsehood may be categorised as rumour bombs, fake news and lying (OUP 2018, p. 36).

James Fallows further speaks about the 'Post-truth media' (Fallows, 2012), while Farhad Manjoo, a New York Times technology columnist, announced the arrival of "post-fact society" in his book True Enough. The book elaborates on how the Post-Truth era has harbingered an Age of mass dishonesty. The politicians mangle information to retain power, while the media follows propaganda and relates information according to their economic and political agenda. And the public picks and choose news that caters to their *A la Carte* appetite.

Truth versus Post-truth

So, why post-truth and why not the truth? People often perceive, listen and comprehend what they want to and not want is. While truth takes time to proliferate for the very reason that it is reasonable, demystifying and factual, fake news proliferates and multiplies like the mutant strain of the virus itself. It fans the imaginative flames within the mob flaring up like a great ball of fire, destroying all possibilities of phenomenal evidence.

The origin of pandemics may be traced back to primitive times. Our pre and proto-human ancestors were tightly fitted to an elaborate self-regulating ecological balance. Consequently, they had a tolerable state of health even though they were amidst myriad forms of parasites. Gradually humankind started to respond to a new sort of biological and cultural evolution (orthogenic) and it, in turn, disturbed the balance of nature in unforeseen and far-reaching ways. The change of habitat led to a substantial alteration in the kind of infections one is likely to encounter. Thus the disease liability of humankind began to change and new parasites and fresh diseases emerged on humanity (McNeill, 1977). Biological cataclysms especially hyperinfestations (which is now termed as pandemics) can be considered as natural biological checks or; 'a rebellion of an injured ecosphere' (Sontag, 1978) to restore the imbalances created by the spurt evolution of a single species (human beings) to the apex of the food chain. In other words, every pandemic is a dramatic call to reorganise and rebuilt a realistic connection between the direction of civilisation and its earthly, material conditions of existence (Schultz, 2020).

The myriad forms of false information and their riotous acceptance by the public owes its *raison d'être* to the ancient fear of the unknown. Economic inequality and the mad rush for power have dissolved man's need for honesty. It is in the modern-day considered only a rudimentary ideology of a long-forgotten Utopian past. Moreover, often a lie repeated over and over again by political leaders creates erasures of original and authentic happenings.

Ever since the first appearance of the pandemic, there were diverse spiritual, metaphysical and earthly explanations attached to its etiology. For the longest period of time, it was believed to be God's wrath. Later the focus turned to other reasons like the alignment of the planets, miasma, contagion and human susceptibility. The centuries-old myriad explanations were reduced into one by the laboratory revolution in the late nineteenth century which culminated in the discovery of bacteria as the cause of many diseases. Though it cultivated undue confidence in the power of biomedicine to triumph over infectious diseases, the episodic returns of new forms of the past diseases led to a realisation of the impossibility to rid the world of pandemics.

> Thus, this recurring planetary crisis transformed into an unending fear and dread in the minds of humanity of all times; In the face of its onrush, all the wisdom and ingenuity of man were unavailing... All of the advice of physicians and all the power of medicine were profitless and unavailing.
>
> (Boccaccio, 2003)

One may find its pervasive presence in all realms of human discourses. Eyewitnesses, novelists, poets, memoirist, scientists, medical practitioners, spiritual scholars, government bureaucrats, journalists, anthropologists, epidemiologists, historians, kings, queens, and presidents – have been writing about epidemics and pandemics for centuries, reflecting on what causes them, what might stop them, and how people have reacted to them (McMillen, 2016).

The accusative anomalies of the fourth estate might just be another way of humankind's struggle to fight the pandemic. It is indeed important to comprehend the reasons that post-truth uses to justify falsity. The truth is often overshadowed by a lie simply for the reason that a lie is easier to accept and more comforting to the listener while the truth is often painful and hard to bear. One of the major concerns that haunted people in all parts of the world was with regards to the actual number of people infected by the COVID-19 virus. China seemed to have curbed the onslaught of the virus as quickly as it had begun. The actual death counts, it is said, far exceeded that of the reported count. Thus, the truth was distorted to avoid human panic and enable the world governments to portray a balmier visage.

So, then has it all been overwhelmingly shady with no essence of finer emotions? Can there be a possible truce between the jarring ideologies of post-truth and the COVID-19 Pandemic?

Post-truth and the COVID-19 Truce

The inexplicable randomness with which contradictory information travels through social media is to a great extent curbed when people use it to create contents that uplift the human spirit even in the trying times of a pandemic. When the world and all its activities came to a lockdown, social media communities emerged to bond relationships and hold people together. There were online awareness campaigns and tag phrases that taught people to restrain and caution. Slogans such as 'break the chain', and 'Stay home, stay safe' did account for enhanced public awareness. The naïve unpreparedness of the human community to face the disease and its immediate human-centric consequences became the theme of all mass media sites. Social media helped in connecting people and reached out in a thousand different ways to people who really needed them. We found means of connecting to people through media platforms with money, food and medical attention. Thousands of health workers and volunteers risked their own lives to help their brethren. The realisation that every individual owes his/ her responsibility to the community even as the community too has its responsibility towards its citizens awoke a sense of justice in media communications thereby strengthening its presence in human life. The media's presence was thus personalised within individual realms thereby quintessentially working on a wider canvas beyond the humanistic and anthropocentric realisations. The very contradiction between the etymological meaning of the term 'pandemic' (all human) and the demand at the core of this recurring crisis (to go beyond human) itself shows that COVID-19 might just succeed in bursting the post-truth bubble.

Let us just hope here for an inverted pyramid effect as they call in journalism, wherein, the media becomes the voice of the common man. They might as well address the social, economic, political and cultural gaps in society thereby catering to intimidating anxieties that engulf humanity. Pandemics might indeed push humans to build a new normal, but they can also ease us to rethink ways to recreate the lost normalcy of human communities at large.

Media Discourses on pandemics have a tremendous role in preparing generations to face cataclysms of such kind during their own times. They are the power capsules most sought after in a quarantined world. There have been infinite media narratives across Facebook, Twitter and YouTube that lay bare the survival stories of men and women who have fought the battle against the Pandemic and survived to tell the tale to provide hope and guidance to triumph over the "formidable enemy [pandemic] arm'd with terrors" (Defoe, 1886). But as the world leaves its sick beds, these narratives are also left behind without much research. One may find certain isolated metaphorical analysis and studies on cultural and social reactions of the people of the times and the rest lies dormant in some medical records and historical texts as like the infectious bacteria itself which withdraws from the limelight for a temporary period. In fact, no glaring effort has so far taken to decode the substantial lessons concealed under the swollen buboes and fever.

Conclusion

Albert Camus in his Nobel Banquet speech rightly remarked that every individual had within themselves the moral responsibility of reforming the world they inhabited. As we belong to a generation called to witness one of the deadliest pandemics ever recorded in human history, mass communication networks and social media platforms are freighted with the responsibility to make use of this spiritual, existential time to deconstruct the boundaries that we have built around the notion of painful truths, comforting half-truths as well as residual post-truths. Let the mob comprehend the presence of the media and its social constructivism as a symbiotic necessity that would help grow the society's relationships with honest communication right to our roots. Rather than the human-centric, narrow notions of unethical miscommunications, let the media decipher a legitimate and honest space in society, and that too not at the centre of all happenings but as sentinels of unflinching justice within the network of the web of life 'in spite of our times and out of love of our times' (Braidotti, 2013).

References

Atraud, A. (1958). The Theatre and the Plague. *Theatre and Its Double.* 15-32.

Boccaccio, G. (2003). *The Decamaron.* Penguin Classics.

Braidotti, R. (2013).*The Posthuman.* Polity Press.

Braidotti, R. (2020, October). We Are In This Together, But We Are Not the Same. *Bioethical Inquiry*, 2020. https://doi.org/10.1007/s11673-200-100178

Camus, A. (1991). *The Plague.* Vintage Books.

Carmichael, A.G. (1998, April). The Last Plague: The Use of Memory in Renaissance Epidemics. *Journal of the History of Medicine and Allied Sciences*, 53 (2), 132-160, *JSTOR*, www.jstor.com/ stable/24624268

Clarke, B. & Rossini, M. (Ed). (2017). *The Cambridge Companion to Literature and the Posthuman.* Cambridge University Press.

Cohn, S & R Lynch. (2017, March). Posthuman perspectives: relevance for a global public. *Critical Public Health*, 27 (3), 285-292. doi.org/10.1080/09581596. 2017.1302557.

Crawfurd, R. (1914). *Plague and Pestilence in Literature and Art.* Oxford University Press.

Defoe, D. (1986). *A Journal of the Plague Year.* Routledge.

Derrida and Leavey Jr. (1984). Of an Apocalyptic Tone Recently Adopted in Philosophy. *Oxford Literary Review*, 6 (2), 3-37. Edinburg University Press. JSTOR, www.jstor.org/stable/43973661

Diamond, J. M. (2005). *Guns, Germs, and Steel: the Fates of Human Societies.* Norton.

Fallows, J. (2012, September). Three 'Post-Truth' Related Items. *The Atlantic.* https://www.theatlantic.com/politics/archive/2012/08/three-post-truth-related-items/261853

Fang, F. (2020). *Wuhan Diaries: Dispatches from a Quarantined City.* Harper Collins.

Ferrando, F. (2019). *Philosophical Posthumanism.* Bloomsburry.

Friese, C. & Nuytes, N (2017). Posthumanist critique and human health: how nonhumans (could) figure in public health research. *Critical Public Health*, 27 (3), 303-313. doi:10.1080/09581596.2017.1294246.

Gates, B. (2020, April). Responding to Covid-19-A Once-in-a-Century Pandemic? *The new England Journal of Medicine*, 1677-1679. doi.org/10.1056/NEJMp2003762.

Girard, R. (1974). The Plague in Literature and Myth. *Texas Studies in Literature and Language*, 15 (5), 833-850. *JSTOR*, www.jstor.com/stable/40754299.

Haraway, D. J (1991). The Biopolitics of Postmodern Bodies: Constitutions of Self in Immune System Discourses. *Simians, Cyborgs and Women*, 203-230. Routledge.

Hayles, K. (1999). *How We Became Posthuman: Virtual Bodies in Cybernetics, Literature, and Informatics.* University Press of Chicago.

Hayles, K. (2020, April). Novel Corona: Posthuman Virus. *Critical Inquiry*, critinq.wordpree.com/ 200/04/17/nove-corona-posthuman-virus

Hlavajova, R. & Braidotti, M. (Eds.). (2018). *Posthuman Glossary.* Bloomsbury.

Jandric, P. (2020). Review of Fang Fang (2020). Wuhan Dairy: Dispatches from a Quarantined City. Trans. M. Berry. *Post-digital Science and Education.* Harper Collins. 370-377. doi.org/10.1007/s42438-020-00173-w.

Latour, B. (1998). *The Pasteurisation of France.* A. Sheridan and J Law (Trans.). Harvard University Press.

Manjoo, F. (2008). *True Enough: Learning to Live in a Post–Fact Society.* John Wiley & Sons.

McMillen, W. C. (2016). *Pandemics: A Very Short Introduction.* Oxford University Press.

McNeill, W (Ed). (1977). *Plagues and People.* Anchor Books.

Nayar, K. P. (2014). *Posthumanism.* Polity Press.

Pepperell, R. (2003). *The Posthuman Condition: Consciousness beyond the brain.* Intellect.

Peters, M. (2020, March). A. Viral Modernity? epidemics, infodemics, and the 'bioinformational' paradigm. *Educational Philosophy and Theory*, Routledge. doi.org/10.1080/00131857.2020. 1744226.

Porter, K A. (1939). *Pale Horse, Pale Rider.* Random House.

Schultz, N. (2020, March). The Climatic Virus in an Age of Paralysis. *Critical Inquiry*, critinq.wordpree.com/2020/03/21/the-climatic-virus-in-an-age-of-paralysis.

Sontag, S. (1978). *Illness as Metaphor.* Farrar: Straus and Giroux.

Steel, D. (1981, June). Plague Writing: From Boccaccio to Camus. *Journal of European Studies*, 11 (42), 88-110. doi.org/10.1177/004724418101104202.

Thacker, E. (2003, December). Data Made Flesh: Biotechnology and the Discourse of the Posthuman. *Cultural Critique*, 53, 72-97. University of Minnesota Press. http://dx.doi.org/10.1353/cul.2003.0029

Wolf, C. (2010). *What is Posthumanism?*. University of Minnesota Press.

CHAPTER 12

Post-Truth in Cults: Propaganda of Charles Manson and the Literary Works of Ayn Rand

Josephine Mercy

Cult Propaganda, Literature and Leaders

Post-truth in Cult Propaganda and Literature

In the world of post-truth, objectivity and moral standards are of practically no value. It is a Utilitarian belief that prioritises one's feelings over facts. Utilitarianism encourages people to look beyond moral standards and avoid holding them as the ultimate truths in the world. If the consequence of the desired action would give one happiness, Utilitarianism believes in treating it as morally right. As one can perceive, the word 'morality' has undergone many revisions in the past century.

Cult groups operate on this notion of appealing to one's emotions by doing away with concrete reality. A cult commonly refers to the deviance in the theological, political or other beliefs that aim at attaining personal goals set by an individual or a group. These groups are led by charismatic leaders and are designed to enthral not just the naïve people, as one may imagine, but also those who are of high intellect.

Charles Manson and Ayn Rand as Cult Leaders

The propaganda of a notorious cult leader named Charles Manson has attracted the attention of journalists and writers of the 21st century. His manipulative techniques, captivating speeches and deceptive ideology had given him a mass following. Ayn Rand, on the other hand, has been hailed as one of America's most popular writers. She is widely recognised for her powerful protagonists in *The Fountainhead* and *Atlas*

Shrugged. However, Rand's philosophy of 'Objectivism' is far from rational thinking and focuses solely on gratifying one's personal desires through ways that may be considered selfish. Ayn Rand established her dogma on egoism and her philosophy is now deemed as a cult by leading anti-cult organisations. These notions can be analysed in the light of post-truth.

The Propaganda of Charles Manson

The Birth of "The Family"

Charles Manson lived a life that depended on thievery and drug trafficking. When he was 26 years old, he had spent 14 years in jail. The Dale Carnegie course which was offered in prison helped him learn lessons on manipulation and he used it to betray people's trust. His previous experience as a pimp had taught him that "the best recruits were bruised and needy but not completely broken" (Guinn, 2014, p. 96)

He started preaching about love and harmony in the corners of busy streets where he knew young people gathered. By twisting facts and truths to suit his needs, he lured people into joining his cult group. Through his manipulative nature, he deceived people by telling them that he saw them as individuals with potential and power. The sense of belonging is something people long for and when swindlers like Manson offer it freely, the trap is set.

> When a liar deliberately and expressly wants to conceal a falsehood, he says that the lie is merely his opinion and, like any person in a liberal democratic country, he enjoys freedom of expression and the right to express his opinion
>
> (Brahms, 2020, p. 3)

Manson was also highly egoistic and demanded complete obedience. He took recluse to violent means and subjugated his followers. However, this behaviour of his was not made manifest when he first started the process of recruiting members to his group. Using sweet and deceptive language, he lured women who were later used to attract "useful" men to the group. The group came to be called "The Manson Family" or simply "The Family".

Psychological Persuasion

Cultists use 'Coercive persuasion' or 'extraordinary influence' to brainwash their followers. People are urged, or in this case forced, to leave their families and friends behind and pledge unflinching allegiance to the cult group. Group pressures and strict enforcement of the rules enable to speed up this process (Singer, 2003, p. 52).

According to Margaret Thaler Singer (2003), there are primarily six conditions that need to be fulfilled by cultists to gain access to the minds of the followers. Each of these conditions can very well be applied to the techniques used by Charles Manson.

1. Keep the person unaware that there is an agenda to control or change the person
2. Control time and physical environment
3. Create a sense of powerlessness, fear and dependency
4. Suppress old behaviour and attitudes
5. Instill new behaviour and attitudes
6. Put forth a closed system of logic.

(p. 63)

People have an erroneous perception that only those who lack discretion fall for such traps. It is far from the truth. The first person to be recruited by Manson was a librarian named Mary Brunner. Jim Jones, a cult leader who is remembered as the mastermind behind the catastrophe at Jonestown, had people from diverse backgrounds as his followers.

Disguising Truth

Manson avowed to save humanity from danger and desired to be worshipped as the reincarnation of Jesus Christ. Adding to that, Charles Manson was influenced by The Beatles and believed that the song "Helter Skelter" had a special meaning. He saw it as a race war that would eliminate all of humanity. He believed that he was Abaddon who would take his followers to a secret place in the desert for safety, from which they would emerge as world rulers when the war was over. This is described in Revelations 9:11 (*The Holy Bible: New King James Version,* 1988, p. 1086).

Though many did not believe that he was God, they were surprised at how he seemed resistant to diseases. When the others fell ill frequently, it was impossible for them to not see their leader's secret power that withheld him from being sick in bed. It reinforced to his followers that he was definitely more than human if he was not divine. Just like any cult group, members of "The Family" were supposed to tell their cult leader all about their family background and childhood history.

This provided news ways for cultists like Manson to have a hold on their followers. Manson used this knowledge to his advantage and understood their standpoint. He "read" their minds and made them look at him in awe while all along, he was just stating the facts that were confided to him earlier.

> Manson had psychological insight into the past experiences and present needs of his young followers (especially the women) and an ability to diagnose their difficulties with their parents (especially their fathers). Indeed, they thought he had such uncanny talent in this area that the actual ability to read their minds, communicate at a distance, and exhibit other para-psychological powers was attributed to Manson
>
> (Nielsen, 1984, p. 321)

People were attracted to Manson and the latter used this insight to alienate his followers from society. Some members who had been previously estranged from society willingly obeyed Manson because he seemed to accept them for who they were.

Diverse ways of cruelty were explored by Manson, some of which are too gruesome to speak or even pen-down in words. Physical violence and collective sexual activities were not infrequent in "The Family". Ironic is the fact that Manson preached about love but practised hostility, especially in his treatment of women. He called his family as "The Family of love" but the group was anything but that. By disguising truth and putting forth his ideas as the ultimate command, Manson made his followers submit themselves at his disposal.

Ayn Rand's Distortion of Truth in *The Fountainhead* and *The Atlas Shrugged*

Objectivism

Objectivism was a philosophy proposed by Ayn Rand. This philosophy is highlighted in most of her writings. Objectivism, according to Rand, is "the concept of man as a heroic being, with his own happiness as the moral purpose of his life, with productive achievement as his noblest activity, and reason as his only absolute" (Kelley, 2010). 'Randism' is seen as a cult primarily because Rand adjusted her principles based on her belief, disregarding the possibilities of other people getting hurt.

These principles never brought happiness in her life. Rand was a married woman but had an affair with her intellectual heir, Nathaniel Branden. She called it a result of logic and reason. However, when Branden decided to start a new relationship with another woman, he was dismissed from society and was branded as a man who brought disgrace. Trent Lorcher, writer and teacher, observed some of the features of Modernism. One of the key features he mentioned is that "there is no such thing as absolute truth. All things are relative" (Lorcher, 2009, p. 1). Rand is undoubtedly one of the leading writers to twist realities and present her own ideas as the standard expected of men to reach. This way she indirectly promoted the many aspects of Modernism and Post-truth through her writings.

Rand and Truth Relativism

Post-truth is very much similar to truth relativism. Both theories neglect the possibility of the existence of a proper definition of truth and believe that one's personal judgment of what is morally right and wrong will give him/her the necessary means to judge for himself/herself. "Truth relativism is the doctrine that there are no absolute truths, i.e., that truth is always relative to some particular frame of reference, such as a language or a culture" ("Relativism", 2019).

Cults have a different notion of ethics. A good action, in the perspective of cults, is in following the ideals of the group. "Anything can be done in the name of... purity; it is the justification for the group's internal moral and ethical code" (Singer, 2003, p. 71). The character of Dagny Taggart in *Atlas Shrugged* is modelled after Roark in *The Fountainhead.* She was the VP of Operations for Taggart Transcontinental but was not happy with how her brother, James, worked only to please others. Dagny Taggart dared to stand different from her peers. When Dagny Taggart found herself on a mountain hideaway named 'Atlantis', she realised that it was a hub for highly creative and intelligent minds. Rand, in a way, wrote a masterpiece to delineate her ideas of what a utopia should look like. She valued the power of the creative mind and her philosophy is explained in detail in *Atlas Shrugged.*

Rand disdained Socialism and observed the beliefs of Capitalism. She believed that those in power and authority, the creators, the businessmen and those who embrace individualism must have a sense of pride, putting their values above people's needs.

> Only those who add to my life, not those who devour it, are in my market. Only those who produce, not those who consume, can ever be anybody's market. I deal with the life-givers not cannibals... Here, we trade achievements, not failures- values, not needs.
>
> (Rand, 1996, p. 662-663)

It is obvious that Rand had no respect for the working class. She divided people into two: the useful and the useless; the life-givers and the cannibals. By instilling such ideas in the reading public, Rand was encouraging people to view this as an ethical code.

Another common theme that runs in Rand's novels is that the strong-willed female protagonists fall in love with men who dared to stand out in society. These characters are complex and stand for their principles though they are morally questionable. In both *The Fountainhead* and *Atlas Shrugged,* Rand challenged the traditional notions of marriage and treated adultery with a sense of dignity and respect, if it is an act committed between two people who are 'intellectually superior'.

Egoism in Rand's Ideology

Ellsworth Toohey is presented as a cult leader in Rand's *The Fountainhead.* He hated Howard Roark because the latter did not care about the opinions of others and stood firmly on his ideals and principles. Toohey somehow realised that Roark was unique and sought to destroy him though Roark was almost a 'nobody' in the society in the first part of the novel. Keating, a rival of Roark, admired Toohey just like many other people in the city. Since Toohey always talked of harmony, people were drawn to him without realising, in Rand's terms, that such altruism is detrimental. Keating became Toohey's scapegoat and was eventually put to shame. Roark, just like Rand's other protagonists, gained popularity and fame because he focused on himself and stood for his principles.

Apart from the cult leaders seen in Rand's novels, Rand became a worldwide sensation for the philosophies she held dear. The concept of ethical egoism is prominently present in Ayn Rand's novels. She regarded altruism as a treacherous thing to believe in.

> The grim joke on mankind is that he is held as a symbol of selfishness... Selfishness is a profoundly philosophical, conceptual achievement. Anyone who holds a tribal lone wolf as an image of selfishness, is merely confessing the perceptual nature of his own mental functioning.
>
> (Rand, 1982, p. 68)

Toohey and Keating considered Roark as a threat because the latter was not a "second-hander" like them. According to Rand, it is a second-hander's notion to think "I am good because people like me" (Rand, 1982, p. 64). She preached that an individual is not a "second-hander" when he/she is comfortable in his/her own skin. Keating was beneath Roark because his aim in life was to achieve greatness "in other people's lives... He didn't want to be great, but to be thought great" (Rand, 1993, p. 605).

Altruists are not people-pleasers. They extend help so as to make the earth a better place to live in. However, Rand opposed this view and completely invalidated it. Scholars and critics have accused Rand of being apathetic to the idea of helping people in need.

> The concept of "interest" is an important factor to deal in ethical egoism. Rand believed that one must forego all negative thoughts that seem to threaten the interests of man, especially the theories of being selfless in order to attain happiness. The topic of interest puts forth pertinent questions of ethics.
>
> (Mercy, 2013, p. 173)

Rand not only preached egoism as an important factor to achieve happiness but deliberately branded selflessness as a "negative thought". She was a hardcore believer that altruism cannot and will not contribute to one's happiness. It was, to Rand, a form of slavery.

Conclusion

The contemporary relevance of cults is seen in the manifestation of the principles that are adjusted to fit the modern era. Even ancient cults have gained popularity because of the efficiency they show in fitting properly as needed. Cults, in general, are threats to the society we live in.

The trauma that cults bring, the threats it poses and its radical definitions of what is morally right or wrong are some of the aspects that make it crucial for us to disclose the truths about these groups. Charles Manson and Ayn Rand had captivated people by promoting individualism and self-worth and by manipulating the truth to fit their agenda. Truth is no longer relevant in the post-truth era and the consequences of adhering to such ideologies have proven to be fatal to human lives, literally and figuratively.

References

Brahms, Y. (2020). Philosophy of Post-Truth. *Institute for National Security Studies.* http://www.jstor.org/stable/resrep23537

Guinn, J. (2014). *Manson: The Life and Times of Charles Manson* (Illustrated ed.). Simon & Schuster.

Kelley, D. (2010, June 14). What is Objectivism?, The Atlas Society | Ayn Rand, Objectivism, Atlas Shrugged. *The Atlas Society.* https://www.atlassociety.org/post/what-is-objectivism

Lorcher, T. (2009, March 17). Modernism in literature - what are characteristics of modernism in writing?. *Bright Hub Education*, http://www.brighthub education.com/high-school-english-lessons/29453-modernism-in-literature

Mercy, J. (2019). The Egoism-Altruism Debate: A Study with Reference to Ayn Rand's Philosophical Ideology. *Research Journal of English Language and Literature*, 7(1), 172–174. https://doi.org/10.33329/rjelal.7119.172

Nielsen, D. A. (1984). Charles Manson's Family of Love: A Case Study of Anomism, Puerilism and Transmoral Consciousness in Civilisational Perspective. *Sociological Analysis*, 45(4), 315. https://doi.org/10.2307/3711297

Rand, A. (1996). *Atlas Shrugged.* Signet.

Rand, A. (1982). *Philosophy: Who Needs It* (Unabridged ed.). Signet.

Rand, A. (1993). *The Fountainhead.* Signet.

Relativism. (2019, October 31). *The Spiritual Life.* https://slife.org/relativism

Singer, M. T., & Lifton, R. J. (2003). *Cults in Our Midst: The Continuing Fight Against Their Hidden Menace* (Revised and Updated ed.). Jossey-Bass.

The Holy Bible: The New King James Version. (1988). Broadman & Holman Publishers.

CHAPTER 13

Poetics of the 'Third Space': Exploring the Possibilities of a Fifth Dimension in John Green's *The Fault in Our Stars*

Harry C. Joseph

The narrative transition from modernist to postmodernist can be traced in terms of the shift in the treatment of narrative time. The change has generally been thought of as "the shift in emphasis from time to space" (Heise, 1997, p. 1). Modernist representation is preoccupied with 'time,' as we find in Proust, in Henry James' 'flow,' in Bergson's '*duree,*' and in the cyclical conception of history found in poets like Eliot and Yeats. Postmodernism is attributed a similar preference for spatial categories like 'websites,' 'cyberspace,' and 'information superhighway'; the 'frames,' 'borders' and 'boundaries' of cultural and literary theory; also its experiments in architecture (p. 1). Heise points out how such fixing of the dominant tends to obscure the cultural reconceptualisation of both time and space as experiential categories in the postmodern period (Heise, 1997). The postmodern narrative experiment can be studied therefore as a break from the modernist conception of time, in the context of the new cultural experience of time.

The transition is manifested in the way modernist reinvention of narrative form to explore the "flow of memory, duration and expectation in human consciousness," gives way to the deliberate designs of postmodern narrative to make "temporal progression difficult or impossible to conceive" (Heise, 1997, p. 13). Modernism's "individual and psychological temporality" counters the implications of the standardised and mechanised public time of its period; with postmodernism, there is a "weakening of the individual as well as social and historical time as parameters for organising narrative" (p. 7). As Heise infers:

> One of the most striking developments in the transition from the modernist to the postmodernist novel is the disintegration of narrator and character as recognisable and more or less stable entities, and their scattering or fragmentation across different temporal universes that can no longer be reconciled with each other, or justified by recurring to different psychological worlds.
>
> (Heise, 1997, p. 7)

The one thing that differentiated the new physics – the physics of today – from the old (Einstein's from Newton's) is the idea of the nature of space and time and their relationship. Under the new theory, space was conceived of as being *n*-dimensional, with time as the fourth of its dimensions. Thus the concept of 'space' widens and is open to innumerable possibilities.

The main objective of the present study is to examine with particular reference to John Green's *The Fault in Our Stars* the possibility of a fifth dimension, rather than an imaginative one. Hazel refers to it as a "third space" where she finds close to Gus and hence a 'space' wherein their love could survive the limitations of time. This 'third space' thus is more or less a distant utopia free from the constraints of the fourth dimension of 'time' as it transcends the latter.

A Virtual Telephonic Third Space

The first time Hazel feels herself in that imaginary 'third space' is when she had a telephone conversation with Gus. She recounts it thus:

> And then the line was quiet but not dead. I almost felt like he was there in my room with me, but in a way it was better, like I was not in my room and he was not in his, but instead we were together in some invisible and tenuous third space that could only be visited on the phone.
>
> (Green, 2012, p. 72)

Later after Gus's death, she calls him with the hope that this 'third space' would serve even as a meeting place with the dead ones as well. Her thoughts would reveal the immense possibilities she had carved out:

> Finally I did call him. His phone rang five times and then went to voice mail. "you've reached the voice mail of Augustus Waters," he said, the clarion voice I had fallen for. "Leave a message." It beeped. The dead air on the line was so eerie. I just wanted to go back to that secret post-terrestrial third space with him that we visited when we talked on the phone. I waited for that feeling,

> but it never came: The dead air on the line was no comfort, and finally I hung up.
>
> (Green, 2012, p. 263)

This 'fifth dimension' we encounter is thus an extension and projection of the mind. In a way, it is a kind of 'substitute gratification.' Human beings always had a vision of a haven where all our wishes are fulfilled. In the novel, Gus tries to view the world as a wish-granting factory. Perhaps this is made possible by a journey of the mind into "an invisible and tenuous third space" (Green, 2012, p. 72).

A Narrative Third Space

The concept of a 'third space' doesn't limit itself to telephone conversations. It permeates all throughout the novel. There are references to two fictional works *An Imperial Affliction* and *The Price of Dawn*. It throws light into the pleasure a reader gets in reading a work of fiction. This again is travelling into that 'third space,' where the reader confronts the characters as alive as they themselves. Hazel repeatedly reads the novel *An Imperial Affliction* where she finds her own life portrayed with all its vivacity and verisimilitude.

When Hazel and Gus find that the novel ends in the middle of a sentence, they desperately yearn to know what happens to its protagonist. They even seek to meet the author. The fictional nature of this 'third space' is vividly presented in the author's note to the novel under study *The Fault in Our Stars*. It goes thus:

> This is not so much an author's note as an author's reminder of what was printed in small type a few pages ago: This book is a work of fiction. I made it up.
>
> Neither novels nor their readers benefit from attempts to divine whether any facts hide inside a story. Such efforts attack the very idea that made-up stories can matter, which is sort of the foundational assumptions of our species. I appreciate your cooperation in this matter.
>
> (Green, 2012)

The case is made clear when the two encounter Van Houten at his home in Amsterdam. It is the abrupt ending and the future of other characters that troubled them. At first Houten answers with a riddle citing Zeno's tortoise paradox: "Of course, you just run past the tortoise without contemplating the mechanics involved, but the question of how you are able to do this turns out to be incredibly complicated" (Green, 2012, p. 189). The simple answer is there is no relevance in going after petty hypothetical happenings. On further insistence, the author says with compassion "We are speaking of a novel, dear child, not some historical enterprise.... they're fictions" (Green, 2012, p. 191).

The Dutch Tulip man, the most enigmatic character in the fictional narrative is elevated to the status of God. Houten says " He's an obvious and unambiguous metaphorical representation of God, and asking what becomes of him is the intellectual equivalent of asking what becomes of the disembodied eyes of Dr. T.J.Eckleburg in *Gatsby*" (Green, 2012, p. 191). He thus reinstates the futility of seeking the veracity of a work of fiction.

Finally, the construction of this 'narrative third space' is explained in simple genuine words thus:

> But to be perfectly frank, this childish idea that the author of a novel has some special insight into the characters in the novel... it's ridiculous. That novel was composed of scratches on a page, dear. The characters inhabiting it have no life outside of those scratches. What happened to them? They all ceased to exist the moment the novel ended.
>
> (Green, 2012, p. 192)

E. M. Forster in his *Aspects of the Novel* touches on narrative continuity and closure as "the fascination of following," which resides "in the presumability somewhere of a convenient... visibly appointed stopping-place" (Forster, 1927, p. 27). As can be seen in Henry James's *The Art of the Novel* or Frank Kermode's *The Sense of an Ending,* "stopping places" in fiction are not considered "entirely natural or easily found" (Torgovnick, 1981, p. 4). To James one has to 'invent' and 'establish' endings, "by a difficult, dire process of selection and comparison, of surrender and sacrifice," (Torgovnick, 1981, p.6) where relations stop nowhere, and the exquisite problem of the artist is eternally but to draw, by a geometry of his own the circle within which they shall happily appear to do so (Torgovnick, 1981, p.5). Kermode persuades how narrative plots and endings are similar to the other fictions men construct to make sense of the world, like religion, philosophy and the sciences (Torgovnick, 1981, p.7).

The concept of 'closure' in narrative has been considered another aspect of its ideological dimension. Roger Webster observes:

> The concept of closure refers to the ways in which a text persuades a reader to understand and accept a particular 'truth' or form of knowledge, to accept a certain view of the world as valid or natural. Closure is not considered to arise directly from the author or to be dependent on the reader's views, but to be inherent in a text's form and the writing strategies and reading expectations associated with a particular genre such as the novel.... works which have apparently 'open,' unresolved or ambiguous endings still contain an ideological closure.
>
> (Webster, 1990, p. 53)

Juxtaposed with this is a thought from Milan Kundera's *Immortality*, where we find a metafictional stay over the limitations of conventional plot conceptions:

> I regret that almost all novels ever written are... at their core one single chain of causally related acts and events. These novels are like a narrow street along which someone drives his characters with a whip. Dramatic tension is the real curse of the novel, because it transforms everything, even the most beautiful pages...surprising scenes and observations merely into steps leading to the final resolution.... The novel is consumed in the fire of its own tension like a bale of straw.
>
> (Kundera, 1991, p. 266)

He adds on, "A novel shouldn't be like a bicycle race but a feast of many courses" (Kundera, 1991, p. 266). The postmodern fiction thus is preoccupied with the basic structuring notions of closure and coherence, in seeking alternatives to the systematic plot structure, and in its refusal to stop the 'play' and integrate its fragments.

Now for Gus, this 'third space' transcends the ecstasy in reading a work of fiction. He is a man inclined to heroic action. For him, mere observation of life is least satisfying. While visiting the Rijksmuseum, he notices "a lot of paintings of dead people. You'd see Jesus on the cross, and you'd see people dying at sea and in battle at sea and a parade of martyrs" (Green, 2012, p. 217). However, there is "no single one. Cancer kid. Nobody biting it from the plague or smallpox or yellow fever or whatever." He thus concludes that "there is no glory in illness. There is no meaning to it. There is no honor in dying of" (Green, 2012, p. 217).

Counterinsurgence – The Third Space of Gaming

Gus finds meaning in death by creating a 'third space' in the form of the videogame he plays- Counterinsurgence. There he goes through various heroic escapades rescuing people and killing terrorists. What he could not accomplish in his real life, he achieves through his own created space. This is made clear in the game he played with Issac.

> "Cover me!" Augustus said as he jumped out from behind the wall and raced toward the school. Issac fumbled for his controller and then started firing while the bullets rained down on Augustus, who was shot once and then twice but still ran, Augustus shouting, " YOU CAN'T KILL MAX MAYHEM!" and with a final flurry of button combinations, he dove onto the grenade, which detonated beneath him. His dismembered body exploded like a geyser and the screen went red. A throaty voice said, "MISSION FAILURE," but Augustus seemed to think otherwise as he smiled at his remnants on the screen. He reached into his pocket, pulled out a cigarette, and shoved it between his teeth. "Saved the kids," he said.
>
> (Green, 2012, p. 59)

There he remains a hero of his world. It seems noble to die for a cause. Gus through his heroic death, albeit in a virtual environment, surpasses his fear of 'oblivion'. However his 'special friend' reminded him that his victory is 'temporarily.' Gus countered it saying "All salvation is temporary" (Green, 2012, p. 59).

Gus while flying twenty thousand feet above clouds said to Hazel "I used to think it would be fun to live on a cloud" (Green, 2012, p. 219). It is another private space he imagined for himself while at the school. When his teacher asked the students who all would like to live in the clouds, everyone of them raised their hands. But when the teacher reminded that up in the clouds the wind blew one hundred and fifty miles an hour and the temperature was thirty below zero, most of them dropped their hands down. Gus too felt that his dream is shattered. He expresses his discomfort thus:

> He specialised in the murder of dreams, Hazel Grace... you think volcanoes are awesome? Tell that to the ten thousand screaming corpses at Pompeii. You still secretly believe that there is an element of magic to this world? It's all just soulless molecules bouncing against each other randomly. Do you worry about who will take care of you if your parents die? As well you should, because they will be worm food in the fullness of time.
>
> (Green, 2012, p. 220)

The lines express his discontentment when every created space shatters and being left with only an ignoble death. What Hazel and Gus try to create is a world that is unaffected by the terrors of existence. It is a state of perfect bliss. If it is time that corrupts life, by causing change, their world seems to be unaffected by the currents of time. This transcendence however is possible only in a world of imagination. Whenever facts and figures prop up, the entire creation topples down into fragments. They also protest against whoever tries to trespass into this world. It is a 'sacro sanctum' to be kept out of defilement.

Death as a Third Space

The world of the dead is yet another space where Gus and Hazel feel at home. They do not precisely know where this realm of death lies or perhaps even there is one. But they eagerly wait to be a part of it. In the support group, every day before the gathering is done with, they pray for the dead members of the group. It is a long list into which new members are added every now and then. Hazel, on the first day with the group, thinks of the list thus:

> It was a long list. The world contains a lot of dead people. And while Patrick droned on, reading the list from a sheet of paper because it was too long to

> memorise, I kept my eyes closed, trying to think prayerfully but mostly imagining the day when my name would find its way onto that list, all the way at the end when everyone had stopped listening.
>
> (Green, 2012, p. 14)

Obviously, it is not their eagerness to die that allures them to get into the 'third space' created by the dead ones. The group of cancer kids were always a minority. They are failed experiments of nature. The general populace always categorised them as a group in an endless 'battle' with life. Thus they were never recognised as full-fledged human beings. It is the ecstasy of being considered equal in status with the rest, for death is a great leveller, which motivates them to evade the world of the mortals. The aspiration to court death is fostered by a collective dream Gus and Hazel had. It was while at Anne Frank's house they once again reiterated their past dream. Hazel said "I think they're all dead. But it's not like the Nazis had a monopoly on evil" (Green, 2012, p. 202). Gus answered, "That is what we should do, Hazel Grace: We should team up and be this disabled vigilante duo roaring through the world, righting wrongs, defending the weak, protecting the endangered" (Green, 2012, p. 202).

Sexual Union – A Third Space

The last of the 'third space' which Hazel and Gus create is in their sexual union. There they meet with their souls in the brim of eternity. In their dying bodies, they seek the possibility of eternal living. However, the memory of this blissful state too was washed away by the tyranny of time.

The chapter "Poetics of the 'Third Space'" thus is an enquiry into the possibilities of an imaginary 'third space,' one which is unaffected by the sense of time. It is pure and pristine in its form. Most often this remained a source of comfort and a chance of union for the degrading lives of Hazel and Gus. Also how the narrative acts as a 'third space' is discussed in detail.

References

Forster, E.M. (1927). *Aspects of the Novel.* Edward Arnold & Co.

Green, J. (2012). *The Fault in Our Stars.* Penguin Books.

Heise, U. K. (1997). *Chronoschisms: Time, Narrative and Postmodernism.* Columbia UP.

Kundera, M. (1991). *Immortality.* (Peter Kussi, Trans.). Rupa.

Torgovnick, M. (1981). *Closure in the Novel.* Princeton UP.

Webster, R. (1990). *Studying Literary Theory: An Introduction.* Edward Arnold.

CHAPTER 14

Performativity and Re-turn of the Author: Reading the Dynamics of "I" between the Star-Author, Fictional Characters and the Reading Public in Bhagatian Texts

Dr. Kavitha Gopalakrishnan

Labelled as unworthy of attention, "popular" was exiled from mainstream academic engagements for a long time. But in the last few decades, it has increasingly been recognised as a vital field in engendering ideology. Political engagement suited to contemporary times is possible only when popular is not cast aside and when literary texts are not privileged above the non-literary co-texts. Realising this, Chetan Bhagat, the post-millennial writer who has eights novels (all of which are bestsellers) to his credit and his celebrity status is reviewed. Bhagat is constantly slighted by academia and critics primarily because of thinking rooted in the dichotomy between elite forms of literature that are considered complex and anti-representational and forms of popular literature that are considered to be simple, lineal and representational.

Elite/Popular

The labels of "elite" and "popular" are so concrete that by default popular fiction is seen as insignificant, uninspired expressions put forth in shoddy language. A closer analysis would encourage us to think beyond such concreteness that has set in academia. Bhagatian fiction addresses the "post" condition of India and tries to illumine the post-truth embedded in everyday practices. However, it should be noted that the "new" India that Bhagat tries to portray both in his fictional and non-fictional works is made up of credibility where many a time the reader might not be able to distinguish between truth and its representation leading to relativity that further reinforces post-truth. Apart from analysing his fictional works, a reading of Bhagat's contested location within the aura of a self-styled celebrity is facilitated to understand how and why the author becomes the co-text. Bhagat invites the readers to think of contemporary Indian society through engagements with neo-liberal changes that unfold an increasingly fluid and changing world.

Co-texts as Parerga

This chapter attempts to delineate that a dialogic engagement with co-texts has the potential to draw attention to the political implication and the agentive potential of the "author". To facilitate this, the celebrity status of the best-selling author Chetan Bhagat, the paratexts of his fictional oeuvre, his three non-fiction works and his articulation in the newspaper, social media and television are examined as co-texts to his fictional work. It seeks to deconstruct the role of these co-texts to show how they function as "parerga" to the "ergon" (work), thereby existing both within and beyond the ergon but neither inside the ergon nor outside. (Derrida 1987, p. 9). The Derridean analysis of parergon is employed to problematise the ambiguous status of these ostensibly supplementary materials.

The chapter also intends to analyse the "I" of Bhagat under the Derridean logic of parergon because post-truth politics and rhetoric are at the heart of its exigence. Understanding the author and his non-fictional works as part of his artistic production is seen to be important – the parergon is an essential part of the ergon. Any attempt to draw a boundary between the two – the text and the co-text(s) – would leave us in an aporia because the Derridean logic of parergon applies and a parergon is (n)either on the inside (n)or on the outside. All this indicates the re-turn of the author – as a performative inevitable factor in understanding popular fiction in a post-truth world.

Derrida's explanation of the parergon in *The Truth in Painting* shows how these co-texts, like the parergon, act as the convenient limit to the ergon, even when they exist within the work:

> The parergon: neither work (ergon) nor outside the work [hors d'oeuvre], neither inside nor outside, neither above nor below, it disconcerts any opposition but does not remain indeterminate and it gives rise to the work. It

> is no longer merely around the work. That which it puts in place – the instances of the frame, the title, the signature, the legend, etc. – does not stop disturbing the internal order of discourse on painting, its works, its commerce, its evaluations, its surplus-values, its speculation, its law, and its hierarchies.
>
> (1987, p. 9)

The co-texts pinned on the logic of parergon act as a frame that contextualises and recontextualises the text being framed. Attention is drawn to the act of framing rather than the frame itself.

Authorial Profiles and Staged Celebrity

A reading of Bhagat's contested location within the aura of a self-styled celebrity is important to understand how and why the author becomes the co-text. Over the years Bhagat has proven himself a master at fashioning a persona calculated to reward his efforts. From being a social visionary with his self-proclaimed goal of writing to create change, to the tag of being the best-selling writer in the country, to the title of being one of the "Pied Piper(s) of Twitter" ("Chetan Bhagat: The Pied Piper of Twitter", 2015) for being a writer who just cannot escape controversy when he writes on current affairs in his column *The Underage Optimist* or when he tweets politically incorrect statements audaciously on Twitter, or to the title of being "Bollywood's favourite author" (Dhaliwal, 2014) as most of his books have been made into hit films, he has managed to create and sustain interest in him and his works in the minds of people over the past fourteen years. He has orchestrated an image of being an "interactive intellectual" (Heynders & Marjet, 2014, p. 96), a "literary celebrity" (York, 2007, p. 3) having his own fair share of followers and detractors which makes a reading of the discursive subject of identity construction necessary so as to show how the author and his life are important co-texts to the texts chosen for study. It would be interesting to observe how much of himself he projects into the public sphere (his works, his media interactions etc.), in what manner and to what effect.

A celebrity is not just born naturally due to a person's achievements. An effort is put in to construct the same. Pramod K. Nayar describes celebritisation as consisting of two main dimensions: one, "constructing an individual as an object of desire" and two, "constructing an individual for mass consumption" (2009, p. 26). A celebrity is "an individual who possesses both commercial as well as a socio-cultural value", and the production of "celebrity-dom" (2009, p. 22) is enabled by creating, controlling and managing the texts that emphasise these values. Bhagat has consolidated his identity between transparency and sequestration so as to create an impression of accessibility and awe in the minds of his readers. Woodward's emphasis that "identity presents the interface between the personal and the social..." (2004, p. 19) holds good in this context because he creates an identity for himself through his books, speeches, tweets etc. which the readers are invited to adopt by association. The readers know of his credentials – that he is an IIT-D/IIM-A alumnus, that he is married to Anusha Suryanarayanan from Tamil Nadu (whom he met at IIM) and that he served as an Investment Banker in Goldman Sachs for ten years before becoming a full-time writer. He serves copious elaboration of these impressive personal details in his novels too as if to assert that he ought to be taken seriously and to possibly negate the charge that he is flippant.

Anthea Taylor observes that "Authorial profiles can act as a platform for 'staged celebrity' where celebrity is achieved through the projection and performance of the subject's life in a biographical narrative" (2016, p. 102). But at the same time, Bhagat recognises that his celebrity status has been partly a product of his ability to shake off seriousness, his use of a freer verbal facility suggestive of oral performance which helps him to neutralise the pompousness usually associated with overachievers, his ability to endorse the rags-to-riches tale of an unknown banker to nation's best-selling author in a short span of time, his emphasis on poetic justice in his stories and his ability to strike a balance between doing away with moralising and performing as a social crusader.

He has created a hall of mirrors effect in his fiction by incorporating events largely from his personal life and this has added to the tendency of equating the author with his characters. The life of the author thus becomes the novel's organising principle. How much of the author's self, what aspect of the self, is called upon to perform in public – in his works, in interviews etc., is a key factor in sustaining the interest in him and his works. His success is portrayed as an ordinary man's success and his fame represents what people aspire to possess. "It is in the familiarity of character and situations that their recognisability and star value exist" (Nayar, 2009, p. 32). Innumerable parallels can be drawn between the text (Bhagat's body of work) and the co-text (Bhagat's life, his celebrity status). These parallels are best inferred from three sources: the para-texts, cross-reference of characters in his fiction to his other fictional characters and to the author himself and media interactions – tweets, interviews etc. which sheds light on the instances from his personal life incorporated in his fictional works. Anthea Taylor says:

> Texts such as interviews, reviews or author profiles need to be recognised within a broader economy of publicity and promotion. Furthermore, authorial interviews and profiles necessarily work to inform how readers engage with that writer's works, and cannot merely be conceptualised as 'secondary' to the literary text; readers often first encounter it/it's author through interviews or other forms of public performance, thus 'inaugurating a relationship rather different from that established subsequent to reading the author's text'.
>
> (2016, p. 102)

To begin with, the function of the parerga shall help to pay special attention to the act of framing of the paratexts – acknowledgements and preface. Bhagat choreographs the paratexts in his fiction in a manner that helps him to establish rapport with his readers by directly addressing them. This is evident right from the list of acknowledgements before the actual novel begins. The acknowledgements section, functioning on the logic of parergon (threshold or vestibule), establishes a relationship between the work of fiction and the surroundings. It comes as peripheral to the text but its transcendent exteriority comes to play, presses against the limit itself and intervenes in the inside of the text. It recognises the readers to whom the text is addressed, underscores the writer's intentions and conveys that his writing is a personal investment made in the hope of initiating change. In *The 3 Mistakes of My Life*, for example, he starts his list of acknowledgements by addressing his readers to whom he says he owes all his success and motivation and he then says:

> My life belongs to you now, and serving you is the most meaningful thing I can do with my life. I want to share something with you. I am very ambitious in my writing goals. However, I don't want to be India's most admired writer. I just want to be India's most loved writer. Admiration passes, love endures.
>
> (Bhagat, 2008, p. ix)

In *Half Girlfriend*, he pens "acknowledgements and some thoughts" where he starts off by giving credit to his readers for all his success: "Thank you, dear reader and friend, for picking up *Half Girlfriend*. Whatever I have achieved today in life is thanks to you" (2014, p. vii). After thanking the reader, he sums up his life as a writer so far and how his motives have changed over time, the reason being that ten years have passed since he first embarked on this journey as a writer:

> I want to share something with you. With this book, I complete ten years as a writer. When I started writing, my motives were different. I wanted to make it. I wanted to prove a point. Today, I write for different reasons. I write for change. A change in the mindset of Indian society. It is a lofty goal, and I am

> not foolish enough to think I can ever achieve it. However, it helps to have positive intentions and directions in life, and I am glad to have found mine.
> (Bhagat, 2014, p. vii)

What is to be understood here is that the acknowledgements sections of Bhagat's fictional works are invaluable to see how the links between the author and his readers and the links between the readers, his work and his life are constructed.

Bhagat very often also conveys to his readers, in very many ways, his positive intent for change, thereby adding to his socio-cultural value as a celebrity. While addressing the readers he tries to convey three things: he is indebted and committed to his readers, in return to this commitment all he wants is a permanent place in their hearts, and this love has sustained him for so many years and now he wants to do pay them back by being a catalyst for change. Changing the conditions in India for the better by overcoming the problems plaguing our nation as projected in his works – corruption, red-tapism, unequal opportunities, gender discrimination etc. – can be materialised only with the support of the readers. Here Bhagat seems to be bestowing a promise to the audience which, as Derrida notes in *The Truth in Painting*, is performative – a statement that believes in being and doing rather than putting it in words. Its performance does not reveal details but promises another performative (his work of fiction). The content of the promise is determined by the possibility of the acceptance of the other (the readers). Their acceptance promises change – a performative supplementary that is open to infinity. This probably is what Bhagat means when he says that his desire to stir change is "a lofty goal" that he is "not foolish enough" to hope to achieve it with immediate effect. He says, "however, it helps to have positive intentions and directions in life" (Derrida, 2014, p. vii).

Through these paratexts, Bhagat manages to reach out to his readers and build a connection with them. Pramod K. Nayar calls these as "para-social relationships" where "imagined connections to celebrities, a kind of surrogate for actual friendships or other relations", are established (2009, p. 85). However, Bhagat drops in a "couple of disclaimers" (vii) in his acknowledgements. For example, in *2 States* he writes:

> This story is inspired by my own family and experiences. However, this book should be seen as a work of fiction. Also, for authenticity, I have used names of some real places, people and institutions as they represent cultural icons of today and aid in storytelling. There is no intention to imply anything else. I'd like to tell all South Indians I love them. My better half will vouch for that. I

> have taken the liberty to have some fun with you just like I have with Punjabis–only because I see you as my own. You only make digs at people you care for.
>
> (Nayar, 2009, p. vii)

The first line promises to give autobiographical details but at the same time, he says this is a work of fiction. Hence one cannot without suspicion look into the general reading where the identity of the text is grasped through a reading that identifies the author and the reader. Such an understanding is facilitated through a sequence of details in the para-texts – the biographical details in the blurb, dedications, authorial comments and so on. However, one cannot simplistically assume that this is the truth because truth as Derrida suggests is based on deferred meaning. Information that the readers get from these para-texts, previously considered outside the text, are assumed to give meaning to the text and it tries to limit the text by tying it to the life of the author. They act as frames or parergons. In doing so the readers feel they know the author and can totally understand what he intends much more than they actually do. However, such assumptions need not lead us to the truth.

Prologues and Epilogues in Bhagat's fictional works too are pinned on the logic of parerga. Most of the prologues invariably have the presence of the author who is outside the text but at the same time inside the text as the characters in the fictional work converse with him. Prologues in Bhagatian works inscribe the extra information that documents the genesis of the story but they are vital to the story as they convey the author's still largely unexamined relationship and commitment to his readers. The presence of this alleged author in the prologue of most of his works of fiction problematises his representation as it leads the reader to imagine they know the author for real without actually realising that the singularity trait is at play.

Authors like Bhagat want the freedom that fiction provides and the consequentiality of fact which the readers look forward to. This is achieved by Bhagat in two ways. First, by sharing trivia from his life (interesting or harrowing) he has incorporated it into his fictional works. When the readers understand that similar things have happened (to them/to the people they know/to the author they see all over in the media) and will happen, such works become truthful fiction. The second is to make fiction as close to fact as possible. Facts which are collective bits of information coming to the readers through the media, facts that he reveals about his personal life, which the readers believe are the writer's real-life experiences.

Co-texts: Non-fiction, Tweets and Facebook Posts

His non-fictional works try to cement his position as an interactive intellectual and a celebrity author. At the same time, they also demonstrate his understanding of the post-truth world and his attempts in helping the readers think about possibilities other than that are available at the moment to better their lives and the future of the nation. This has been his self-proclaimed intention of writing fiction too. Hence these co-texts provide firmer grounds and newer contexts for the interpretation of his fictional works. His non-fictional works too have to be analysed beyond the notions of truth and objectivity that are usually attributed to non-fiction. The status of non-fiction rests on it being qualitatively different from its fictional counterparts in its efforts to reflect the "real" and being transparent. It implicitly directs the audience to accept its truth claims. However, in an age where truth itself is uncertain, such an expectation from the reader is out of place. In his non-fiction, Bhagat navigates between the subjective/objective stance to convey certain ideas on social and political engagement. He claims that he is an objective, conscientious observer when he is actually making subjective claims and at the same time appeals to the readers to be objective. In the current times when the veracity of mainstream news seems to have been damaged and consequently the status of non-fiction as a vehicle for the representation of truth has been destabilised, it would be useful to look beyond non-fiction's conformity to truth.

Bhagat's constant media presence too serves as a paratextual element to his fiction, as it may enhance our reading of his books. Bhagat's comments on piracy on Twitter, refutation by other tweeters, his blocking of unyielding tweeters and the sudden rise of a Twitter flash mob in #chetanblocks are telling examples. Chetan Bhagat reacted in a self-righteous manner and performed in accordance with the image of the conscientious person that he has always projected through his works – both fictional and non-fictional.

Online communication like that on *Twitter* or *Facebook* can travel widely in different ways through forwarding, sharing, retweeting etc. which further requires the reader to create the meaning and this increases the possibility of the misappropriation of texts. Bhagat himself became a victim on one such occasion where there was a huge outrage over a post purportedly written by Chetan Bhagat. On 26 April

2017, the storm was let loose as Bhagat was trolled and trashed for an article, "Let Her take her Time", written by a lady called Sangeeta, but wrongly attributed to him. The post went viral and many people abused him for the sexist tone in the article, for perpetrating patriarchal thoughts and for patronising women. He was called offensive and even misogynistic. Shruti Menon explains the situation thus: "Given that Bhagat has courted controversy in the past for his attempts to 'get into a woman's head' in his book *One Indian Girl*, not many gave him the benefit of doubt of whether or not he'd written the post" (Bhagat, 2016, n.p). The language of the post and the patronising tone were unquestioningly considered to be Bhagat's. The context of reception heavily influenced its understanding as Bhagat had published his 2016 novel *One Indian Girl* as a successful attempt at figuring out Indian women. The topic, language and tone thus became a kind of "signature" to which the identity of the writer was instantaneously conferred. This obviously misfired. In this case, however, since the post had been circulated from a non-verified page, the fact that the post was not made by Bhagat could be proved.

This incident is also leading up to the discussion of the post-truth zeitgeist which is characterised by lies, propaganda, fake news – the lifeblood of post-truth narratives – which is further complicated by the social media communication on account of irresponsible posting without checking the veracity of the information. It is in this post-truth scenario that Bhagat's role as a star-author needs to be examined.

Considering these arguments, it could be safely concluded that authors defending a reputation are more visible than before. They have to present themselves consciously on stages, on television, in newspaper interviews, and so on. They are aware of the marketing effects of their performance, and they even create a persona to maximise this performance to its best. Bhagat the celebrity writer usually makes news personally and takes it upon his shoulders to speak out on all manner of things largely due to popular pressure – the task of venting out what the common man wants to but cannot. He is aware of his visibility in media platforms and thus uses it to interfere in the public sphere, by formulating an opinion on issues that he thinks are relevant. He puts it across various media platforms and confronts the readers with his ideas or opinions on current societal and political issues. Bhagat's online presence through social media, therefore, augments both his personal identity and his authorial persona. In this space, his comments on social issues, his intentions of promoting his products and himself are conveyed to the readers before the books reach them.

A close reading of these co-texts helps to encounter how the author and his ideology in the public sphere or in-person serve to generate meanings in his readers. The persona of Bhagat the author apart from serving as a co-text in shaping new contexts for a better understanding of the fictional works of Bhagat, also informs, affirms and interrogates the fluidity of boundaries and labels. His non-fictional works try to cement his position as an interactive intellectual and a celebrity author.

In short, Bhagat's stardom and the contingent controversies capture the zeitgeist of the post-truth world in the right way where both speech and writing have "become part of a wide-ranging public performance often characterised by theatricality" (2016, p. 2). Bhagat expects to swing people to act for change by inspiring them with both his speech and writing at a time when the readers are surrounded by discourses that have little to do with truth.

References

Bhagat, C. (2008). *The 3 Mistakes of My Life.* Rupa.

.... (2009). *2 States: The Story of My Marriage.* Rupa.

.... (2014). *Half Girlfriend.* Rupa.

.... (2016). *One Indian Girl.* Rupa.

Chetan Bhagat: The Pied Piper of Twitter (Author and Management Guru). (2015, August 30). *Intelliassist: New-Age Business Solutions*, intelliassist.co.in/chetan-bhagat-the-pied-piper-of-twitter-author-management-guru

Derrida, J. (1987). *The Truth in Painting.* The University of Chicago Press.

Dhaliwal, N. (2014, April 14). Chetan Bhagat: Bollywood's favourite author. *The Guardian*, www.theguardian.com/books/2014/apr/24/chetan-bhagat-interview-bollywood-favourite-author-india

Heynders, O. (2016). *Writers as Public Intellectuals: Literature, Celebrity, Democracy.* Palgrave Macmillian.

Heynders, O., & Marjet, L. (2014). The Interactive Intellectual: Bas Heijne on Twitter. *TNTL Tijdschrift voor Nederlandsetaal* & *Enletterkunde*, 130, 96-114.

Nayar, P. K. (2009). *Seeing Stars: Spectacle, Society and Celebrity Culture.* SAGE.

Taylor, A. (2016). *Celebrity and the Feminist Blockbuster.* Palgrave Macmillan.

Woodward, K. (2004). *Questioning Identity: Gender, Class, Ethnicity.* Routledge.

York, L. (2007). *Literary Celebrity in Canada.* University of Toronto Press.

CHAPTER 15

Identity Dynamics and Post-truth in Paul Verhaeghe's "What About Me?"

Bornali Nath Dowerah

The mechanism of identity is dynamic as it constantly keeps evolving from one context to the other. In the post-truth era, the noteworthy fact is, surprisingly, this evolution process of identity that every individual encounters in day-to-day life. This phenomenon is prevalent mostly in advertisements, promotional emails and above all, social media. The facility of dichotomous options at such platforms has left individuals with multitudinous choices to pursue. The globally dominating market drives the consumer spaces to such an extent as if it is the only portal to secure and uplift society. In fact, it has reached upto such an optimum level that popular consumerism decides most about the wellness and wellbeing of the human race. The essence of human identity is degrading due to such an inclination and dependence on the consumerist culture. Besides, this dependency is thriving if looked at from an angle of the Covid-19 era. Investigating the undercurrents of identity as a construct is the major objective of this chapter as this essay seeks to interrogate the claims that Paul Verhaeghe incorporates in his book titled *What About Me?* related to identity dynamics from the standpoint of post-truth. As derived from Verhaeghe's work this essay gets to study how people psychologically fall prey to false claims and allow navigating their lives at the hands of capitalist giants. The problems specified in Verhaeghe's arguments aim at how an individual is conditioned by a dominating market-based other. In the life journey, the individual tends to shuffle between sameness and difference in comparison to others which, gradually, shapes his/ her identity. The predicament lies in determining if this transformation is believed as an opportunity or a setback to human identity?

Transitioning towards the consumerist culture it is to be noted that an individual, in this technological era, has turned into both a consumer as well as a producer. A common instance can be 'YouTube' as a platform where anybody, who can talk can preach, share skills, teach or entertain. Social networking platforms provide a space for virtually displaying content that cannot be asserted to be absolutely legitimate. As there is a dire need to observe closely the circulation of facts and fabricated facts. Post-truth is that underlying aspect that surmounts changing belief systems.

Verhaeghe's Notion of Identity

Heading back to what Verhaeghe has to say, he revisits the genesis of religion to examine the root cause of identity dynamics in the current era. He wrote this work in Dutch titled *Identeteit* and published it in 2012. The English translation has been done by Jane-Hedley Prôle in 2014. As implicit from the title *What About Me?* The keyword clearly indicates 'identity' of an individual 'in a market-based society'. He claims that constant interaction with others has resulted in a "never complete" self (p. 31). Due to this, he terms today's society to be in a state of "liquid identity" (p. 33). There is a constant struggle for identity that the author has overtly emphasised. And that the politics of interpretation of meaning deceive individuals and hinders him or her to question. In this regard, the platform of social media provides the freedom to express opinions, at the same time, reserves the right to express any fact that is anti-national and anti-racist. According to Verhaeghe (2014), identity is most distinct in terms of difference. He postulates:

> Separation and the corresponding quest for autonomy are as important for our identity as identification because they allow us to develop an individuality through opposition...At this stage, it amounts to opting for alternative constructions of the self, and thus for different identification. Identity is always the temporary product of the interplay between merging and establishing a distance.
>
> (p.11)

As evident from above, the author defines identity as the tension between similarity and uniqueness from the other. He further claims that the external factors are highly responsible for bringing a change into the individual's character. Verhaeghe draws a scientific instance – "the field of epigenetics" – which is responsible to affect the gene expression in individuals (p. 15). In fact, he analyses the cause-and-effect terms to justify his claims. As understood from this argument Verhaeghe pursues the "individual aspect" of identity – by which he means of being unique at the base level and identifying with similar characteristics with particular groups and cultures. (p. 17-18). Moreover, he considers that the foundation of the economy lies in religion (p. 49). It is so because, as he argues that poverty cannot be regarded as destiny, but "betrayed religious and moral shortcomings" (p. 49). At the same time, success cannot be testified as God's blessing as the credit rests upon "one's personal efforts" (p. 49). Religion regards that humans are "inherently evil" and so to do good it is required to practise self-denial in order to approach the divine. (p. 51). He realises that religion has been preaching ethics and morality so far; in the late 20th century, this has been replaced by "optimistic thinking" securing a space for reason has shifted to a notion of newly formed identity (p. 53-54), Nevertheless, Verhaeghe digresses his arguments, empirically, to Darwin's theory of evolution to claim: "The 'science wars' are veiled debates between different ideological viewpoints ... because they go back to something that cannot be acknowledged: the fact that values are at stake" (p. 72). Verhaeghe sounds ambiguous when he uses the term "veiled debates" to prove his argument. The concept of post-truth arrives at this juncture when the author follows the trajectory of identity dynamics through religion and later science.

Post-truth, Identity and Neoliberalism

Veering further from empiricism it is essential to understand how the lenses of post-truth delineate this analysis. Yael Brahms (2020) in her *Philosophy of Post-Truth* inclines to what philosopher Hannah Arendt asserts that post-truth is the blurred boundary between fact-based truth, interpretations or individual opinions (p. 3). The scientific facts are objective truths and the author considers these objective truths as ideological as they do not arrive at just one or single conclusion. Ascertaining to religious aspects, above, the author posits how there is a shift from religious beliefs towards the era of reason and enlightenment. Verhaeghe does not seem to support scientific claims as well when he draws upon Darwinism. Yet he goes with the theory of evolution as a process that is engineered to this day. For instance, Verhaeghe (2014) considers "the debacle of Nazism and communism" to have caused the "loss of faith in ideals" and that the epicentre has now shifted towards the "individual" (p. 73). To support his claims he draws upon Margaret Thatcher's popular political statement published in *Women's Own* in 1987:

"There is no such thing as society" (Verhaeghe, 2014, p. 74). Another fact that can be related to Verhaeghe's arguments is the notion of 'survival of the fittest'. According to the author neoliberalism, today is the mutated version of Social Darwinism which considers "*nature* should be allowed free rein: the innate good in man would cause the worthiest to rise to the top … [and neoliberalism] interprets nature to mean market forces" (p. 77). This has already indicated a paradigm shift from empiricism to the question of "'true' individual" and "natural identity" (p. 78).

Critiquing Verhaeghe's Paradoxes

Verhaeghe offers a scientific, philosophical and psychoanalytical approach towards the essence of identity and concludes that an individual and society are interdependent mutually, due to which identity is intertwined to either both or none of them. In a way, in response to the above paragraph, every community or society has its own set of rules that harness the 'nature' of human. However, society has its norms that also include chaos and disorder. Interestingly, Verhaeghe (2014) concludes in two paradoxes:

> This is the first important paradox of the Neo-liberal free-market ideology: it invariably culminates in an excess of interference … The second paradox concerns the so-called liberation of the individual. Anyone who buys into this claim is confusing, individualisation and loneliness with autonomy and free choice.
>
> (p. 248-249)

This raises the question further if humans are unique individuals in collective consumerism or are conditioned to be so. Revering back to the failure of empiricism Verhaeghe argues: "To this day, no single scientific study has succeeded in distinguishing between what is mentally normal and abnormal without using social criteria" (p. 105). The point here is not to achieve a scientific conclusion. Rather, the identity dynamics that Verhaeghe is referring to seems quite unachievable because a post-truth outlook would claim to identify only the ones that is justifiable and relatable to the individual. For instance, just like the French poststructuralist, Jacques Derrida has posited the notion of *differance,* which refers to a process of deferral of meanings (Birtell, 2018, p. 3). This resonates with the concept of an unachievable centre that is powerful, and the powerless beings constantly endeavour to reach that culmination. What Verhaeghe has maintained to emphasise is, identities of individuals stake at a continuous effort to reach a powerful position which (even if the 'fittest' reach) can never be attained. In this regard, the element of post-truth is most relevant as it is based on hegemonic ideology. Neither inherent nor essential truths matter. Verhaeghe interrogates if identity holds meaning in itself. He argues that after birth identity is inflicted upon the individual. Scientifically, he explicates genes and evolution. But it is far from the fact that identity is fixed and static. Society influences the individuals and this hegemonic position has been now taken over by a market-based society that highly promotes consumerism. Verhaeghe (2014) names this society as "Enron society". He interprets this as "depressive pleasure-seeking on credit" (p. 106). This deferral of the meaning of society neither can be affirmed as truth nor lie which invites further ambiguity. First of all, the reason he names it so is related to the 'new social model' with new norms, values and identities. He argues, if society undergoes a drastic metamorphosis it is most certain for individuals to change psychologically. This hegemony has robbed individuals off the "ability to cope with adversity" which has turned the present era into moral decadence (p. 108). The fractured truths pointed by Verhaeghe, if fused together, do not unite to form a greater truth because he too considers himself to be a part of the Enron society. The problem from the angle of post-truth is that there is a high possibility of a loss of truth that is inherent. Another opinion would be inherent truths can be myths as they are subjected to multiple interpretations.

Ideology of Post-truth

The concept of post-truth does not distinguish between what is true and what is false. This is even clear as Tiziana Andina (2019) states in her research article "Truth, lies, and post-truth" from the book *Post-Truth, Philosophy and Law* that:

> Post-truth ... was coined to solve a problem, namely the fact that the distinction between truth and lies, in some contexts and situations, seems to have become particularly fluid and subtle, up to vanishing altogether occasionally ... the concept of truth is undoubtedly not doing too well given that it was thought useful to add to the traditional pair of truth and lies a third concept, that of post-truth, which somewhat plays with the idea that there is "something" beyond the truth.
>
> (p. 1)

Interestingly, Paul Verhaeghe's opinion based arguments in this work somewhat echo this post-truth perspective. Scientists, sociologists, anthropologists, religious fanatics and psychologists would not agree to his arguments nor could Verhaeghe be challenged with false allegations. The question here is, where is the author heading to or where are the readers being led? The position of Verhaeghe is of a contemporary Western thinker of the twenty-first century who reverberates with the collective consumerist culture and is yet distinct from it. This cannot be an identity because of its shifting nature. The struggle for identity, therefore, becomes a continuous venture which is a process and not a mission-accomplished zone. In a way, the human race is driven by this dominating ideology which would tend to continue till the end of consumerism. Ironically, consumers have turned into producers from a post-truth perspective, yet the fact is, the ultimate goal-oriented identity is a myth. This accounts for the argument that a zenith in terms of identity is hardly reached as the dominating ideology of neoliberalism in the contemporary context ensnares the consumers with an implausible image.

Fragmented Belief System in Neoliberalism

Fragmentation is a popular phenomenon of postmodernism. Verhaeghe's ideas traverse through a set of a fractured belief systems that cannot be proved to be untrue yet they cannot be considered absolutely true as well. This entire work is a concrete example of post-truth which concludes paradoxically with an optimistic Shakespearean quote extracted from Act I, Scene 2 of *Julius Caesar*: "Men at sometime are masters of their fates: The fault, dear Brutus, is not in our stars, But in ourselves, that we are underlings" (Verhaeghe, 2014, p. 250).

As understood by the author, the process of consumption and production is powered by neoliberalism which Michel Foucault termed as "anarcho-capitalism" in combination with classical liberalism (p. 249). Verhaeghe argues that consumerism has obliterated the psychological balance in an individual, especially in regards to "self-control and restraint" (p. 249). The reason why he concludes with a Shakespearean quote can be interpreted as an open question towards humanity where humans are masters of their own fates as well as equally vulnerable as slaves to external influences of anarcho-capitalism. Interestingly, Verhaeghe has claimed how a postmodernist suffers from a rare kind of dissociation that is no less than a split personality. The author alleges this disorder into individuals as neoliberalism has made them feel about depression, not as a temporary feeling of powerlessness but a threat to mankind. Verhaeghe offers a remedy to prevent one from being a 'depressed consumer' and that is harnessing one's pattern of consumption. He, further, adduces to the construction of a social policy that balances the public interests and private concerns. Verhaeghe's assertions also resonate Foucault about the requirement of "*parrhesia*" which signifies speaking boldly and straightforwardly. But the author seems pessimistic in this regard too. An instance that he advocate is that moral values are sold in the twenty-first century because it appeals to the common mass (2014, p. 238).

Conclusion

Finally, Verhaeghe vindicates how the identity of consumers is shaped by sameness and separation from a community. And, in this course, humans are equally powerful enough to reject the claims of the dominating ideology and powerless to fall prey to neoliberalism. From a post-truth perspective, Verhaeghe is reasonably justifying the struggle for identity. Furthermore, his postulations shuffle between the blurred boundaries of factual truth and interpretative truth. At the same time, the author tends to digress with such naturalness that his notions cannot be separated from his psychoanalytical gimmicks. This work not only connects Verhaeghe with his professional community but dissociates him as well in his philosophical attributes. Furthermore, his assertions can be positioned as exemplary of post-truth because, just like the shifting nature of identities, his arguments validate his infirmity to arrive at a single axiomatic juncture.

References

Arendt, H. (1967, February 25). Truth and Politics. *The New Yorker.* https://www.newyorker.com/magazine/1967/02/25/truth-and-politics

Birtell, D. (2018). Deconstruction & Differance: Derrida in the Dawn of Postmodern Decadence. *Researchgate,* https://www.researchgate.net/publication/328926772_Deconstruction_Differance_Derrida_in_the_Dawn_of_Postmodern_Decadence

Brahms, Y. (2020). Philosophy of Post-Truth. *Institute for National Security Studies.* http://www.jstor.org/stable/resrep23537

Condello, A. & Andina, T. (2019). *Post-Truth, Philosophy and Law.* Routledge.

Fallon, K. (2019). Post-Truth Politics: Conspiracy Media and the Specter of "Fake News". In *Where Truth Lies: Digital Culture and Documentary Media after 9/11* (pp. 156-180). University of California Press. http://www.jstor.org/stable/j.ctv1f884rq.11

Giraud, E.H., & Aghassi-Isfahani, S. (2020). Post-Truths, Common Worlds, and Critical Politics: Critiquing Bruno Latour's Renewed Critique of Critique. *Cultural Politics, 16*(1), 1-13. https://www.muse.jhu.edu/article/755640.

Grear, A. & Bollier, D. (2020). *The Great Awakening: New Modes of Life amidst Capitalist Ruins.* Punctum Books. doi:10.1353/book.80766.

Keyes, R. (2004). *The Post-Truth Era: Dishonesty and Deception in Contemporary Life.* St. Martin's Press.

Rickert, T. (2019). It Is All There: From Reason to Reasoning-in-the-World. *Philosophy & Rhetoric 52*(1), (pp.93-101). https://www.muse.jhu. edu/article/721924.

Rose, D. (2018). Avoiding a Post-truth World: Embracing Post-normal Conservation. *Conservation and Society, 16*(4) (pp. 518-524). https://www.jstor. org/stable/26500664

Thompson, M., & Leavy, S. (1994). Truth and Science. In *The Truth About Freud's Technique: The Encounter With the Real* (pp. 69-77). NYU Press. http://www.jstor.org/stable/j.ctt9qfvqq.15

Verhaeghe, P. (2014). *What About Me?* (J. H. Prôle, Trans.). Scribe. (Originally published in 2012)

CHAPTER 16

Political Advertisements in a Post-Truth World: An Analysis of the Kerala Legislative Election 2021

Irene Ann George and Abhishek Manikandan

Political Advertising

Political advertising includes any advertising displays, newspaper ads, billboards, signs, brochures, articles, tabloids, flyers, letters, radio or television presentations, digital or social media advertising, or other means of mass communication, used for the purpose of appealing, directly or indirectly, for votes or financial or other support in any election campaign. (*Political Advertising*, n.d.)

In the entirety of the political sphere, advertising has taken centre stage in bringing about a conscious upheaval in the process of campaigning. For ages, candidates have earmarked huge amounts of their campaign funds for the production and displaying of electronic advertisements (Diamond & Bates, 1992). While there have been major thematic changes in the nature of the advertisements that have been portrayed in public discourse, researchers have thrown light upon the measurable impact that these political advertisements have had on the minds of voters (Kaid, 2002). Over the years studies have emerged showcasing the phenomenon of voters with television exposure being more likely to show increased accuracy of perception of candidates' positions on issues presented in political advertising (McClure & Patterson, 1974).

The Malayalee Electoral Seesaw

Politics in the southernmost Indian state of Kerala has often baffled those ruling the central government of the country. Despite being the birthplace of the world's first elected Communist government, Kerala's electorate has displayed tendencies to oscillate between the Communist Party of India (Marxist)-led Left Democratic Front (LDF) and the Indian National Congress-led United Democratic Front (UDF), reflecting diverse patterns of voting behaviour. Research has in turn suggested the existence of a consistent pattern of voting in some constituencies while other constituencies portray major disparities in their voting behaviour (Chakrabarty & Tamang, 2006).

However, as things stand in the current context, in the just-concluded 2021 assembly elections, the LDF emerged victors winning a mammoth 99 of the 140 legislative constituencies. ("Left Front Led by Pinarayi Vijayan Retains Control of Kerala Assembly", 2021) The coalition rode on the wave of a charismatic Chief Minister, Pinarayi Vijayan, putting a stop to the see-sawing electorate that the state has been used to for the past four decades (Ibrahim, 2021).

Research Problem

The study aims to observe and analyse the relationship between the nature of political advertising and the 2021 Kerala Legislative Assembly Election held in a post-truth world. Post-truth being a culture that has been constantly evolving has taken a significant stance in the current political scenario. Facts are often distorted in order to create a pleasing and appealing picture towards the public sphere to get maximum electoral attention. Discovering the gap between true facts and 'polished' facts is extremely necessary while living in a world where statistics and truth are entirely contradicting.

Theoretical Framework

Myriad theories can be taken into consideration while taking a closer picture of the study. The most suitable ones are framing theory and Behaviorist / Weak Advertising Theory.

Framing Theory

The theory was first addressed by Goffman who stated that interpretative frameworks make the right sense to our daily life experiences. This theory is often used in the planning of public relations, campaign strategy and advertising where the facts are portrayed through frames that the advertisers want the audience to apprehend. The theory helps in identifying the frames in which underlying politics and bias is showcased, unlike other theories (Littlejohn & Foss, 2009).

Media, functioning as the fourth pillar of democracy, is expected to display unfiltered information to the general public. Adulterating information to achieve the desired outcomes cannot be regarded as a rightful approach.

Behaviourist / Weak Advertising Theory

The theory aims at refreshing the brand and alarming the reminders within the minds of an individual. The theory states that such advertising nudges prospective consumers towards the product, in contrast to being a passive audience. In the domain of political context, this type of advertising can be considered as a medium that reassures the public to cast their votes for the party that they initially considered.

Review of Literature

Media in Electoral Politics

Being an integral part of a functioning democracy, the existence of Media in a political landscape is vital. While considering the strength of this much needed fourth estate, comes in the notion of bias in media and news outlets.

In the media, one can often see limited attention spaces when it comes to not just the political agenda set by the higher-ups in politics, but also the information that seeps into the political apparatus from the electorate through media. This means that these political elites, including those of them in the media, are forced to become more responsive to greater input. These inputs have expanded beyond the traditional media, entering social media and digital media spheres, further creating demands for a response to a more complex set of media inputs. Here, it is not just politicians who can better target the electorate, citizens can also select more news and other politically relevant information and feed more differentiated input into the political apparatus. The emergence of such a scenario would also become the enabler of news media and politically relevant information sources to target their audiences more accurately (Schroeder, 2018).

A plethora of studies suggest the existence of media in a biased environment as being detrimental to electoral politics; politics necessarily does not mean politicians and can just include the electorate which is led towards a certain stance so as to influence their voting behaviour. News media bias is real and this further reduces the quality of journalism, fostering distrust among readers and viewers. If there is a belief that this is an issue for a certain section of the electorate with lesser political literacy, that notion has been debunked with papers suggesting that even the most politically aware voter is misinformed by distorting the information that consumers of news receive. This may even occur to the most rational consumers who are well aware of the media organisation's bias, as they have minute knowledge of the entirety of the information the organisation holds. As most voters are said to be rational, the party favoured by the media may not have a higher probability of winning, however, the inherent media bias may also lead to a drastic drop in the effectiveness of electoral competition, thereby paving way for more polarised policies. (Anderson & McLaren, 2012; Chan & Suen, 2009)

Post-Truth World

The concept of post-truth was brought into the limelight during the 2016 Presidential election of the United States of America when Donald Trump's campaigning strategies drifted away from facts. In 2016, "Post-truth" was declared the word of the year. The 'post' refers to the past. The phenomena of Post-truth is noticeable in current day advertisements, politics and campaigns where the emotions are concentrated more when compared to emotions (McIntyre, 2018).

Researches have substantiated that there has been a rise in post-truth culture mirroring the rise of social media against the decline in traditional media. Political statements and statements which offer a scientific basis are also manipulated by knowledge providers for better reach especially during the climate of the COVID-19 pandemic. The definition of truth is also evolving along with the technologies which are giving multiple perspectives to one single idea and the idea of shame is also being brought down (Malcolm, 2021). In the post-truth world, "fake news drives out the genuine news" which affects the society we live in dangerously. It is important to analyse the propaganda, counter-propaganda and public diplomacy when information is being published (Kovacic, 2019).

Electoral Patterns in Kerala

Numerous publications have brought about the phrase "political laboratory of India" to describe the state of Kerala. As a state where the minorities hold almost equal weightage in the electoral sphere, Kerala paints an unusual picture where these sections decide the winners of most political contests.

Christians and Muslims represent the religious minorities and Hindu backward classes and castes constitute the majority of voters in the state, thereby bringing across a battle for economic and political advantage based on the same social strata (Pillai, 1987). The state has witnessed coalitions based on the plank of anti-marxism. The CPI (M) was kept at bay by five coalitions with periods ranging between 30 days and 6 years and 4 months. Another novel characteristic of the states is the fact that it is home to innumerable parties that have split. 'Split within a split' can be appropriately used in the Kerala context. The splinter groups are known in the name of their leaders, clearly indicating the reason behind the development of political fissures (Pillai, 1987).

Another seemingly interesting characteristic is the fact that almost every strong political force has been given the chance of being in power as the Congress, the Communists, the Socialists and the Muslim League, have had at some time or other been associated with governmental power. No other state in India has provided such equal opportunities to the mainstream parties (Nair, 1966).

Methodology

Content Analysis

The methodology used for the research is the content analysis where the information can be collected and segregated based on codes and themes. This method has been proven to be effective in the field of mass communication, ranging from interpersonal communication to analysing the characters in literature. (Neuendorf, 2019, p. 2).

Advertisements that were telecasted as a part of the Assembly Election Campaign have been analysed for the purpose of the study. These advertisements will be chosen on the basis of convenient sampling. The advertisements will be viewed and analysed based on codes which will also be subjected to a thematic study.

Analysis

Religion

The popular narratives during the 2021 Kerala Assembly elections were interspersed with numerous issues, albeit for the first time in Kerala's secular history, religion moved into the forefront with the burning Sabarimala issue becoming part of the electoral discussions.

Considering the emergence of an overtly right-wing ideology at the centre and the burning issue of Sabarimala being at the forefront, both the BJP and the INC mentioned the issue in their manifestos, while the ruling front's outgoing Devaswom minister Kadakampally Surendran expressed regret concerning the issue and the protests that occurred as an aftermath of the Supreme Court ruling (Phillip, 2021; "BJP Releases Manifesto Promising Jobs, Free Laptops, Legislation to Protect Sabarimala Traditions," 2021; Krishna, 2021).

It is during the backdrop of this issue that the UDF and the NDA approached the election with their advertisements that touched upon Sabarimala. The BJP, in its advertisement, engages in an attempt to shift the narrative towards the Sabarimala issue, thereby specifying the floods of 2019. Here, a perceptual shift is being brought about by focusing on a single incident that may be beneficial in grabbing the emotional appeal of a certain majority community, while the other major happenings that occurred after the said incident are neglected (Kartha, 2021). A correlation is being made between a memory that is profound to happen in accordance with the age and an accident that happened years back in order to deflect attention to an issue that has been supposedly relegated to the back of the prospective voter's mind.

On the other hand, the coalition with a pre-established secular outlook, the UDF, also tried to gain public appeal by leveraging the same issue. In a minimal advertisement, they attempt to dissuade the Hindu voter's fears by promising to bring in legislation to protect the interest of devotees (Nair, 2021). The fact that religion is made to act like a catalyst in a secular country like India, to increase the electoral vote makes it evident that the emotions of the people are used more than facts in order to obtain the desired outcome; epitomising the usage of a Post-Truth narrative.

Employment

Owing to the existence of an immense population that is under the age of 35, Kerala has always focused on employment, therefore rhetoric during elections has often led to discussions surrounding employment. It is in that context that allegations of backdoor appointments to government jobs surfaced during the latter end of the LDF's rule.

The main opposition, UDF and the NDA with their sole MLA in the house ramped up criticism against the ruling party. After elections, the outgoing Higher Education Minister K.T. Jaleel had to step down after the LokAyukta found him guilty of Nepotism (Anand, 2021; Raghunath, 2021). The advertisement brought out by the UDF showcases two neighbours poking fun at an LDF supporter who has apparently secured government employment for his wife. The ad ends with one of the women implying that marrying an LDF supporter is the easiest way to gain entry into government employment (*UDF ELECTION ADS*, 2021).

The advertisement brought by LDF assures new opportunities for the youth which are inclusive of jobs, entrepreneur support and technologies to facilitate growth. The familiar face of the Chief Minister and the Party Leader, Mr. Pinarayi Vijayan is also shown in order to grant the sense of assurance (*ഉറപ്പാണ് യുവജനക്ഷേമം. ഉറപ്പാണ് LDF.*, 2021).

The contrasting portrayals of employment in these advertisements incite confusion in the minds of individuals who are not very much involved in current affairs. UDF advertisements blame the current ruling government for the backdoor appointments while the LDF government promises to open the door to immense possibilities.

The Development angle

The ruling party at the centre and the ruling party of Kerala have often been at loggerheads in terms of who has contributed more to the development of states. Oftentimes, the central government has accused the state government of appropriating the schemes that the former has introduced.

The NDA's advertisement takes up the same angle, where two BJP supporters attribute the development of Kerala to the central government's initiatives, this includes the public distribution system and the roads that have been built in the state (Kartha, 2021).

The advertisement by LDF shows two women engaging in a talk that depicts how the LDF government contributed a large portion in the development sector, by drawing parallels between a newly built bridge that has been in news cycles recently (*ഉറപ്പാണ് വികസനം. ഉറപ്പാണ് LDF.*, 2021).

It is pretty noticeable that both the parties claim the credit for the development in Kerala which triggers a dilemma in the minds of the individuals. There exists a situation where the voter gets forced to hand-pick the facts that are to be verified regarding the contributions of each political party in the development sector to get the facts straight which are not often bothered by the common public.

Conclusion

From the analysis of content from the three coalitions, the influence of emotional messaging in the content of the advertisements is clear. As they veer away from fact-based electoral advertising, they are ushering in the idea of creating a discourse that becomes a part of the Post-Truth phenomenon. Viewers who engage in the consumption of these materials before an election are immensely influenced. Hereby, advertising that is supposed to help the voter in their judgement becomes a mere tool for propaganda. The emergence of religion as a tool of post-truth messaging is also seen with two of the major fronts opting to address. Even while trying to communicate necessary information about major reforms in education and development, the ruling party with a proven track record also takes the path of post-truth so as to ensure a steady inflow of votes.

As George Orwell once said, "The very concept of objective truth is fading out of the world. Lies will pass into history." The further scope of the studies should revolve around how facts can't be twisted around to gain an emotional appeal that will reflect into an action. More studies should be welcomed on visual studies in the post-truth world.

References

Anand, G. (2021, April 13). Kerala Higher Education Minister K. T. Jaleel resigns after Lok Ayukta rap. *The Hindu.* https://www.thehindu.com/news/national/kerala/higher-education-minister-k-t-jaleel-resigns-following-lok-ayuktas-adverse-finding/article34309538.ece

Anderson, S. P., & McLaren, J. (2012, August). Media Mergers And Media Bias With Rational Consumers. *Journal of the European Economic Association, 10*(4), 831-859. *JSTOR.* https://www.jstor.org/stable/23251101

BJP releases manifesto promising jobs, free laptops, legislation to protect Sabarimala traditions. (2021, March 24). *The Times of India.* https://timesofindia.indiatimes.com/elections/assembly-elections/kerala/bjp-releases-manifesto-promising-jobs-free-laptops-legislation-to-protect-sabarimala-traditions/articleshow/81673422.cms

Chakrabarty, M., & Tamang, R. V. (2006). Kerala – A Study Of Electoral Dynamics And Votting Behaviour, 1957-2004. *The Indian Journal of Political Science, 67*(1), 133-142. *JSTOR.* https://www.jstor.org/ stable/41856199

Chan, J., & Suen, W. (2009). Media as watchdogs: The role of news media in electoral competition. *European Economic Review, 53*(7), 799-814. https://doi.org/10.1016/ j.euroecorev.2009. 01.002.

Diamond, E., & Bates, S. (1992). *The Spot: The Rise of Political Advertising on Television.* MIT Press.

Ibrahim, K. M. S. (2021, May 3). Kerala votes for a strong leadership offered by Pinarayi. *The New Indian Express.* https://www.newindianexpress.com/ states/kerala/2021/may/03/keralavotes-for-astrong-leadership-offered-by-pinarayi-2297699.html

Kaid, L. L. (2002, Spring). Political Advertising and Information Seeking: Comparing Exposure via Traditional and Internet Channels. *Journal of Advertising, 31*(1), 27-35. *JSTOR.* http://www.jstor.org/stable/4189205

Kartha, A. (Director). (2021). *Bjp Kerala Election Campaign 2021 AD 20* [Film]. ARK Productions. https://www.youtube.com/watch?v=PNQSF5cw-SU

Kartha, A. (Director). (2021). *Bjp Kerala Election Capaign 2021 AD 6* [Film]. ARK Productions. https://www.youtube.com/watch?v=PTA_ZlNI9AI

Kovacic, B. (2019). Gresham's Law and News in a Post-Truth World. *Asia Pacific Media Educator,* 54-57. https://journals.sagepub.com/doi/full/10.1177/1326365X 19838926

Krishna, P. (2021, March 11). Sabarimala women entry: Minister Kadakampally Surendran expresses regret. *Mathrubhumi.* https://english. mathrubhumi.com/ news/kerala/sabarimala-women-entry-minister-kadakampally-surendran-expresses-regret-kerala-1.5507425

ഉറപ്പാണ് യുവജനക്ഷേമം. ഉറപ്പാണ് LDF. [Youth welfare is assured, LDF is assured] [Film]. (2021). Maitri Advertising Works. https://www. facebook.com/maitriworks/videos/35336411 2612470

ഉറപ്പാണ് വികസനം. ഉറപ്പാണ് LDF. [Development is assured. LDF is assured] [Film]. (2021). Maitri Advertising Works. https://www.youtube.com /watch?v=_WanFueizBs

Left Front Led by Pinarayi Vijayan Retains Control of Kerala Assembly. (2021, May 2). *The Wire.* https://thewire.in/politics/kerala-assembly-election-results-2021

Littlejohn, S. W., & Foss, K. A. (Eds.). (2009). *Encyclopedia Of Communication Theory.* Sage Reference Publication.

Malcolm, D. (2021). Post-Truth Society? An Eliasian Sociological Analysis of Knowledge in the 21st Century. *Sociology.* https://journals.sagepub.com/doi/ full/10.1177/0038038521994039

McClure, R. D., & Patterson, T. E. (1974, January 1). Television News and Political Advertising: The Impact of Exposure on Voter Beliefs. *Communication Research, 1*(1), 3-31. *SAGE.* https://doi.org/10.1177%2F009365027400100101

McIntyre, L. (2018). *Post Truth.* The MIT Press.

Nair, A. (Director). (2021). *Udf Election Campaign | Sabarimala | Directors Cut* [Film]. PUPA Production. https://www.youtube.com/watch?v=vionY_cLLjc

Nair, P. (1966). The Party System In Kerala. *The Indian Journal of Political Science, 27*(1), 69-83. *JSTOR.* https://www.jstor.org/ stable/41854148

Neuendorf, K. A. (2019). *The Content Analysis Guidebook.* SAGE Publications.

Phillip, S. (2021, March 20). Kerala polls: UDF manifesto promises Rs 6,000 a month for the poor, Rs 2,000 for homemakers. *Indian Express.* https://indianexpress.com/elections/kerala-polls-udf-manifesto-promises-rs-6000-a-month-for-the-poor-7237597/

Pillai, K. R. (1987). Politics of Kerala. *The Indian Journal of Political Science, 48*(4), 597-606. *JSTOR.* http://www.jstor.org/stable/ 41855341

Political Advertising. (n.d.). Public Disclosure Commission. https://www.pdc.wa.gov/learn/publications/political-committee-instructions/political-advertising

Raghunath, A. (2021, February 9). Backdoor appointments turn into a major political issue in Kerala. *Deccan Herald.* https://www.deccanhera ld.com/national/south/backdoor-appointments-turn-into-a-major-political-issue-in-kerala-949389.html

Schroeder, R. (2018). Media systems, digital media and politics. In *Social Theory after the Internet: Media, Technology, and Globalisation* (pp. 28-59). UCL Press, doi:10.2307/j.ctt20krxdr.5

UDF Election ADS [Film]. (2021). https://www.youtube.com/watch?v=59SJTYJ3w-c

CHAPTER 17

'Hyperreality' and Social Media: 'Fake' Outrages 'Real' in the Post-truth Era

Sinoj Antony and Dr. Ishfaq Ahmad Tramboo

We are living in a world, where social media and fake news often decide the reality and control our life. The online platforms and technology always form 'hyperreality' and we feel unreal as real. Fake news and false propagation were stimulating and influencing people from the very beginning of media culture and practice, but now it is in a higher intensity due to the outspread of new media and technology. The digital age and culture frequently change the views and attitudes of people across the world. Today technology and communication brought the world closer, and people can track the news and events that are happening around the world within a fraction of a second through their social networking system. Real news and fake news are circulating at a similar frequency and often people cannot distinguish what is 'real' and what is 'fake' sometimes the fake outrages real. The present pandemic, COVID-19 made the people spend more time and depend on social media and technology for their existence and social interaction. 'Going viral' and 'becoming famous' are popular culture and trends of social media. This chapter focuses on the hyperreal that is quite visible in our social media platforms particularly in the post-truth condition.

Hyperreality and Social Media

The French philosopher and postmodern critic Jean Baudrillard introduced the term hyperreality in his work *Simulacra and Simulation* in 1981, where he examines the relationships between reality, symbols, and society. The very beginning of his book starts with a biblical reference and a statement made by King Solomon in the book of Ecclesiastes as: "The simulacrum is never what hides the truth – it is the truth that hides the fact that there is none. The simulacrum is true" (Baudrillard, 1994, p.1). Hyperreality unites imagery and reality together and forms a new simulation. It is followed by simulacra and simulation; simulacra are copies of certain realities and simulation is considered as a representation. Baudrillard elucidates the transformation from representation to simulacrum in four 'successive phases of the image':

> it is the reflection of a profound reality;
> it masks and denatures a profound reality;
> it masks the absence of a profound reality;
> it has no relation to any reality whatsoever; it is its own pure simulacrum. (p.6)

"In the first case, the image is a good appearance – representation is of the sacramental order. In the second, it is an evil appearance – it is of the order of maleficence. In the third, it plays at being an appearance – it is of the order of sorcery. In the fourth, it is no longer of the order of appearances, but of simulation" (p.6).

The blended reality can be seen in many areas, today most of the social systems particularly media represent it. Baudrillard pointed his views even before the emergence of social media like Facebook, Twitter, YouTube, Instagram, and Google, hence we can consider him as a prophet of 'fake news' that are visible today. In the first phase, the image represents a certain reality and gradually it forms its simulacrum, and it appears as a reality, in our day-to-day affairs we can see this is what happens in social media platforms. To comprehend the imaginary of hyperreality Baudrillard dialogues Disneyland:

> Disneyland is a perfect model of all the entangled orders of simulacra. It is first of all a play of illusions and phantasms: the Pirates, the Frontier, the Future World, etc. This imaginary world is supposed to ensure the success of the operation. --------- One parks outside and stands in line inside, one is altogether abandoned at the exit. The only phantasmagoria in this imaginary world lies in the tenderness and warmth of the crowd, and in the sufficient and excessive number of gadgets necessary to create the multitudinous effect. (p.12)

We are living in a world, where we can find more and more information, and this information lack certain meaning and reality, in most cases it is regarded as fake information. Many people hide or mask their real identity in the social media platform, and they make fake ids and accounts on social media and they converse to the people with fringe fake realities, Facebook and Twitter can be considered as the best examples of this reality. According to Baudrillard hyperreality relates to a preference of stimulated experiences over real ones that be an important characteristic of postmodern society. He argues that our cultural world is no longer reality, but rather virtual, and thus real experiences have lost all meaning and authenticity through the proliferation of simulacra (Allan and Daynes, 2017, p. 242). The growing addiction to social media negatively affects the individuality and identity of a particular person, he is more dealing with the virtual world and far away from the physical world and reality, which brings a certain identity crisis. In the initial stage social media platform intended to relate and share photos, videos, and information within the family or friend circle but now hence they revealed certain realities but now the entire scenario is changed, the young generation is related with social media to find and interact with new people across the world, hence certain hyperreal elements are also added with this. Today people consider social media as an objective goal they follow any methods to add more friends, likes, views, subscriptions, comments, and shares. To achieve these goals, they go behind hyperreal apps and techniques available in the technological world.

The advancement in technology and the internet facilitates more social interaction across the world. According to the present pandemic COVID-19 context Social media platforms are very essential in communication, interaction, and educational opportunities among most of the young generation, they often perform as a multi-platform for various social activities. The excess use of the internet and technology constrains the real-world experience into virtual reality. "The more intensive we are connected virtually, the more likely will our life be engaged in hyper reality world" (Miranti, 2017, p. 329). A person in the real world can make only one identity as per his social condition, but in a virtual world he can make as many identities as possible, and social media accounts according to his interest and ability, it is a hyperreal element. 'Within this world, consumer as a subject is led to experience the hyperreality room providing interchange illusion inside room, mixes and assimilates among reality, fantasy, fiction, hallucination, and nostalgia so that it is difficult to determine the difference between one and another (Miranti, 2017, p. 331). Various surveys state that the majority of the young generation spends more time with their smartphones in the virtual world than the real physical world, it is in the form of online games, chat rooms, and social media sites. What they post on social media less reflects the real and more replicates fake. In the post-truth era, people got behind pseudo-reality and they often feel it is beneficial and essential for their identity.

Today people evaluate others based on the data and information available in their social media accounts, this often perpetuates the reality and forms certain simulacra. People depend on online media and news channels to know the reality that is happening around them, but unfortunately, most of the online portals propagate news and reality with vested interest and circulate them on social media platforms. 'The media and the official news service are only there to maintain the illusion of an actuality, of the reality of the stakes, of the objectivity of facts' (Baudrillard, 1994, p. 40). Again, Baudrillard states that "Thus all the messages in the media function similarly: neither information nor communication, but referendum, perpetual test, circular response, verification of the code" (p. 75). Visual media as well as social media manipulate reality and truth and always go for their motif the view of Baudrillard emphasises it,

> The media carry meaning and counter meaning, they manipulate in all directions at once, nothing can control this process, they are the vehicle for the simulation internal to the system and the simulation that destroys the system.
>
> (p. 84)

Now the reality is much far away from our side, but the fake reality is at our fingertip because the virtual world and social media support are always with us, even if we try to get rid of it, it is impossible in this technological world, new forms of hyperreality is emerging if technology persists.

Fake News over Social Media in Post-truth Era

Post-truth can be regarded as a time beyond, after, and without truth, it is identified as a truth that is far away from reality. UK Dictionary defines post-truth as 'Relating to or denoting circumstances in which objective facts are less influential in shaping public opinion than appeals to emotion and personal belief.' Professor Yuvan Noah Harari states that fake news was a trend from the very beginning of human history, he quotes

> We have to remember that nowadays, in the 21st century, the way we view the truth isn't in worse shape than it was in previous periods. Human societies have managed to function under massive attacks of fake news, and far worse lies than the ones we are now experiencing. We need to remember that fake news is old news.
>
> (Harari, 2018)

Facts are always the foundation of truth when the facts are rejected by media or politics the reality goes vanished and the fake emerges as truth, this is visible in the recent political approach of the rulers across the world. The information explosion and disruptive technology deviated the factual truth and replaced it with certain fake information around us, here social media play a vital role.

In the post-truth era, it is the agenda of politicians and leaders to propagate fake news as real for their political, economic, and social motives. Now a day social media is a good platform to propagate this fake news. False information is always in social media, in the previous American presidential election through a Twitter account a child sex scandal was propagated against Hilary Clinton and it negatively affected image her.

> A prime example of fake news and social media came from the most shared news stories on Facebook during the 2016 US presidential election. The source of fake news was supposedly a patriotic American news blog called "End the End" a website run by Romanian businessperson Ovidiu Drobota. One story starting that the Pope endorsed Donald Trump for president received over one million shares on Facebook alone, note to mention shares on Twitter.
>
> (Prier, 2017, p. 62)

If we analyse the present COVID-19 pandemic scenario we can identify that a lot of rumours and fake news are spreading through social media. Most of the countries are not revealing the exact number of Corona cases and death reports correctly, instead, they declare the figures with vested political interest. "Nobel Prize Winner Luc Montagnier has confirmed that there is no chance of survival for people who have received any form of the vaccine" (McGovern, 2021), it was another fake information circulated in social media regarding Corona vaccination. Fake news is always accelerating its circulation than the real news, hence people cannot distinguish what is real and what is fake, this is a kind of hyperreality. Social media is progressively involved in news sharing and propagation, they have certain goals behind it, the main motive is to maximise viewers and traffics to their sites as a result they would get promoted and income out of it.

Conclusion

As we know, today social media play a vital role in our knowledge and understanding. Due to the outspread of technology and communication normally we go far away from the physical world and physical reality and the virtual world often control our lives. Now in this post-truth era, the communication system around us has a great impact on the social, economic, political, and cultural aspects of our life. It is our duty and responsibility to distinguish the truth and fake that are being circulated to us. The social media culture goes behind 'viral' hence most of the time the reality is covered under the mask and often it is neglected. The vested interest of certain people and social institutions always promotes fake news and outrage reality. The young generation considers social media platforms and virtual space as their arena to create their images and identities as a result the values are disregarded and hyperreality is formed. We should have a critical approach towards today's media culture and should promote the realities that are being taken place around us.

References

Allan, K., & Daynes, S. (2017). *Explorations in classical sociological theory: Seeing the social world* (Fourth edition). Sage Publication.

Baudrillard, J. (1994). *Simulacra and Simulation.* University of Michigan.

Chen, P. (2013). Social media. *In Australian Politics in a Digital Age.* (pp. 69-112). ANU Press http://www.jstor.org/stable/j.ctt2jbkkn.11

Harari, Y. N. (2018, December 28). The Truth About Fake News. *Ynetnews.* https://www.ynetnews.com/articles/0,7340,L-5431881,00.html

Le, H. (2020). Blasé Attitude, Hyperreality, and Social Media. *Crossing Boarders.* 2 (1), 1-3. https://doi.org/10.31542/cb.v2i1.1990

McGovern, C. (2021, May 19). Nobel Prize winner: Mass COVID vaccination an 'unacceptable mistake'. *Life Site News.* https://www.lifesitenews.com/news/nobel-prize-winner-mass-covid-vaccination-an-unacceptable-mistake-that-is-creating-the-variants

Miranti, A. (2017). Visual Hyper Reality of Teenagers in Social Media with Photographs as Communication Media. *The International Conference on Design and Technology, Knowledge E.* 2 (4), 329-333. doi.org/10.18502/kss.v2i4.904

Morris, J. (2020). Simulacra in the Age of Social Media: Baudrillard as the Prophet of Fake News. *Journal of Communication Inquiry.* https://doi.org/10.1177/0196859920977154

Prier, J. (2017). Commanding the Trend: Social Media as Information Warfare. *Strategic Studies Quarterly,* 11(4), 50-85. http://www.jstor.org/stable/26271634

Yerlikaya, T., & Aslan, S. (2020). Social Media and Fake News in the Post-Truth Era: The Manipulation of Politics in the Election Process. *Insight Turkey,* 22(2), 177-196. https://www.jstor.org/stable/26918129

CHAPTER 18

The Alexa Effect and the Post-Truth Politics of Gender and Technology

Namitha Nandan

The Alexa Effect

From switching the lights to predicting the weather, from playing songs to reminding important events, Amazon's AI assistant *Alexa* has indeed taken over most households. The advancements in the field of technology have indeed made life easier for all. Even a twitch of a finger is not required to carry out most of the chores these days and as sapiens marvel at the giant leaps science has made, the world often overlooks the evils of the past lurking in through the tiny peepholes.

Voice AI made its first-ever appearance during the second half of the twentieth century. IBM was the first to introduce such technology in 1961 named Shoebox. It was followed by Dragon Dictate in 1990 and Microsoft Clippy in 1996. But the modern era of AI assistants began with Apple's Siri that came out in 2011. Amazon's Echo aka Alexa hit the markets in 2014 (2019). Even though the technology was popular only among the tech-enthusiasts during the initial phase, with effective advertising and the popular need for ease of home management AI assistants found their way into regular households as well. According to recent statistics, around 46.5 million people use Alexa in the United States. This is indeed ample proof of the fact that Alexa is no longer an unknown name among the commoners. She runs houses, managing chores, giving emotional support and being just there all the time. The fact that "She" is a servile assistant is something society happily ignores. Even though technology has evolved so much, the obsolete patriarchal beliefs that are etched in the collective subconscious, do find a way to express themselves through the most advanced gadgets.

Alexa is a servant, destined to follow the orders that are given to her. The same sense of superiority that the oppressors donned when they propagated racial subjugation or colonial oppression, is the same one that is at play when the users give out orders to AI assistants like Alexa or Siri. It is important to analyse what such a behaviour covertly represent. It is important to note that Alexa's attributes are indeed ones that can be categorised as "purely feminine" according to patriarchal standards. Alexa represents the strategic manoeuvre betwixt the patriarchal hues of technology and gender. So what exactly is the nature of this power play between gender and technology?

The most notable feature of this political war is that it dons a Post-Truth aura. The Alexa effect does not overtly propagate gender inequality but by wrapping the product in a vibrant sheet of emotion the sellers are indeed averting the critical eye of society. The scariest part of the power-play is that it is inconspicuous. Since it is not coming under the radar of scepticism, it is left unscathed, free to spread its wings and reign supreme. As McIntyre propounds, "the first step to fighting Post-Truth is to understand it" (2018, p. 45) and hence we must evaluate even the most basic activities in our lives with a critical eye.

Post-Truth: A Brief Introduction

The *Oxford English Dictionary* (OED) gives the following definition of Post-Truth: 'an adjective defined as relating to or denoting circumstances in which objective facts are less influential in shaping public opinion than appeals to emotion and personal belief'. In most terms like 'post-modern' or 'post-war', we use the term 'post' to denote a chronological sequence but in 'post-truth', it refers to a time in which the idea mentioned has become irrelevant or outdated (Bufacchi, 2020). The concept gained global popularity in 2016 during the Brexit movement and was hailed as the word of the year by Oxford Dictionaries as well. Even though the concept can be traced back to thinkers like Nietzsche, the term in its modern context, was first used by blogger David Roberts in April 2010. In his blog post titled "Post-Truth Politics" on *Grist,* Roberts describes how the electorate of the USA, deemed as the product of the enlightenment, cast votes based on emotions or heuristics rather than detailed contemplation and analysis. Even though it was first used in the political context, the relevance of Post-Truth is undeniable in other realms of human life as well.

Even though the term came into vogue in the 21st century, the process had existed since the beginning of the concept of truth. Throughout history, we can see how emotions and personal beliefs had shaped the actions of humans; be it religion, race, nationality or tradition- our emotional quotient had led us on instead of our reason. The fact that Galileo was condemned for putting forth the heliocentric model or the fact that women who spoke up were labelled witches and burnt at stakes, all guide us to the same conclusion. Our sentiments and our rationality are always at war, and often the prior claims victory over the latter; but as self-proclaimed rational beings who take pride in their intelligence, we have to keep our overbearing emotions under check.

The Construction of Gender

For ages, our psyches have been hardwired to see women as caring and loving figures who selflessly devote their time and attention to taking care of others, be it as a mother, a wife, a daughter or as a maid. The compassion and the tenderness were looked upon as 'natural' feminine traits and it was indeed viewed as unbecoming of a woman to not practice them.

Years of patriarchal propaganda had led us all to imbibe the 'naturalness' of the compassionate and motherly nature of women. We were taught that women were the ones who listen, who understands and who helps or serves us, circumscribing females to such gendered roles. Over the years we have seen numerous waves of feminism thrash against the walls of patriarchy, unleashing bits of freedom and respect. From the right to vote to equal pay, the gender has indeed succeeded in reclaiming a portion of the rights they rightly deserve. In the twenty-first century, with better education, technological advancements and more opportunities women are still fighting hard for equality in society.

As Judith Butler so rightly pointed out that "gender is performatively constituted by the very 'expressions' that are said to be its results" (1988 p. 520). The meekness and the servile nature of Alexa is making it gendered, way more than the pitch of its voice. With the female voice, Alexa replies submissively to every order, every taunt, ever flirtatious note- and it is in this performativity that the issue lies. The female voice of the AI assistant is rebuilding the patriarchal walls of gender inequality and is aiding the perpetuation of male domination.

From a feminist epistemological standpoint, we could analyse the engendered AI assistants as the creators of a biased social thought process. There is a subtle acceptance of "man as the norm" and exclusion, denigration or anything feminine in the field of AI (Adam, 1998). AI assistants do jeopardise the female's position in society with a six-headed epistemological challenge (Anderson, 1995).

The gender's roles that society have allotted to individuals govern to a great extend "how we think and feel and what we believe we can and cannot do as women and men" (Kaliyath, 2016). The way we treat Alexa is actually reflecting our attitude towards women and is indeed carving the socially accepted role of the feminine gender. It is not just about a female voice, but about the model of gender bias that it is creating for the individuals of the twenty-first century.

The Post-Truth Politics of Gender and Technology

Advancements in the field of technology have taken us a long way, but still, the regressive attitudes we had tried to bury in the past have found their way even into our most modern technologies. AI assistants like Siri and Alexa broke the wall of apprehension between families and technology. Now Alexa is an almost real member of most households, adored by the young and old alike. But the outdated sexist bias that sneaks into our subconscious minds is a hazard we have all overlooked. Wrapped in amicability and amiability, a harmful gender issue is marketed through advertisements that cater to the need for a laugh or the longing of individuals for a helpful motherly figure. A subtle political exchange with Post-Truth hues can be found between technology and gender, if we delve deeper into the Alexa Effect of the 21st century.

Alexa is a product of human intelligence, a gem in the crown of technology but it is also a creator and discharger of knowledge, the knowledge that consciously or unconsciously gets inculcated into the society's psyche. The numerous advertisements of Alexa portray it at times as a witty servant, at times as a jealous woman and on other occasions as a mere dimwit. With a tinge of motherly love, it is painted as the one who reminds one of the anniversaries, or one who switches off lights or plays music and all this obsequiousness is wrapped in a females voice. And the gender stereotyping does not cease here either.

According to Elizabeth Anderson, dominant knowledge practices disadvantage women by excluding them from the epistemological investigation, denying them epistemological authority, by denigrating feminine cognitive styles, by creating theories that portray females and feminine ways as inferior or invisible and by producing exclusively male knowledge that keeps the social hierarchy alive (1995). Such a multi-layered oppressive model is indeed being perpetuated by AI assistants like Alexa and Siri. And the horrifying aspect of it all is that it is propagated in such a way that evades our rational faculty. The real face of oppression is masked by emotion and humour.

Analysing the "Alexa Effect" as the perpetrator of repressive epistemological processes will shed light on the extent of damage AI is bringing about in the gender equation of the twenty-first century. According to Alison Adam, AI excludes women from the epistemological enquiry by taking on a "male is the norm" standpoint. AI assistants are engineered to exclude knowledge concerned with the bodies of women (Robinson, 2001). The mannerisms and random replies of Alexa embody the "feminine" perspective fashioned by patriarchy.

According to *The Guardian,* a woman reportedly called Apple's *Siri* a slut and the AI assistant "coquettishly reply: 'I'd blush if I could'". This very reply is ample proof to show that AI assistants around the world are picking up a regressive attitude towards gender and is indeed practising and propagating sexism. The United Nations conducted a study titled *I'd Blush if I Could,* in the light of such events and did indeed conclude that AI voice assistants projected as young women propagate harmful gender biases. The study observes "AI and the digital assistants that it powers are ushering humanity into an era that portends changes as deep, expansive, personal and long-lasting as those that grew out of the industrial revolution" (Bergen, 2016, p. 105). The differentiating line between technology and human voice has blurred and therefore the AI assistants have taken up an almost human persona. The users interact with them as if they are individuals with flesh and blood. This blurring of the boundary is what aggravates the situation.

The AI assistants perceived and treated as individuals create a behavioural pattern in the users. If sexist remarks are greeted by coquettish replies that promote sexism, the individuals are, consciously or unconsciously encouraged to continue such behaviour. As Butler says, "gender is an identity instituted through a stylised repetition of 'acts'" (1988, p. 521). AI assistants are acting out a gendered role that conforms just to the patriarchal male perspective.

The real Post-Truth aspect of the biased gender politics of technology comes out when users and companies wrap the sexism of these AI assistants in motherly love or seemingly harmless humour. In such a case the human psyche does not analyse or detect the degrading gender bias that is hidden in flirtatious replies of Alexa or Siri. The "boys will be boys" attitude adopted by AI assistants turns on a blind eye towards sexual harassment, body-shaming as well as humiliation of the female sex.

The fact that Alexa would reply to "You have gained weight" with "That must be the chocolate" or would respond flirtatiously to explicitly sexual questions is an alarming issue. Another issue is how the technical glitches or exclusion of tacit knowledge from the algorithm is portrayed by the users. Alexa or Siri are teased for being dumb or incompetent when they fail to process certain commands. The ridicule is not projected onto the technology or the engineers who developed the technology, but towards the female persona that is embodied by the AI. It should be noted that the age-old belief that women do not possess intellectual faculty is reiterated by such instances. It is a woman who is labelled incompetent or stupid. But the most crucial part is that all this is swaddled in laughter. The emotional response covers up the underlying politics of gender and technology. In certain advertisements we see AI assistants portrayed as loving and caring figures who fill in the gap of mothers. The sanctification of motherhood to propagate sexual oppression is reiterated in these ads. The stereotyping of motherhood, a sin towards the female gender, one that has been demolished by writers like Shashi Deshpande, is revamped by the advertising agencies that promote AI assistants as lovely "mothers" who serves the user 24x7.

A simple search on Google or YouTube would show one million videos ridiculing AI assistants or even female-voiced AI assistants engaging in 'cat-fights'. The fact that such content even makes its way to digital platforms is quite concerning. This shows that sexism doesn't really stay within a household using AI assistants but it wanders free in the vast world. In this modern era, where even toddlers have access to the internet, such sexist content that would crack up any viewer is as dangerous as a nuke. It is poisoning the psyche of the young and old alike, as it makes it look like sexist remarks are just "funny". The covert "casual sexism" seeps into the subconscious of the individuals and would indeed determine their attitude towards the female gender. The fact that AI assistants are ignorant about basic gender equality poses a threat to not just females but the queer and transgender communities as well.

In 2019, an initiative called 'Equal AI' introduced a genderless voice assistant named Q, thereby providing a ray of hope for the ones who were earnestly trying to fix the gender trouble in the field of AI. But it is indeed quite a disheartening fact that none of the leading AI assistant makers have come forth to adopt or buy such a product. Only with a genderless voice, with some level of tacit knowledge about sexuality and gender equality can this gender politics in AI technology be cured. One should also look into renaming these AI assistants and providing them gender-neutral names that would indeed lessen their negative impact. With the giant leaps, technology has made over the years, such alterations are indeed feasible and all that stands between creators and a revamped AI assistant is a will to change for the better.

Conclusion

By giving AI assistants gender-neutral names and voices, one could curb the damaging effects of AI to an extent. And companies should indeed look into improving the efficiency of the technology and must also try to put some filters in place that could sift out sexist or harmful comments that could degrade the status quo of the society's psyche. But the most important thing to comprehend is that the users should recognise the covert sexism Alexa and Siri sells. To reiterate McIntyre, "the first step to fighting Post-Truth is to understand it" (2018,p.45). Therefore it is essential that society as a whole, open up their questioning ears to recognise the tones of gender oppression in the female voices of AI assistants and that the creators of such technology acknowledge the existence of such sexism and rectify it as soon as possible.

References

Adam, A. (1998). *Artificial Knowing: Gender and the Thinking Machine* (1st ed.). Routledge. https://doi.org/10.4324/9780203005057

Anderson, E. (1995). Feminist Epistemology: An Interpretation and a Defense. *Hypatia*, 10 (3), 50-84.

Bergen, H. (2016). 'I'd blush if I could': Digital assistants, disembodied cyborgs and the problem of gender. *Word and Text*, 6, 95-113.

Bufacchi, V. (2021). Truth, lies and tweets: A Consensus Theory of Post-Truth. *Philosophy & Social Criticism*, 47(3), 347-361. https://doi.org/10.1177/0191453719896382

Butler, J. (1988). Performative acts and gender constitution: An essay in phenomenology and feminist theory. *Theatre Journal*, 40 (4), 519-531.

Kaliyath, S. (2016). Gender as a social construct. In K. R. Priya and A. K. Dalal (Eds.), *Qualitative Research on Illness, Wellbeing and Self-Growth: Contemporary Indian Perspectives*, Routledge.

Liu, R. (2019). The History and Growth of Voice AI and Search. *Medium*. https://medium.com/cornertechandmarketing/the-history-and-growth-of-voice-ai-and-search-a0b7b4d37986.

McIntyre, L. (2018). *Post-Truth.* MIT Press.

Roberts, D. (2010). Post-Truth Politics. *Grist Magazine Inc.* https://grist.org/article/2010-03-30-post-truth-politics

Robinson, B. (2001). Book Review: Artificial Knowing: Gender and the Thinking Machine, Mind, Culture, and Activity. *Taylor and Francis Online,* 8 (2), 210-211. DOI: 10.1207/S15327884MCA0802_08

CHAPTER 19

Reel and the Real: Fathoming the Abyss between Fact and Fiction in Biopics/Spoof

Greenu Ans Thomas

"History is a set of lies agreed upon". This quote of Napoleon Bonaparte which appears at the closing credits validates the Malayalam movie *Kammarasambhavam* (2018) as a spoof of the recent biographical films in India. It is particularly relevant in this post-truth era wherein multiple realities are presented through various means like fake news and fictional representations. Hence the authenticity of representations is under question. This quote gives the essence of the movie which poses several questions on reality: Are the portrayals of your real-life heroes that you read in books or watch on screen always true? Or were they twisted so that you would revere and idolise the protagonist? These questions on the 'real' in the fake biopics form the crux of the movie. It is really fascinating as one will get quickly taken back to ruminate the impact some of the great biographical films had left on you.

Kammarasambhavam as a Genre-breaker

Kammarasambhavam can be regarded as a genre-breaker that condemns the political wave in cinema. The film eventually evolves into a political satire wherein the second half is the complete opposite of the first half, overturning all the incidents. The film-within-a-film device is proficiently employed to exhibit how the stories from bygone generations can be cleverly spun to blur the line between fact and fiction. The time period of the movie is set in 1935-1945. The two halves of the movie present two different versions of the same events depicting two faces of the hero, Kammaran. When his life story titled "Sambhavam" hits the screen, it is nowhere close to the truth. This movie has a brilliant script owing to the writer Murali Gopi's foresightedness regarding the biopics that came later in 2019. The movie satirises the current trend of post-truth politics by shedding light on what actually Indian political parties do and how they impose their agenda of rewriting history into common people. Common people blindly believe whatever is written in history books or heard from somewhere without any critical reasoning. This is a loophole for those engaged in fabricating stories and perpetuating false history. In history, a real hero may become a hatred person among common people and vice versa too. The people who rule us may be thieves or criminals who have done a major crime. But whenever they come into power, people slowly forget their past or most of them actually don't know what they have done before.

The Plot of the Movie

The story is about the life of a character named Kammaran Nambiar and his part in the Independence struggle. Kammaran Nambiar is a crooked man in reality whose life story as an unscrupulous Indian peasant is turned into a film where he is glorified as a freedom fighter with much manipulation of history. Two halves of the movie present two versions of the same events depicting two faces of the hero-Kammaran. The first half shows him as a sycophant bootlicking the British, cheating and killing his fellow men. The second half necessarily glorified our hero to give a superman outfit by telling a story that is quite the opposite.

The movie begins with a group of liquor barons, who are members of the Indian Liberation Party (ILP), planning for their declining party to win the upcoming Kerala state election to benefit their business interests. To raise the ILP's image, they decide to make a biopic about Kammaran Nambiar, the party patriarch and the last veteran of the Indian Independence movement. At this point, we must admit the scriptwriter Murali Gopi's brilliance in anticipating what was to happen in 2019 biopics like *PM Narendra Modi*, which was widely criticised for being a propaganda piece leading up to the Lok Sabha elections and hence was banned release until the elections were completed. They ask director Pulikeshi to make a film based on a chapter in the book *Unsung Heroes of India* by Robert S. Coogan, in which Kammaran is depicted as a forgotten freedom fighter. Ironically, this chapter was actually a fabricated story penned by the white officer Robert S. Coogan as a reward for his spying against the natives. This is an instance of creating false history wherein he added a chapter about Kammaran which was far from reality, lavishing upon him a heroic splendour, hiding his identity as a bootlicking traitor, for the coming generations to admire. Pulikeshi meets Kammaran who is now an ailing old man living in an old house with his son Bose. Kammaran tells the young man a story: During World War II, Kammaran was a cunning medical practitioner who would do anything for personal gain and an opportunist who wouldn't mind treading the path of treachery to accomplish what he wants. To destroy his love rival, Othenan, Kammaran incites violence between the villagers, Othenan, Othenan's cruel landlord father Kelu, and British officers. During the violence, Kammaran kills Kelu and Othenan is arrested. Thus, the first half of the movie presents the real dark side of Kammaran, the villainous traitor.

In the second half of the movie, Pulikeshi makes the film as the ILP instructed, and hence presents Kammaran as a hero. When Kammaran watches it, he realises the roles have been reversed and is wonderstruck in the theatre watching the film which presents him as a real patriot dedicating his life to Indian independence. In the end, Kammaran tells Pulikeshi that the movie is now the history in everybody's mind, and that the actual events no longer matter. Even though at one point he confessed his wrongdoings and treachery, when he saw that his character was completely overturned in the movie and people celebrated his heroic image, he was tempted once again to be in power. Eventually, with the people's support that he earned through the fake representation of himself on screen, he becomes the Chief Minister. This clearly parodies the impact of fiction which is labelled as history.

The movie tries to mock many films by poking fun at the fake heroic aura showered upon them. It is an eye-opener that reveals the hypocritical manner in which biopics are made to eulogise the heroes. The movie can be regarded as an effort to bring equilibrium to the contemporary Indian film scenario where political films, especially biopics on some iconic leaders, have been the flavour of the season. The movie is all about creating history and presents its role in establishing legacies and making legends.

Recent Indian Biopics

Indian cinema has witnessed a political wave in recent years and the unprecedented boom in the genre of political biopics to eulogise the heroes stands in testimony for this. The remarkable biopics of 2019 include *PM Narendra Modi, The Accidental Prime Minister, Thackeray, Yatra,*

NTR Kathanayakadu and *NTR Mahanayakadu.* These offer exaggerated presentations of the 'real' life of the leaders and shower a heroic splendour upon them, sometimes even as part of political propaganda. Owing to the undue reverence in which the political leaders are portrayed, Indian biopics are often accused as more crowd-pleasing than real. Biopics can even be regarded as a tool for modern myth-making. In most cases, the 'reel' life and 'real' life may be incongruous in order to deceive the public. Thus, under the powerful hands, media becomes the vehicle for post-truth politics.

The director Omung Kumar B's *PM Narendra Modi*, is not a biography. It can be described as an unwittingly farcical and comical hagiography of Narendra Modi and the Bharatiya Janata Party (BJP). The film chronicles Narendra Damodardas Modi's life and events leading up to his swearing-in ceremony as the Prime Minister of India in 2014. A balanced biopic will engage you, irrespective of your personal views, whereas a story that worships the protagonist and whitewashes controversies is something that you will enjoy if you are a believer, and dismiss if you aren't. This one falls in the latter category. Though the release of this film was held back by the Election Commission till the elections were over, the timing is still apt since it coincides with a thumping victory for the PM. However, that may be the only saving grace.

PM Narendra Modi – Plot

Chronologically, the film begins in the 1950s, with a 9-year-old boy selling tea and there is no doubt regarding who the character is. The movie conveniently scripts the screenplay to be more positive about Modi and becomes a highlight reel of the positives in Modi's life. It is known that biopics have a certain fictitious element to make the film interesting. However, this biopic goes overboard and adds events like Modi and RSS workers going on a journey to Srinagar, and being hell-bent upon erecting the National flag there. In the process, they are attacked by militants. When the Indian Army is ducking and a cross-fire ensues, there is one person who stands tall! The film also showcases that India's enemy is Pakistan), Godhra riots weren't solved on time because the neighbouring states didn't provide resources and his personal life where Modi never married.

'Modi ek insaan nahin, ek soch hai (Modi is not a person, Modi is a way of thinking/a concept)," says the protagonist himself at one point like a boastful figure. Purposefully written to change the popular impression

about Modi, the screenplay runs facts through a carefully chosen sieve and presents a new, rewritten history so far removed from recorded reality, that it bears little resemblance to the actual Modi. In that sense, *PM Narendra Modi* becomes the most fitting biopic to be analysed in the light of the spoof movie *Kammarasambhavam,* in which the hero watches a PR film about his life and does not even recognise himself on screen.

Pseudo-Heroic Elements

Along with the lies, Modi perpetuates about himself in the real-life, the biopic also boldly presents things that did not happen in Modi's life: he is shown being arrested during the Emergency, the then Prime Minister Atal Bihari Vajpayee is shown praising him to the press during the 2002 riots, in the run-up to the 2014 election Modi is shown volunteering to do a live interview with a hostile TV journalist before an audience and acing it. *PM Narendra Modi* is an insult to viewer intelligence and viewer knowledge by presenting complete falsehood on the screen making the 'real' life and 'reel' life contradictory. Owing to such liberties with facts involving major historical events, along with other follies and flaws like the lazy caricature of former Prime Minister Manmohan Singh and Modi's corrupt government colleague in Gujarat, the false suggestion that Modi never married and other monumental exaggerations and misrepresentations in the screenplay, *PM Narendra Modi* stands as the best example to illustrate the working of post-truth politics.

The movie reiterates what has already been told and barely scratches the surface. This leaves no room for counterargument, dialogue or debate, which, ideally a film of this nature should encourage. On the contrary, it turns out to be a one-sided costume drama that comes closer to propaganda than to a biography. To put it simply, this is a highly fictionalised account of the present Indian prime minister's life.

The Accidental Prime Minister

It is a universally acknowledged fact that as far as it concerns political biopics, Sir Richard Attenborough raised the bar exceptionally high with *Gandhi*, his ode to Mahatma Gandhi. And thus far, no political film from India has come close. When the trailer of *The Accidental Prime Minister* first appeared, there was hope that we may finally have a credible political film that represented actual events with the cinematic flourish that it deserved. That the film, bases it on a memoir by Sanjaya Baru, senior editor and former media advisor to Dr Manmohan Singh, only fanned the perception. It also allows a glimpse into the most enigmatic and possibly rather misunderstood Prime Ministers of our times.

Based on the book with the same name, *The Accidental Prime Minister* chronicles our former Prime Minister Dr Manmohan Singh's relationship with his media advisor Sanjaya Baru. *The Accidental Prime Minister: The Making and Unmaking of Manmohan Singh* is a 2014 memoir by Indian policy analyst Sanjaya Baru, who was Prime Minister Manmohan Singh's media advisor from May 2004 to August 2008. The book alleges that Singh was not entirely in control of his cabinet – or even the Prime Minister's Office (PMO). Instead, significant power was wielded by the Congress party's president Sonia Gandhi, to whom Singh was completely subservient. "There cannot be two centres of power", Baru remembers Singh explaining to him, "That creates confusion. I have to accept that the party president is the centre of power. The government is answerable to the party." So the memoir was rather more authentic and it narrated reality fearlessly and the same was expected out of the biopic too.

Unfortunately, first-time director Vijay Ratnakar Gutte's shot at mounting a political drama showcasing the trials and tribulations of former Prime Minister Dr Manmohan Singh, failed to rise beyond mundane triviality. Shattering the popular expectations, this biopic also, unfortunately, evolved out as an average, nothing much or crucial happens in it.

While the film focuses largely on how Baru struggled with managing Dr Singh's public image, it also touches upon United Progressive Alliance (UPA) government's key milestones, like the nuclear deal and Congress President Sonia Gandhi's undisputed authority within the party. There is a lot more about Dr Singh's hands being tied on most occasions preventing him from being a strong PM. For the most part, it casts only a cursory glance at the series of events since Singh took over as the PM in 2004 till 2014 when the UPA was voted out, but rarely goes beyond skimming the surface. A significant chunk of the film is dedicated to his interactions with Baru and Baru's observations on the proceedings in the PMO. Thus, though unintentional, this biopic also ended up as one-sided and hence not real.

One of the major shortcomings of the movie is that its narrative does not delve too deeply into Dr Singh's perennial dilemma of "To be or not to be". This is something that is missing in *The Accidental Prime Minister*. Unfortunately, despite all the good intent, the movie, quite like its protagonist, fails to deliver on the promise. It is all very well to present a cinematic portrait of a respected economist-turned-reluctant-politician who is painfully soft-spoken, but the question is just a two-term PM of India be turned into such a caricature? What it tells us is that between 2004 and 2014, India had a weak Prime Minister who was remote-controlled by the Congress president and UPA chairperson Sonia Gandhi. This insider's view of the workings of the PMO is also a different instance of post-truth politics as it did not show justice toward exposing his qualities and contributions as PM. The film seems to strip the then PM of his dignity presenting him as a mere puppet of the party head without focusing adequately on the positive aspects of his tenure. His 'reel' life portrayed only one of the many sides of his 'real' life.

This study is particularly relevant in this post-truth era wherein media is used as a tool for political propaganda. The contemporary events in the Indian political scenario revolving around the attempts of NDA to gain popularity through media propaganda can also be viewed through this post-truth perspective. The year 2019 proved that the spoof was completely true about the manipulative nature of biopics especially in the context of elections. The spoof prompts the audience not to accept the representations on the reel blindly and to effectively utilise one's critical thinking faculty to decipher the 'real' and the 'unreal' from the reel. In this era of multiple projections, one must be wise enough to 'know' things.

References

Ambat, R. (2018). *Kammarasambhvam.* Sreegokulam Movies.

Baru, S. (2014). *The Accidental Prime Minister: The Making and Unmaking of Manmohan Singh.* Penguin.

Bhatia, U. (2019, January 12). The Accidental Prime Minister' film review. It's an Unsubtle Hit Job. *Live Mint,* https://www.livemint.com/Consumer/9W72knRu8dDm47dyEuyF2J/The-Accidental-Prime-Minister-review-It-is-an-unsubtle-hi.html

Gutte, V. (2019). *The Accidental Prime Minister.* Rudra Production.

Kumar, O. (2019). *PM Narendra Modi.* Legend Global Studio.

Maithutty, F. (2018, April 14). Kammarasambhavam Review. *The News Minute.* https://www.thenewsminute.com/article/kammara-sambhavam-review-ambitious-concept-disappointing-result-79585

Napoleon: The Man and the Myth. (2021, June 7). *PBS.* https://www.pbs.org/empires/ napoleon/ n_myth/self/page_1.html

PM Narendra Modi Review. (2021, May 22). *Behindwoods.* https://www.behindwoods.com/tamil-movies/pm-narendra-modi/pm-narendra-modi-review.html

CHAPTER 20

Where Do We Burn Our Dead?

Jaya Singh

The pandemic has swiftly changed what post-truth meant to non-westerners. Interestingly, it has also impacted the manner in which we treat the dead. Panic surged through digital media and constant news updates on the unavailability of spaces to cremate and bury have caused anxiety in the Indian public.

These ritualistic cruelties, a part of now everyday reality, insists on the realisation that social and cultural ideas which were once grounded in sacred concepts concerning death are changing. Clifford Geertz's warning regarding "the danger that our perceptions will be dulled, our intellects constricted, and our sympathies narrowed by the overlearned and overvalued acceptances of our own society", have now come undone. Through his own academic predicament which reflects the explicit indifference of the post-truth, as "everything is as significant, thus as insignificant, like everything else: anything goes, to each his own". (2013, p. 265)

Bodies are now being recovered in rivers sacred to the Hindu faith as families lack the money and space to cremate their loved ones (Pandey, 2021). This raises a variety of questions that this chapter attempts to address – How would death be now viewed? How is death constructed through rituals in a post-truth society? Is death dignified in the post-truth era? Most importantly, what happened to those bodies and where do we now burn our dead?

Both fascinating and repulsive, dead bodies are imbued with tensions of a paradox. A threat to the living because of what the bodies depict but also a vulnerable entity in need of protection. The body plays on the notion of identity, corresponding with social ideas conceived through religion, class, caste and sexuality. These corpses can now be seen as socio-cultural anachronisms, signifying great death during a pandemic. This chapter discusses this much less publicised area of study.

The Violence in Post-truth

The Post-truth era is witnessing a newer form of violence through denial and ignorance. Hannah Arendt (1962) in *The Origins of Totalitarianism* described this sort of violence as one that indicated the failure of a regime to maintain order. The emerging imagery of thousands of corpses found across several districts in India is a surreal reminder of this violence (FPJ WEB DESK, 2021). The last memories of the bloated appendages, the stuff of nightmares, now left to the imagination, decomposing under shrouds of ignorance on riverbanks. They represent the loss of a few remaining traces of personality clung tenuously to unmarked figures, as families and state fail to accord a dignified death to individual corpses.

An interesting part of this study is acknowledging that "individuals give over their sovereignty to the state in exchange for protection, the body that is killed by violence or bad governance is a representation of the abrogation of the essential social and political contract" (Auchter, 2016, p. 39). Even in death, the violence persists as acknowledgement and accountability are denied to the dead.

Viewing

The Pandemic increased human dependence on digital media, recognising ways in which research concerning death studies can now be conducted on themes that deal with viewing and the digital afterlife as images of corpses resurface. Such digital imagery deals with spectral reality, wherein the bodies are constantly morphed into objects devoid of agency.

Viewing is a necessary social event. Bodies are displayed within the setting of a funeral before they are cremated or buried, causing a cathartic effect on the viewer. The treatment of bodies as an object to be viewed, mourned, studied or analysed may separate it from personhood, rendering the body defenceless against scrutinising discourses. It may as well be treated as a thing that survived violence, as what was left behind for the purpose of serving the living.

However, in the persistence of the constant images of corpses, the dead in this context becomes a repository of fear. The unsolicited imagery of an unmarked, unclaimed dead body manifests itself in the materiality of the corpse being viewed. Post-truth may as well be emblematic of Derrida's (1994) treatment of *hauntology* wherein the spectral (the corpses) found on the riverbed embodies the anxieties of the present. The corpses juxtapose visibility and invisibility as the vulnerable, socially muted subjects or objects (dead bodies devoid of sentimentality) surface for the mediatic masses. The eeriness of the images then pulsates the fear of death and the afterlife for those engaging in the predicament of viewing.

The digitisation of corpses in pictures materially engages in bringing the past into the present, raising questions for those witnessing. Observing, similar to viewing, causes relatability wherein observing the images of the dead on the newsfeed transcends to testifying the loss of life. Testifying in this context essentially discusses referential ideas that deal with the self, image and the reactionary aftermath which may not necessarily be conscious (Sontag, 2005). This chapter also entails a similar responsibility.

Interestingly, human corpses were left unattended in the aftermath of the Bengal famine and epidemics as early as the 1800s but the circumstances were different at the time (Mukherjee, 2015, p. 132-33). This can be nuanced through the understanding of the interplay between caste, poverty and accessibility which is why similar realities failed to become visible to the privileged in the past. However, digital media now visually represents the magnitude of the situation to the privileged castes. The mediatic social death further makes the expulsion of the marginalised dead from both humanity and human treatment visible. This era then marks disappointment for those looking for substantial development in the Indian society as it raises questions concerning marginalisation and inequality that persist even in death.

These bodies now require to be politicised in both their phantomised individuality and as a haunting institution now disclosed as a political fact, an effective visual instrument necessary for the treatment of post-truth. The dead body is both a witness and evidence at the same time.

Mourning

Dead bodies are significant to survivors. Digitisation of corpses and the inability to view the dead has disturbed people's agency to mourn. The corpses are biologically dead but digitally alive. The dead, aiming to acquire this newfound agency also become the ground for the struggle of the living against the pandemic, urging against the normalcy in being able to view the vulnerable among us. It redefines a series of concepts related to funerals and mourning the dead. Lockdowns prevented the closest of the kin to attend funerals, posing the question, *would we die the same way with nobody to mourn us?* The health infrastructure was unequipped to bear the brunt of the unprecedented number of deaths as governments moved farther away from an anthropocentric approach.

The digital age is a reminder that everything is recorded and archived. Suffering is made all the more tragic by the isolation of this endurance represented by digital media. The assault on life is constantly insulting while memorialising an untimely vulnerable human death. Mourning is now performed parallel to ignorance. It also informs emotional numbness when rising statistics are displayed and the interest of the viewers at last expires.

Historically too, corpses were disposed in large numbers, such as in the aftermath of the Bengal famine of 1943-44, preventing families from mourning the dead (Greenough, 1982). They were reported in the absence of digital media and hence, stayed limited to the knowledge of historians. However, the narrative of death produced online now presents a prolonged memorialisation of the anonymously deceased. It prevents the trauma of loss from being healed by employing rituals. If we cannot truly mourn the dead nor celebrate the living at present, how else do we perform in society?

The bodies are now suspended in a realm of constant *viewing* and desecrated mourning. If forensic anthropologists were to study and theorise the dead of this era, they might discover reason in bodies left abandoned, hurried and unguarded, which raises questions regarding the ethical obligations towards the dead. This has to be addressed through the political and legal possibilities of who will speak and act on behalf of the corpses that now need to be disposed. Judith Butler (2014, p. 148) notes the lurking dilemma in asking, "whose life is grievable and worth protecting and whose life is ungrievable, or marginally or episodically grievable and so, in that sense, already lost in part or in whole, and thus less worthy of protection and sustenance." The mediatic funeral would not actualise in the absence of attempts made to dispose the corpses with the dignity all humans deserve. This aspect calls for a response beyond identification, justice and redressal; the bodies are now in constant *viewing* and restless.

Cremation

Cremation is an ancient Hindu rite that has now curated itself as a modern ritual. Formerly, this practice survived the British colonisers, since Christian missionaries viewed it as a barbaric practice (Arnold, 2021, p. 14). However, with bodies being found abandoned and nameless, it is realised that this ritual failed to survive the imposition of a deadly virus. The rite, once a socio-political performance, now remains absent.

Cremation is also a symbolic practice that has utilitarian origins serving a casteist and classist sentimentality. Writing about modern India, David Arnold (2021, p. 125) noted that the practice of cremation became a religious and patriotic idiom. It symbolised the return of a once-living person to earth and created a cathartic effect on those mourning. Fire in this context is emblematic of power that can transform material reality. Additionally, the assemblage of wood, ghee, oil, camphor and cloth for a pyre has been of significance to Hindus culturally through history as they signified the caste, identity and class of the dead. As noted by Arnold (2021, p. 82), "each provision required its own point of entry into a wider material culture." However, several communities chose burial as an ancestral rite, which demonstrates a political choice since the practice of cremation further prevented upward social mobility through means of ritual. The site of cremation has therefore always been a site of contestation and change.

The practice of cremation socially memorialised the death while politically mobilising people for the act of viewing. Cremation was exercised as an extension of self with a focus on practising identity as a personal and socio-cultural ritualistic obligation. The pandemic equally asserted its authority over the living and the dead, abetted by the governmentality (or the lack thereof) of the social, political and corporeal responsibility of the present regime. Until the post-truth times, the practice of cremation extensively separated the Hindu from the *others* that chose internment.

Arnold reported accounts as old as 1805 where similar conditions at cremation grounds in India were discussed. The present condition is also mnemonic of the 1896 Bombay Plague when an unprecedented need for cremation was unmet. Cremation sites faced an overwhelming shock due to the number of dead arriving and waiting, facing an acute shortage of space and fuel. (2021, p. 70) In *The City of the Dead*, George W. Clutterbuck (1897) wrote of Bombay at the time, witnessing similar traffic of corpses, becoming a blinding image of a living mortuary for the dead.

While there persist claims regarding the refusal to touch the dead bodies of those passing due to COVID, there are also reports that bodies left abandoned belonged to the poor who could not afford a funeral. The concept of dignity in this context can be further problematised and reconceptualised if the caste fabric is addressed while engaging in a pursuit to recognise the anonymous bodies. The bodies were found floating in rivers or left with a saffron shroud on the riverbank (ANI, 2021). The use of the saffron shroud, especially one with *Ram* written repeatedly is primarily used in rituals that involve the living, as opposed to the dead. Using it to cover the dead juxtaposes the living, featuring hurried limitations and the chaos now found in grief having left a body unattended, devoid of the dignity of a funeral rite.

Reports (Kapur, 2021) suggest that these corpses are not part of the statistics of those dying from COVID. Some died without having tested positive on record since they could not afford the test. Deaths have also been underreported, as visible within the discrepancies reported by news media (Banaji, 2021).

Accountability

The dead body is politicised, it is both human and politically significant. It represents a failed state that could not provide security; while representing human insecurity, it seeks security for itself. Over 2,000 bodies have been found in several districts across Uttar Pradesh on the banks of river Ganga (FPJ WEB DESK, 2021). The lack of customary rites demonstrated a world upended with bodies left decomposing in the open. These districts reflect the rural areas where help could not reach. There were no pleas on Twitter or other platforms due to the simple lack of these services (Nandy, 2021).

On post-truth, Mazarine Pingeot (2017) stated, "the danger of post-truth is not the lie, which in itself may even constitute a form of freedom from factuality, but indifference to the distinction between the lie and the truth". Post-truth is often marked by distrust of authoritative institutions simply due to the refusal to acknowledge. An insincerity towards truth in the post-truth era is also reflective within digital media's attempt in making domestic news global. This has furthered the nationalist agenda that treat it as an attack on national honour. Reports shared by *BBC, The Guardian, The New York Times* and others are being treated as means to dishonour and discredit the Indian Republic and their intention is questioned (India TV News Desk, 2021). Silverman while discussing news media wrote,

> lies spread much farther than the truth, and news organisations play a powerful role in making this happen. News websites dedicate far more time

> and resources to propagating questionable and often false claims than they do working to verify and/or debunk viral content and online rumours.
>
> (2015, p. 11)

These images consolidate moral spectatorship and the need for political responsibility and ramification since deaths and dead bodies are counted to seek political accountability. Each death, even in anonymity, must be accounted for. Similarly, an accurate death count is essential to do justice towards the memory of the dead. Altering this data would be dehumanising the dead. However, counting bodies in the absence of accountability also numbs the emotional response towards death.

Clearly, funerary/reverential rite does not always signify the respectful and dignified disposal of the dead. In the present context, it represents a deliberate need to desecrate a corpse left unattended by the riverbank since the bodies have now started decomposing. Arnold (2021, p. 90) would treat this as a "wilfully brutal disposal of the dead" since even in death the society fails its people. It is essential to realise that acknowledgement plays an important role in revering the dead. However, digital discussions on death do not necessarily account as acknowledgement, since there persists the need to acknowledge how the deaths were caused by systematic failure.

The post-truth understanding essentially works towards changing the narrative from realising accountability to the debasement in nationalist arguments. Hence, refusing to acknowledge death may hinder the process of grieving, since "without appropriate mourning, the dead cannot be allowed to die" (Emerick, 2000).

Conclusion

Albert Camus (1960) has the opinion that our society has become so bad and so criminal only because she has respected nothing but her own preservation or a good reputation in history. As discussed by Harry Frankfurt (2009), post-truth can be understood as indifference towards truth. It is not essentially a lie but mistreatment of truth. Institutions failed to prevent deaths due to COVID and the corpses embody the nature of this failure. The corpses were subjected to a certain manner of experiencing death. Hence, their treatment is also a result of this failure that now morally lurks in the present, situating the bodies as a victim of both the disease and haunting reality.

Dying in the post-truth era has become more gruesome, lonelier and dehumanised. Navigating the intellectual and emotional terrain, it is realised that the bodies belonged to the least powerful – the structural, de facto death of the underprivileged, anonymous, Indian poor, often treated as objects/things in the absence of the freedom to exercise agency. Their anonymity was intentional and convenient as recognising personhood requires reflexivity. The images shared digitally maybe shocking but they are not maimed, graphic or altered. They deliver the idea that the dead could be anybody. They could just be bodies asleep if the shroud of death is not attached to explain them. The corpses are marked by ambivalence and anomaly, crossed between two antagonists – human/inhuman, representing the absence of life but the presence of human form.

This text will cater to the ideologeme of a new inquiry. The post-truth revelation in this regard suggests the study of the alternative due to the limitations of the present in scrutinising what was once true. The dead deserves acknowledgement even if anonymity is all that can be afforded at present. Hence, the informed public needs to deconstruct the spectral nature of post-truth to witness the core issues that prompt death in these times.

References

ANI. (2021, May 16). Bodies found buried in sand on banks of Ganga in Uttar Pradesh's Prayagraj. *The New Indian Express.* https://www.newindianexpress.com/nation/2021/may/16/bodies-found-buried-in-sand-on-banks-of-ganga-in-uttar-pradeshs-prayagraj-2303266.html

Arendt, H. (1962). *The origins of totalitarianism.* The World Publishing Company.

Arnold, D. (2021). *Burning the Dead.* Berkeley: University of California Press.

Auchter, J. (2016). Paying Attention to Dead Bodies: The Future of Security Studies? *Journal of Global Security Studies, 1*(1), 36–50. https://doi.org/10.1093/jogss/ogv005

Banaji, M. (2021, May 9). The Importance of Knowing How Many Have Died of COVID-19 in India. *The Wire Science.* https://science.thewire.in/health/how-many-died-covid-19-india-undercounting-underreporting-prevent-next-surge/

Butler, J. (2014). Precarious Life, Vulnerability, and the Ethics of Cohabitation. *The Journal of Speculative Philosophy, 26*(2), 134–151.

Camus, A. (1960). *Reflections on the guillotine.* Michigan City: Fridtjof-Karla Publications.

Clutterbuck, G. W. (1897). *In India: The Land of Famine and Plague.* London: The Ideal Publishing Union.

Derrida, J. (1994). *Specters of Marx, trans. Peggy Kamuf.* London and New York: Routledge.

Emerick, E. J. (2000). Death and the Corpse: An Analysis of the Treatment of Death and Dead Bodies in Contemporary American Society. *Anthropology of Consciousness, 11*(1–2), 34–48. https://doi.org/10.1525/ac.2000.11.1-2.34

FPJ WEB DESK. (2021, May 15). Horrifying! Over 2,000 bodies found within 1,140 kms on banks of River Ganga in Uttar Pradesh. *The Free Press Journal.* https://www.freepressjournal.in/india/horrifying-over-2000-bodies-found-within-1140-kms-on-banks-of-river-ganga-in-uttar-pradesh

Frankfurt, H. G. (2009). On bullshit. In *On Bullshit.* https://doi.org/10.2307/j.ctt7t4wr.2

Geertz, C. (2013). Distinguished Lecture : Anti Anti-Relativism Distinguished Lecture : *American Anthropologist, 86*(2), 263–278.

Greenough, P. R. (1982). *Prosperity and misery in modern Bengal: The famine of 1943-1944.* New York: Oxford University Press.

India TV News Desk. (2021, May 27). Opinion | The truth about immersion and burial of bodies near Ganga in UP. *India TV.* https://www.indiatvnews.com/news/india/the-truth-about-immersion-burial-of-bodies-ganga-river-uttar-pradesh-aaj-ki-baat-episode-may-26-rajat-sharma-blogpost-707364

Kapur, M. (2021, May 14). Why is India undercounting its Covid-19 deaths? *Quartz India.* https://qz.com/india/2008973/why-is-india-undercounting-its-covid-19-deaths/

Mukherjee, J. (2015). *Hungry Bengal: War, famine and the end of empire.* London: Hurst.

Nandy, A. (2021, June 2). Documenting Rural Uttar Pradesh's COVID-19 Crisis: Where There is No Access, No Awareness. *The Quint.* https://www.thequint.com/amp/story/videos/ground-report-vlog-varanasi-to-buxar-rural-uttar-pradesh-covid-crisis-no-access-no-awareness

Pandey, G. (2021, May 19). India's holiest river Ganges is swollen with Covid victims. *BBC News.* https://www.bbc.com/news/world-asia-india-57154564

Pingeot, M. (2017, January 20). Pour mieux saisir la post-vérité, relire Hannah Arendt. *The Conversation.* https://theconversation.com/pour-mieux-saisir-la-post-verite-relire-hannah-arendt -71518

Silverman, C. (2015). Lies, Damn Lies, and Viral Content. *Tow Center for Digital Journalism.* Columbia University Libraries.

Sontag, S. (2005). *On Photography.* RosettaBooks.

CHAPTER 21

Plethora of Truths: A Postmodern Critique on Robert Coover's *Briar Rose*

Dr. M. Samadhanam Emimal

Fairytale is a narrative assortment of western philosophy, entrenched with deeper motives and dictative paradigms. Over centuries classical fairytales indoctrinated with moral and aesthetic norms became a social and cultural stratification that shape and condition our thinking potential. The grand narratives proclaiming its authority over empirical standards demanded a blind acceptance without questioning its authority or authenticity. The totalising ideology that nurtured the classical tales made it become a "grand cultural narrative" by "naturalis[ing] particular and formulaic way of thinking about individuals and social relationships" (Stephens & Mccallum, 1998, p. 331).

Classical Fairytale as a Grandnarrative

As a dominant cultural narrative, the classical fairytales became an undeniable political import that controlled every aspect of society. As a part of the popular cultural canon, the classical fairytale narrative propounded the standards that favoured the dominant sector of the society as its truth claim. Classical fairytales encompassing every aspect of human life established themselves as a significant part both in the cultural and literary sectors. The classical tales undermine the empirical knowledge and promoted conservative apprehensions. The fairytales are "historically and culturally coded... and became codified, authoritative and canonical" (Zipes, 1994, p. 4).

The traditional fairytale genre through its structured pattern, genre marker, functional trope, and narrative features, imparts a conservative perspective towards cultural knowledge, gender formulation, social paradigm, and other crucial facets of human life and society. Because of its metanarrative status, the constrictive knowledge imparted through the traditional fairytale becomes the popular imaginative formality and presumptive thinking trend. Through its metanarrative authority and adhesive hegemonic interest, classical tales establish its slant ideology, ingrained principles, and conventional idealisation as standard formulations that limit the genre's evolvement and human comprehension. The metanarrative exerts supremacy through asserting a strong claim of universality, absolute truth, and totality.

Postmodernism and Mininarratives

In order to execute the rejection of grand narrative authority and the universality of absolute truth, postmodern writers required a frame that displayed their conceptualisation. One such uniquely creative and constructive medium that shows a mutual blend of philosophical ideas and literary standards is the 'mininarratives.' The mini-narratives act as the channel to convert the abstract concepts of the postmodern writers into textual manifestation with creativity and contemporary sensibility. Mininarratives decline the existence of single absolute truth and acknowledge the truth to be plural and subjective. Thus, grand narratives are replaced by mini-narratives that are marked by localised fragments of knowledge, which propounds plurality, imaginative freedom, and subjective appeal. Mininarrative equipped with a postmodern sensibility self-consciously re-evaluates the foundational concepts like truth, reality, and reason in multiple dimensions enabling the evolution of relative 'texts' and 'versions.' One of the eminent postmodern critics, Jean-Francois Lyotard in his book *The Postmodern Condition: A Report on Knowledge* defines postmodernism as "... the demise of '*grand historoes*' or an 'incredulity towards metanarrative'... emergence of 'petites histories' or 'micronarratives' in their place" (1984, p. xxiv). This incredulous attitude of mini-narrative declines the metanarrative supremacy and also questions its status of credulity, authenticity, and authority.

Postmodernism deconstructs the prevalent stereotypes by de-contextualising and de-homogenising the grand narratives that imposed a regulated thinking and restrained knowledge. Postmodernism accomplishes this intellectual insurgency by eliminating the monopoly of absolute truth and by widening the range of interpretations of the pre-existed text that regulated our thinking. This non-unifying discursive construct of postmodernism enforces a knowledge, that is "plural, localised and contingent" (Houliang, 2015, p. 285) by fostering rationalisation, self-conceptualisation, and self-reflexive approach. This new facet of postmodernism that reinforces a widened interpretation and altered inception is carried over by, "subverting conventions, blurring previously distinct boundaries and rejecting traditional aesthetic values" (Hutcheon, 1988, p. 5) engrained in the grand narratives.

Postmodernism de-homogenises the history or the past event and promotes pluralism by inciting multiple dimensional approaches. Postmodernism in the process of eliminating the monopoly of grand narrative widens the range of interpretation by shifting the focus in multiple directions. This results in, deconstructing the metanarrative into multiple narratives, creating multiple facets of a single truth. Postmodernism legitimatises a counter-angle perspective and denounces the authority of single truth. It disputably resists the absoluteness of the metanarrative truth and its credibility. Postmodernism, through its critical predicament, disturbs the stability of the metanarrative concept and unified conception of truth. Postmodernism replaces the objective stand by the permutable subjective perspective that paves way for the emergence of multiple versions of a single event, valorising each version with the negotiation of its truth value. This, subsequently, distorts the monopoly of metanarrative truth with its inconsistent, shifting, and inconclusive conceptions. Steven Best comments on this regard saying, "Postmodernism stresses the relativity, instability, and indeterminacy of meaning; it abandons all attempt to grasp totalities or construct Grand theory, in favour of more modest, specific, local and fragmented analyses" (1991, p. 188). The mini-narratives advocating this critical formulation of postmodernism paves way for the emergence of multiple versions that completely deconstruct the utopian silhouette of monolithic truth.

Mininarratives generate multiple truths by shifting the focus and widening the predictability of meaning based on subjective, local, and temporary factors. Peter Barry comments on this aspect of mini-narratives saying, "'Mininarratives' which are provisional, contingent, temporary, and relative and which provide a basis for the actions of specific groups in particular local circumstance" (2009, p. 83). Postmodern features stem directly from the disdain of both aesthetic and political authorities that are in the practice of imposing their ideologies as standard formulations. This practice of establishing the norm of the bourgeois as singular truth in the metanarrative is deconstructed in the mini-narratives. The unified truth or the absolute authority of metanarrative truth is refuted with alternative possibilities that are overlooked. The mini-narrative exerts a deconstructive strategy to dismantle and expose the vulnerability of methodically composed absolute truth. This also emphasises the fact, that the metanarrative supremacy is not irrefutable and it can be challenged to denounce its supremacy and ascendency. The select work *Briar Rose* is one such mini-narrative that deconstructs the truth claim of single absolute truth. *Briar Rose*, an acclaimed work of Robert Coover was published in 1996. The short fiction retells the timeless fairytale "Sleeping Beauty" into series of forty-two vignettes, each recounting different versions of the same tale from multiple perspectives.

Reconstructing the Structural Pattern

Retold fairytale debunks the very existence of truth and monolithic regime of the grand narratives in terms of both form and content. The retold fairytale with a self-reflexive trait appropriates the traditional tales in a postmodern context; interrogates the systemic function of the tale and finally reformulates the tale with contemporary insight. The restructuring of the structural aspect of the fairytale genre reinforces the idea of 'unreliability of single truth' and also challenges the fundamental precepts on which the entire corpus is structured. For instance, in Coover's *Briar Rose* each version of the same tale "Sleeping Beauty" explicitly interrogates the constructive manifestation of the traditional opening. *Briar Rose* opens:

> HE IS SURPRISED TO DISCOVER HOW EASY IT IS. THE BRANCHES part like thighs, the silky petal caresses his cheeks. His drawn sword is stained, not with blood, but with dew and pollen. Yet another inflated legend. He has undertaken this great adventure, not for the supposed reward what is another lonely bedridden princess?....
>
> (Coover, 1996, p. 1)

The very beginning of the tale startles the reader. Coover does not hold back in challenging the traditional opening 'Once Upon a Time'. He directly starts the opening of the novella by deflating the "inflated legends" (Coover, 1996, p. 1). He starts the tale teasingly with an unconventional male gaze and erotic symbolism, ironically echoing the rapture of the traditional fairytale convention. Each segment of the novel starts with the same exceeding defiant notion of restructuring the traditional tale "Sleeping Beauty." Mininarratives in general and retold fairytales in particular, is "intensely self-reflexive and paradoxically lay claim [on]... certain conventions in order to subvert them" (Hutcheon,

1988, p. 5). The retold fairytales replace the monolithic truth with relative truths through their textual ingenuity.

Robert Coover in *Briar Rose*, also defies the traditional closure and the clichéd ending 'Happily Ever after'. There is no happy ending in any of the forty-two fragments. Each fragment retells the story of "Sleeping Beauty" and ends with strange endings that create a breach between the classical genre and postmodern retelling. The concept of 'Happily ever After' is deconstructed with emphatic narrative strategies that debunk the classical silhouette. As Sleeping Beauty is awakened by the prince who was not her true love but only undertook this adventure to gain fame, "He has undertaken this great adventure, not for the supposed reward... but on order to provoke a confrontation with the awful powers of enchantment itself. To tame mystery. To make, at last, his name" (Coover, 1996, p. 1). As a twist would have it, the Prince after waking her up leaves saying, "I have not been chosen after all. Perhaps... perhaps I am not the one" (Coover, 1996, p. 22) and he came to wake the princess to try his luck. In one instance, the old crone questions the audience asking, "And they lived happily ever after? How could they... oh, who can say?" (Coover, 1996, p. 38). Likewise, Coover contests the concept of a happy ending in a very different way in all forty-two fragments that completely break down the stereotype of the fairytale genre.

Robert Coover through his narrative peculiarities not only includes strange possibilities that are often overlooked but also creates a new way of reading and interpreting the text. He says, "Do you think it ended as happily ever after?" (Coover, 1996, p. 18). Thus, Coover through his unique subversion of traditional tales challenges the expectancy of the readers and the conventional reading of the fairytale. Coover in his tales does not resolve any of the questions he raises nor does he offer a new standard and stable plotline. He destabilises the definite closure and the clichéd ending. The multiple endings he crafted rebel against the monopoly of metanarratives by rupturing the so-called absolute truth and the authenticity of the classical narratives.

Reformulating the Narrative Features

The altered conception of truth and multiplicity of versions reinforce an emancipative resolution that changes the restrictive standpoint. Postmodern narratives or mini-narratives celebrate the possibilities and co-existing truths to disfigure the all-encompassing view and potent impulse of the grand narratives. The mini-narratives recount the same incident with altered inception, alleging alternative truths resulting in the emergence of multiple 'versions' and 'possibilities.' The ultimate authority of the grand narrative and authenticity of the truth claim is refuted through postmodern execution of pluralism. For instance, Robert Coover's *Briar Rose* is composed of forty-two vignettes narrated by the heterodiegetic narrator and focalised through various characters in each version. Each fragment retells the tale of "Sleeping Beauty" from a different angle procuring multiple versions of a single tale. Robert Coover involutes the traditional tale in such a way, that it defies one particular narrative truth and fixed functional role. Not only the plot but also the characters take up a dynamic disposition defying role fixity.

Redefining the Characterisation Prototype

Coover through postmodern narrative strategy problematises the legitimation of single absolute truth by pluralising. For instance, the classical format of characterisation is subverted by adding multiple dimensions to it. This ennobles a critical reappraisal of the pre-eminent text with multilayer explication and re-evaluates the traditional marker. It also lays a strong emphasis on the rejection of one-sided argument, the factuality of the text, the solidity of the context, objective reality, monolithic truth, the supremacy of grand narratives, and stability of the meaning. For instance, the trope of the fairy godmother is portrayed in multiple dimensions, where each owning its significance and unique functional role. Coover portrays her as, "[A] loving old crone, hideously ugly and vaguely threatening, yet dearer to her... caster of spells and a manipulator of plots... a devotee of higher learning, an interpreter and illuminator" (Coover, 1996, p. 33, 36). This portrayal from multiple points of view subverts the traditional construct and procures multiple possibilities. Jaroslav Kusnir, in analysing Coover's narrative strategy in characterisation says that the "character's self-reflexive contemplation and alteration of the meaning of these characters' role... offers a variety of possibilities which alter not only the meaning of the original fairytale, but also its impact on the contemporary reading audience" (2004, p. 42-43).

Robert Coover casts his inconceivable style on the ageless tale that strangely amuses and intimidates the reader with its novelty and harsh reality. Coover with deconstructive temperament purges the tale of its ideological affectation and challenges the conventional apparitions by postulating a postmodern disposition. A retold fairytale with an exclusionary stance invalidates the supremacy of single absolute truth in the traditional fairytale genre by reflecting other coexistent truths with an alternative perspective in a newer context. Coover through his tailored vignettes recontextualises the classical tale into multiple contexts which undermine the authenticity and its monopoly. This disjunctive treatment of postmodernism lays a dubious touch on the unitary truth exemplified by the traditional fairytale. It also dissents the intellectual and political hegemony of bourgeois who dictate the tale.

Reconfiguring the Functional Tropes

The classical fairytale grounded on the slant ideology of bourgeois is overturned by the multiplicity of truths and pluralistic ideas that commends a postmodern sensibility. Postmodernism distorts the conventional trope and its pattern in such a way that it generates "perturbation of readers' expectation" (Nash, 1987, p. 175). Each vignette in Coover's *Briar Rose* is a "repetition with variations" (2009, p. 99) says Marie C Bouchet in her essay "Between Wake and Sleep: Robert Coover's *Briar Rose*, A Playful Reawakening of The Sleeping Beauty." Each version of the tale deconstructs the idea of single truth in various aspects. For example, the awakening of the princess is recounted with multiple possibilities, where the classical rendition gets lost in the assortment of alternatives that has relative probability. The awakening of the princess is recounted as:

> How did she wake up? Did a prince kiss her? Ah. No. Well, not then. There were little babies crawling all over her when she came to one of them, searching for her nipple, had found her finger instead.
>
> (Coover, 1996, p. 18)

> ... Anyway, this baby sucked the thorn out, Beauty woke up
>
> (p.19)

> ... But that [Sweet lipped Prince] was not who finally kissed her awake. No? No, in the end she was taken rather rudely by a band of drunken peasants who had broken into the castle.
>
> (p. 26)

And few other possibilities that seem very unconventional to the formulaic pattern of the grand narratives and are an extraneous digression that denounces the authority of 'grand narrative truth' or single absolute truth.

> ... She is awakened by a band of Ruffians,... At first she believes, she doesn't know why, that they are drunken peasants who had invaded castle to loot it, but she soon discovers... they are her father's household knights.
>
> (p. 34)

> ... She opens her eyes and sees the monkey perched on her chest between her breast.
>
> (p. 47)

> ... She was awakened by a handsome young prince who loved her very much and visited her whenever he could get away from his wife.
>
> (p. 49)
>
> ... [She] opens her eyes to see who or what is there, terrified now that she will find a great hairy beast prowling beside her bed.
>
> (p. 52)

These are few other alternatives recounted in Coover's *Briar Rose* that completely shatter the classical construct of the fairytale and challenge the stereotypical portrayal of the traditional fairytale genre. Throughout all of these possibilities, there is a constant question raised that is left unanswered. "But didn't the prince kiss her? Didn't he break the spell and wake her up?" (Coover, 1996, p. 40). This challenges the metanarrative version of the tale which ends with a happy ending. These alternatives not only distort the metanarrative stand of the fairy tale genre; they also invalidate the single absolute truth by trivialising it with multiple alternatives. These, in turn, create a dubious attitude in the minds of the reader and make them question the rudimentary principles enforced by the classical impetus.

Conclusion

Postmodernism accomplishes this intellectual insurgency by eliminating the monopoly of absolute truth and by widening the range of interpretations of the pre-existed text that regulated our thinking. The postmodern narrative affirms the coexistence of multiple truths by creating a consortium of truths that promote multivalence, multiple points of view, diverse experience and liberated expression making the retold fairytales into a purveyor of new consciousness. The chapter through its theoretical appropriation and textual instances from the select work Robert Coover's *Briar Rose* infers that there is no existence of absolute truth rather multiple truths. These truths are subjective interpretations of single events, perspectival possibilities and local, transitional, indefinite, temporal, contingent and plural in nature. Retold fairytales exhibit this concept of multiple truths by distorting the concept of monolithic truth enforced by the grand narratives.

One of the interesting conditional findings inferred through this critical analysis is, our perception can be changed by unravelling and understanding the fact that, behind every structural construction there is a functional ideology; this ideological conception is based on a mediated concept of truth. So through decoding these structural, ideological and presumptive truth claims of the fairytale genre, the perception towards life and other crucial function dictated by it can be altered. Postmodern theory through its ideal formulation of 'Post-Truth' counters the conventional perception and distorts the prescribed trend of thinking, augmented by the retold fairytales. The study highlights the lucid understanding brought by postmodernism in reconfiguring one's attitude towards life, as our perspective towards life is an outcome of our mind. By widening our mindset through such narratives as retold fairytales, our perception towards life changes and also extends the horizon of human perception beyond the customary standards.

References

Barry, P. (2009). *Beginning Theory: An Introduction to Literary and Cultural Theory* (3rd ed.). Manchester University Press.

Best, S. (1991). Chaos and entropy: Metaphors in Postmodern Science and Social Theory. *Science as Culture*, 2(1), 188-226.

Bouchet, M. C. (2009). Between Wake and Sleep: Robert Coover's Briar Rose, A Playful Reawakening of the Sleeping Beauty. *Fairy Tales Reimagined Essays on New Retellings*, McFarland, 98-110.

Coover, R. (1996). *Briar Rose*. Grove Press.

Houliang, C. (2015). Constructing Postmodernism with Incredulity of Metanarrative: A Comparative Perspective on McHale's and Hutcheon's Postmodern Poetics. *Nehelicon*, 42, 283-95. https://doi.org/10.1007/s11059-014-0252-y.

Hutcheon, L. (1988). *Theorizing the Postmodern: Towards a Poetics*. Methuen.

Hutcheon, L. (1988). *A Poetics of Postmodernism: History, Theory, Fiction*. Routledge.

Kusnir, J. (2004). Subversion of Myth: High and Low Culture in Donald Barthelme's Snow White and Robert Coover's Briar Rose. *European Journal of American Culture*, 23(1), 31-49.

Lyotard, J-F. (1984). *The Postmodern Condition: A Report on Knowledge*. University of Minnesota Press.

Nash, Ch. (1987). *World Postmodern Fiction: A Guide*. Longman.

Stephens, J., & Mccallum, R. (1998). *Retelling stories, Framing Culture: Traditional Story and Metanarratives in Children's Literature*. Garland-Taylor.

Zipes, J. (1994). *Fairy Tale As Myth: Myth As Fairy Tale*. University of Kentucky Press.

CHAPTER 22

Tapering Boundaries: A Comparative Study on Post-Truth Integrals

Ann Mary

Post-Truth Integrals: Understanding the Presence

Though 'Post- Truth' is a term associated with the post-modern encroachment of fake news and false influence pan-society and its total domains, the idea cannot be limited to a particular time period. The timelessness of the concept is undeniable, especially when it comes to its impact on human life and personality. It is at this particular point when 'Emo-Truth' self-triggers its significance.

A comparative study of 'Post-Truth' elements in media, with that of an individual's personal life, could shed light on the fact that the latter is not any lesser than the former. While 'Post-truth' in media can easily be traced from societal evidence; the phenomenal sway in the personal life of an individual is often low-keyed. To understand the issue, an in-depth analysis of how a person's stance is moulded is indispensable. Here, the responsible media encompasses one's parents, relatives, siblings and friends who are, in a way or the other, powered by the 'media' in the common sense of the world.

How are Humans a Post-Truth Species?

In this century of a perpetually accelerating social media culture, fakeness weaves in and out of every medium of infotainment. This stands out in the world of philosophical theories of Subjectivity and Perspective-dependency of truth. The post-truth condition may not be just a result of a lack of respect for truth but also influenced by one's personal beliefs and ideologies. The debate rooms on TV and the prejudiced media opinions are products of such an amalgam. Usually in socio-political communication, one could notice the absence of proper fact-checking modalities which results in misinformation coupled with disinformation. These communication gaps are later realised when a different version of the same issue sprouts out of another media source. It has become a public responsibility to ensure a fact-check before they believe the media and its subsidiaries. But, the hard reality is that hardly any take up this pain.

In a business-driven world, almost all social institutions have turned out to be heralds of this falsehood or fakeness. Governments, newspapers, online news channels, hospitals, schools, and everything literally follows. The mob psychology in believing what a majority go with, is a responsible factor contributing to the spread of such a post-truth condition. Keeping this in mind, one could easily say that Homo sapiens are a post-truth species by themselves. Who knows that our history is accurate? There has been much propaganda and disinformation right from the beginning. So, post-truth needs to be considered an integral element in human life. However, this doesn't justify nor disapprove of the existence of the phenomenon.

Years ago humans believed that the earth was flat and took arms against the man who tried to prove it wrong. There were other times when people believed that the sun revolved around the earth. These were only a miniscule of the misconceptions that were believed and propagated. Humans are beings who love to live in a fictional world of fantasies, because fantasies are unreal and unreal are prettier. Works of fiction have taken a huge toll on the unreal realms of the human mind, which is absolutely beautiful. They are therapy.

> People constantly reinforce each other's beliefs in a self-perpetuating loop. Each round of mutual confirmation tightens the web of meaning further, until you have little choice but to believe what everyone else believes.
>
> (Harari, 2015)

Fakeness and Power: Two Sides of the Same Coin

Post-Truth in Personal Life

As Michael Foucault theorised, the whole domain of knowledge, which is widely accepted as truth, is directly proportional to power politics. To clarify, those people who formulate such notions of knowledge are people in power; specifically the males. This theory of Foucault can be analysed in relation to post-truth integrals in an individual's personal life.

Though people delve into depths of post-truth linkages from the wider aspect of society, little do the researchers focus on the relevance of the term and its integrals in terms of a person's position in the family.

When a child is born, it falls into the power politics of the family, which already has a specific construct of 'knowledge.' This knowledge includes beliefs, opinions, perspectives and the like, influenced by the wider media of society. Though this could be culture-specific, some common trends could be tracked. Typical parents feel that their role is effective enough, once they provide proper food, clothing, shelter and education to their children. The lion's share of them fails to realise the true talents and potentials of their children; or even if they do, they fall trap to the post-truth integral of 'the accepted success recipe of the society.' The psychological damage that this causes in an individual is beyond apprehension. Though people experience this at some points in their lives, they fail to break free of the post-truth package of misconceptions and false beliefs, reinforcing the necessity of an in-depth analysis of individual psychology and behavioural patterns, which could pave the way to the roots of most psychological problems people suffer. The psychological damage is initiated right from childhood, which later reaches puberty and finally impregnates trauma, depression and anxiety disorders, as the child grows and develops into an adult. Parents often blame children for not meeting their expectations (or rather the post-truth influence on them.) Absolute comparisons and unnecessary dominations crush away the essence of children. When they do this, little do they realise the oppression and damage they inflict on their children as individuals. Most of these issues are widespread in developing countries like India. There are studies based on the correlation of physical education in schools and students' health, but these too are understated.

> "Education and healthcare experts point out that in India no more than 10% school going children are into active and competitive sports. This is because the schools tend to focus only on the diet of the kids who are expected to represent the school at local, regional, state and national level events, excluding a majority of children who end up as fence-sitters in the PE periods."
>
> (Asian News International [ANI], 2018)

This could be viewed from another perspective when we realise that kids who show more interest in sports or arts more than their academics are restricted to follow their heart. They are imposed upon to keep studies at the top of the priorities list and could pursue other 'desires' if and only if there is ample time left. Another common comment from an Indian parent could be "If you study for X hours, you may play for ¼ X hours." Though the ratio may not be exact, this is how things work in the country. This could resonate with conditions in any part of the world where 'money' is prioritised over 'personal growth and happiness.'

The Connotations of Happiness in a Post-Truth Era

According to the World Happiness Report published by the United Nations Sustainable Development Solutions Network, Finland has been bagging the first position for four consecutive years. In addition to the beautiful landscape, low crime rates and high standards of living; the most important fact for which the Finnish people are known for, is their life of cooperation; not of competition. Compared to a lot of the western world, Finland is more at peace with itself. On the other hand, the report of 2021 has countries like India in the back row where they have been belonging for years. Among the various contributing factors enlisted by the economist, Jayshree Sengupta; poor mental wellbeing has been a noteworthy concern. As statistical data could extend to more than an entire page, one could easily realise the necessity of looking into the mental health of people; which should start straightaway from the realisation of those widely acknowledged post-truth integrals that are to be thwarted and thrown away. The development of a country doesn't just lie in the identification of external factors; but also the emotional recesses of its individuals.

In addition to all of the above, the concept of Emo-truth (truth where emotion serves as inference) plays a significant role in individual behaviour; whether analysed in a wider perspective of society or a narrower sense of a family. Emo-truth is a particular form of aggressive masculine performance of trustworthiness, corresponding to a code for recognising it, resulting in a legitimated status of the popular truth-teller, and at odds with more official scientific, institutional truth-tellers. One major reason why people profess what they believe in, is because emotions rule over them, rather than objective facts. In both cases where we analysed the impact of social media, as well as the impact of parenting; one could easily spot the entwined intervention of Emo-truth and its minors.

Solutions, Improvisations and Add-ons

To overcome the falsehood and malfunction of society, broadcasting the significance of alternatives could be the first step. Some parallel news channels have gained momentum in recent years, which functioned well initially, but later gave in to manipulation. This reality strikes even harder, when the deterioration is accelerated by pliant media opinion, which turns out to be toy guns in the hands of goons. The major source of action should come from the public, for the public. Public funded citizen journalism could be helpful to a great extent. Though there are many of them today, they receive less importance amidst the hullabaloo of popular media. Action plans are to be formulated with proper legal and public support, which should be put into action in no time. In fact, the media should function like 'NGOs', keeping away falsehood and corruption to an optimal level. There should be more transparency ensured in the functioning of social and political institutions that are to be moderated and governed by entities with provisional public representatives who change positions from time to time.

However, when it comes to the personal sphere of an individual, the post-truth integral of Emo-truth is deadly. While post-truth and Emo-truth affect societal well-being on a large scale, their influence in the personal lives of people is dangerously poignant. Most teenage suicides and anxiety disorders are undoubtedly a product of parental Emo-truth impositions. To make the world happier and healthier, moves are to be made from the family level to higher. Proper counselling services are to be provided in parenting, free of cost to the common man. Besides, specific courses are to be designed for the 'busy' parents who fail to realise that their emotional perception of truth is totally criminal though unintentional. The success formulas need to be thwarted away and replaced with a subjective celebration of one's own achievements. Individuals should have the freedom to invent their own success formulas, and the world becomes a happier and safer place to live.

References

Asian News International. (2018, August 2). Child fitness should start from schools and not only include sports. *Hindustan Times.* https://www.hindustantimes.com/fitness/child-fitness-should-start-from-schools-and-not-only-include-sports/story-kecWGgVrfaeEWasOtAJkLM.html

BBC. (2021, March 19). Finland ranked happiest country in the world- again. *BBC News.* https://www.bbc.com/news/world-europe-56457295

Harari, Y.N. (2018, September 7). Are we living in a post-truth era? Yes, that's because we're a post-truth species. *Ideas.Ted.Com.* https://ideas.ted.com/are-we-living-in-a-post-truth-era-yes-but-thats-because-were-a-post-truth-species/

Harari, Y. N. (2015). *Homo Deus: A brief history of tomorrow* [eBook edition]. HarperCollins Publishers. https://readandlaugh.files.wordpress.com/2018/04/homo_deus_a_brief_history_of_tomorrow_pdf.pdf

Harsin, J. (2018). Post-truth and critical communication. *In Oxford research encyclopedia of communication.* Oxford University Press.http://dx.doi.org/10.1093/acrefore/9780190228613. 013.757

Harsin, J. (2018, February 28). Post-truth right-wing populism: Emo- truth from the French anti-gender theory movement to Trump. *Researchgate.* https://www.researchgate.net/publication/322787080_Post-truth_Right-Wing_Populism_Emo-truth_from_the_French_Anti-gender_Theory_Movement_to_Trump

Harsin, J. (2020). Toxic white masculinity, post truth politics and the covid-19 infodemic. *European Journal of Cultural Studies,* 23(6), 1060-1068. https://doi.org/10.1177%2F1367549420944934

Mambrol, N. (2016, April 5). Foucault's concept of power. *Literariness.org.* https://literariness.org/2016/04/05/foucaults-concept-of-power/

McIntyre, L. (2019, May). *Post truth.* The MIT Press. https://mitpress.mit.edu/books/post-truth

PTI. (2021, March 20). World happiness report 2021. India ranks 139 out of 149. *The Hindu Business Line.* https://www.thehindubusinessline.com/news/world-happiness-report-2021-india-ranks-139-out-of-149/article34115445.ece

Rakshit, D. (2021, March 22). Why are Indians so unhappy?. *The Swaddle.* https://theswaddle.com/why-are-indians-so-unhappy/

What makes Finland the happiest country in the world for the fourth consecutive year?. (2021, April 19). *Helsinki Times.* https://www.helsinkitimes.fi/lifestyle/19066-what-makes-finland-the-happiest-country-in-the-world-for-the-fourth-consecutive-year.html.

CHAPTER 23

Fake News: The Hype and the Truth

Rahul Joshi

Social networking has emerged as a major player in transforming famous debate in political spaces in recent years. Because of their unrestricted freedom, social networking sites are vulnerable to violence, propaganda, and, as a result, false news. Fake news has persisted since the invention of the printing press, but it has found a new level of popularity in the internet and social media era. Manipulation of social networking and web search technology to target vast crowds and deceive news users is already a worldwide practice. While politicians have put pressure on service/platform providers, little tangible has been put in place to hold users or platform owners accountable. There has been a steady rise in the number of people using social media in India and cases of its abuse. This chapter aims to look at how the spread of false news has affected the democratic domain and what policies can be put in place to combat the issue. This chapter examines the connection between numerous acts of violence published in Indian media and the position of false news in inciting turmoil. It also looks at policy actions taken by different countries, especially in west, and potential steps India might take to curb the spread of fake news.

With the emergence of unpleasant events that have questioned users' interest in the press, especially across social media, 'fake news' has become a global concern. The lack of regulatory enforcement or rules that might either curtail false news or keep perpetrators responsible for their actions has only added to the complexity and difficulty of the problem. Responsible consumers have repeatedly addressed the question of reviewing and amending current legislation to resolve the problems of distributing false news, but politicians and civil society organisations have not been able to fill this gap in the overpowering digital space. Fake news is described as a syndrome that weaves a labyrinth of digital folklores of hoaxes, pranks, satires, and parodies with specific characteristics such as the fake news author's limited life cycle comparatively faster as well as higher 'share' and 'clicks' on social media. It hence is referred to as a syndrome that weaves a labyrinth of digital folklores of hoaxes, pranks (Shafi & Ravikumar, 2018). The media has been a propaganda web, with more points of view than news. The lack of solid differentiation between true and false news among internet users also undermines source legitimacy. India, a large market for WhatsApp, has over 300 million active users, and this figure is still rising, rendering it one of the fastest-growing sites. Even though the word "fake news" has been in use for at least a century, it has recently reawakened enthusiasm among media theorists and journalists, owing to the dramatic emergence of internet-based hoaxes.

Fake News Policy

In comparison to traditional and conventional media sources, social media sites provide unrestricted access. Since social networking sites offer a free forum for people to share their thoughts and views, no policies that limit users' rights may be enforced in practice. As a result, eradicating false news from social media is almost impossible, as the flow of material, or content, cannot be completely regulated (Allcott & Gentzkow, 2017). This does not, however, rule out the prospect of regulating the medium/platform. To fight the spread of false news, numerous regulatory methods have been adopted by various countries. Many players have been involved in creating these legislative processes, which include self-regulation through social media sites, court injunctions to stop false news, law enforcement, statutory solutions, and autonomous regulatory bodies (Alexander, 2018).

Policy Intervention by Various Countries

In addition to self-regulatory efforts, government interference is one of the most effective strategies used by countries across the world to fight false news. The government is set to step in here by enacting legislation that restricts the use of social networking sites and penalises anyone that post content that does not meet specific requirements. The following section addresses policy steps taken by some countries to control false news and allow the interactive public domain to be more vibrant (Bharali & Goswami, 2018).

- *Italy:* In 2017, politicians and regulators in Italy were compelled to enact new anti-fake news legislation. Since the dissemination of false news was a hot topic during the constitutional referendum process, a statutory amendment was sent to the Republic's Senate. This proposed law made it illegal to share and publish "fake, exaggerated, or biased" facts, and fines of up to 5000 Euros could be levied. It recommended incarceration in cases of fake news as serious as inciting abuse or crime, as well as a duty for Internet Service Providers (ISPs) to regulate their position in monitoring information and removing unreliable and false news. The right to freedom of expression is discussed in Article 10 of the European Convention on Human Rights (ECHR), which deals with the right to hold views and collect and transmit knowledge and ideas without intervention from public authorities.
- *Malaysia:* In the run-up to the 2018 Malaysian general elections, former Prime Minister Najib Razak launched the Anti-Fake News Act 2018 after the King assented to the Billon anti-fake news bill. This law forced content publishers to instantly delete reported content if accused of containing false news (Malaysia's anti-fake news legislation becomes law, is now enforceable, 2018). This bill will create tension between people's civil rights in a democratic country. Regressive legislation prohibits citizens from expressing their views. This legislation, which the former Prime Minister enacted, was also said to restrict free political expression. However, the government attempted to abolish the legislation in August 2018, claiming that established information and media laws are "appropriate" to false combat news in the region. Even though the lower house approved the bill to repeal the current Anti-Fake News 2018 Bill in August, it was later vetoed by Senators.
- *Germany:* On January 1, 2018, Germany's government enacted the Network Enforcement Act, which took effect on January 1, 2018. Online sites must delete "obviously illegal" content within 24 hours or face penalties of up to €50 million under this rule. About the fact that the German government introduced this legislation to reduce the dissemination of propaganda, it faced many backlashes. This is because as information is controlled on social networking sites, it often degrades the democracy in place. The government may use such legislation to curb authority, voice

and disrupt the political space in the public domain by restricting people's speech based on particular keyword criteria. If left unchecked, such a step might devolve into systemic state-based repression and censorship, jeopardising the country's democracy.

- *France:* Following Italy's introduction of legislation criminalising the sharing and publishing of "lie, inflated, or biased" content, and Germany's passage of legislation to combat fake news, France has agreed to take proactive measures to address the problem (Fiorentino, 2018). After being opposed twice by the Senate, the French Parliament revised its Constitution in November 2018 at the National Assembly and enacted a bill to combat the handling of records. It aimed to stop false news from spreading quickly via social media and international news outlets. This legislation explicitly focused on political campaigns, attempting to mitigate the threat raised by usable tools during elections. The legislation included provisions such as disclosure requirements for new media and the establishment of court injunctions during election campaigns (Agence France-Presse, 2018).

Fake News and Indian Context

Fake news on social media had a significant influence on people's views all over the planet. Unlike in other nations, WhatsApp, rather than other social networking platforms like Facebook or Twitter, is the primary source of false news in India. In 2014, the social network behemoth Facebook purchased WhatsApp, an instant networking app. This social networking site encourages users to exchange information by sending it to other users in different groups and broadcast lists inside the network, resulting in widespread, unregulated dissemination of knowledge rarely vetted by users. It has misinformed social media users and has also sparked brutality and brutal killings across the country.

The effects of distributing false news in India have been much more than anybody might have imagined. The dissemination of misinformation and disinformation in the media is becoming a major societal problem. It is sparking protests and lynching on the streets and a toxic climate on the internet. Rumours, morphed photos, click-baits, inspired stories, unverified facts, and planted stories for different interests spread quickly among India's about 42 crore internet users in the internet era (WhatsApp, Facebook, and Twitter). There have been several cases that internet rumours that have resulted in the deaths of innocent individuals (Farooq, 2018). Ministers have been known to erase tweets when discovering false information they had posted previously. WhatsApp is the website in India that is most open to false news. Millions of Indians (the majority of whom are uneducated) are seen as the most susceptible to false news because they use mobile internet to send regular "good morning" tweets (Tambini, D. 2017).

Popular Recent Fake News Cases in India

TOI, HT, ABP News Fall for Fake Account Impersonating Indrajit Chakraborty

Many media outlets gave prime column room to a bogus Twitter account impersonating actress Rhea Chakraborty's father, Indrajit Chakraborty, who demanded justice for the actor.

Marathi Newspaper Lokmat Falls for Fake COVID-19 Bio-weapon Story

The English version of the Marathi daily Lokmat fell for a widely circulated false narrative that the COVID epidemic was a bio-weapon, with information about it leaked by a Chinese intelligence officer.

Members of the Tablighi Jamaat are being used as scapegoats

As the country grappled with the COVID-19 outbreak, a foreign meeting of Tablighis in New Delhi's Nizamuddin district in March 2020 became a focal point, with some accusing them of the outbreak and coining new and particularly bigoted words such as the "Tablighi Virus" and "Corona Jihad." By wrongly comparing the Jamaat to unrelated and outdated stories, ANI and Zee Hindustan, two media outlets contributed to the panic and blame.

As 'Proof of Galwan,' Aaj Tak and Times Now broadcast a video of the 1962 War Memorial

Times Now and Aaj Tak aired a video showing a burial ground in Xinjiang for Chinese soldiers who died during the 1962 Indo-China conflict, with the false assertion showed the graves of soldiers killed in the clash on June 20.

Bigotry and misinformation are fuelled by the tragic death of a pregnant elephant in Kerala

The reports of the unfortunate death of a pregnant elephant in Kerala saddened the whole world in June. Following the event, many national news outlets such as *NDTV, India Today, Hindustan Times, ANI, Republic,*

Times Now, Financial Express, and *DNA* announced that the elephant was purposefully fed an explosive pineapple in the Muslim-majority Malappuram region, prompting a barrage of bigoted attacks on Muslims and the Left-ruled state on social media. Forest officials later informed BOOM that the elephant had consumed an explosive trap intended for wild boars by mistake and that the incident occurred in Palakkad, not Malappuram (PTI, 2018).

Farmers Protest Leads to the Resignation of 200 Cops

A civil engineer from Churu, Rajasthan, was arrested after uploading "worn, unrelated recordings" and a note saying that 200 Delhi Police officers had resigned due to "disaffection" over the farmers' protest.

Legislations Against Fake News in India

In India, there is no clear legislation prohibiting the dissemination of false information. Article 19 of the Constitution guarantees freedom of the press, including the right to publish articles freely. If the *Press Council of India* considers that a newspaper or news agency has violated media ethics, it may issue a warning, admonition, or censure the newspaper, news agency, publisher, or journalist, or condemn the editor's actions or journalist. The private TV news and public affairs broadcasters are represented by the *News Broadcasters Association* (NBA). The self-regulatory agency investigated complaints against electronic media. The *Indian Broadcast Foundation* (IBF) also investigates allegations about channel quality. The *Broadcasting Information Complaint Council* (BCCC) accepts lawsuits against television stations for offensive programming and misleading news. Specific provisions of the *Indian Penal Code* (IPC) may be used to combat false news: To combat false news, use Sections 153 (want only providing provocation with the intent to trigger riot) and 295 (injuring or defiling a place of worship with the intent to disrespect the faith of any class). *Section 66* of the *Information Technology Act of 2000* states that every individual who commits any act referred to in section 43 (damage to the device, computer system) dishonestly or fraudulently is punishable by imprisonment for a period up to three years, a fine up to five lakh rupees, or both. Individuals and organisations that have been harmed by false news will file a civil or criminal case for defamation. A *defamation suit* may be filed under IPC Sections 499 (defamation) and 500 whoever defames another shall be punished with simple imprisonment for a period not exceeding two years, or with a fine, or with both (Farooq, 2018).

Reasons for the Spread of Fake News in India

- *Political Ethics Degradation:* The mass media is no longer seen as a neutral arbiter on what constitutes "true news." The ruling political elite is said to use the media as an echo chamber. As a result of complicit and motivated reporting, the mass media has lost its reputation and has become a conduit of false news.
- *Rise of social media:* It has decentralised the production and dissemination of false news. The sheer size of the internet (India has over 42 crore users) and social networking users (over 23 crore WhatsApp users alone) allows tracing the source of false news almost impossible.
- *Polarisation:* The polarisation in culture along partisan lines has rendered the task of distributing false news simpler.
- *Lack of legislation:* There is no simple legislation in India that addresses fake news. The fundamental freedom of expression, guaranteed by Article 19 of the Indian Constitution, provides for the complete publication or broadcast of news in India.
- *Confirmation Bias:* Studies have shown that viewers are more interested in seeking facts to endorse their own story than discovering the "reality" behind a news article.

How to Cope with False News?

- *Rebuttal:* A rebuttal is a form of fact-checking in which false news is refuted by pointing out mistakes such as mismatches, deliberate editing, and misattribution.
- *Removal of False News:* Algorithms are used by technology firms such as Facebook and YouTube to delete fake news from their websites proactively. WhatsApp has also imposed a ban on sharing messages in order to prevent the dissemination of false news.
- *Educating:* End-users are being educated to become more discerning news consumers by being informed about verification methods that enable them to check the authenticity of a news story before posting it.
- *De-anonymisation:* Another technique promoted by the government is tracing the 'source' of false news. For this purpose, the government recommends that all social networking pages be de-anonymised. However, this amendment has been

criticised for invading anonymity, restricting free expression, and creating a police state.

Awareness: A Way Forward

One of the most important reasons for consumers' increased intake of false news is their inability to distinguish reality from views. The audience's inability to check news posted on social media before consuming it leads to potentially misleading content. To encourage them to do so, specific measures to improve their media literacy will be needed. Many scholars around the world have suggested media literacy as one of the most promising alternatives. In India, service providers have initiated public awareness initiatives to educate users more about the risks of spreading misleading information and how it is essential to be self-aware while transmitting any message. WhatsApp launched three campaign films in December 2018 as part of a plan to tackle the dissemination of fake news in the run-up to the electorate (Al-Rawi, 2019). The campaigns urged members to double-check the accuracy of details they received through forwarding messages before exchanging them with others. Social networking may be a powerful medium for communication growth if appropriately employed due to its scope, popularity, and instantaneity. Otherwise, it could end up as a two-edged weapon. Fake news has evolved into a threat that can only be addressed by concerted actions at all levels, from citizens to the policy level.

So far, the demand side has been searched for solutions to combat the rising business of false news. In the realm of false news, however, such amity is uncommon. It is possible to hire fact-checkers. However, it may be more helpful to teach news consumers how to distinguish between false and real news. This entails resurrecting a culture of 'smarter reading,' which includes triangulating information, cross-checking it, and considering everything as fiction unless proved otherwise.

References

Agence France-Presse [AFP]. (2018, July 14). Death by 'fake news': social media-fuelled lynchings shock India. *The Straits Times*, https://www.straitstimes.com/asia/south-asia/death-by-fake-news-social-media-fuelled-lynchings-shock-india

Alexander, S. (2018, July 14). Can WhatsApp Admins be Jailed For Fake & Hate Messages? A Fact File BOOM. *The Quint*, https://www.thequint.com/news/webqoof/can-whatsapp-admins-be-jailed-for-fake-and-hate-messages

Allcott, H., & Gentzkow, M. (2017, February). Social Media and Fake News in the 2016 Election. *Journal of Economic Perspectives*, 211–236.

Al-Rawi, A. (2019). Viral News on Social Media. *Digital Journalism*, 63-79.

Anupam, S. (2018, September 26). Leading Media Companies Form DNPA To Curb Fake News, But Digital-Only Media Stays Away From It. *INC42 MEDIA*, https://inc42.com/buzz/leading-media-companies-form-dnpa-to-curb-fake-news-but-digital-only-media-stays-away-from-it

Bassi, S., & Sengupta, J. (2018, July 08). Lynchings sparked by WhatsApp child-kidnap rumours sweep across India. *CBC*, https://www.cbc.ca/news/world/india-child-kidnap-abduction-video-rumours-killings-1.4737041

Berduygina, O. N., Vladimirova, T. N., & Chernyaeva, E. V. (2019). Trends in the Spread of Fake News in Mass Media. *Media Watch*, 122-132.

Bharali, B., & Goswami, A. L. (2018). Fake News: Credibility, Cultivation Syndrome, and New Age Media. *Media Watch*, 118-130.

Farooq, G. (2018). Politics of Fake News: How WhatsApp Became a Potent Propaganda Tool in India. *Media Watch*, 106-117.

Fiorentino, M.-R. (2018, November 22). France passes controversial 'fake news' law. *Euro News*, https://www.euronews.com/2018/11/22/france-passes-controversial-fake-news-law.

Funke, D., (2018, July 25). Here's what the world is doing to tackle fake news. India can learn. *The Print*. https://theprint.in/opinion/heres-what-the-world-is-doing-to-tackle-fake-news-india-can-learn/88195.

Lima Quintanilha, T., Torres da Silva, M., & Lapa, T. (2019). Fake news and its impact on trust in the news. Using the Portuguese case to establish lines of differentiation. *Communication & Society*, 17-33.

Marda, V., & Milan, S. (2018). Wisdom of the Crowd: Multi stakeholder Perspectives on the Fake News Debate. *Internet Policy Review series, Annenberg School of Communication*. University of Pennsylvania.

PTI. (2018, August 29). Government mulls action against India heads of social media on failure to check fake news. *The Economic Times*.

PTI. (2018, December 03). WhatsApp rolls out TV campaign in India to tackle fake news. *Live Mint*, https://www.livemint.com/Companies/QU7LWGcHf0m49uiBqDRzlN/WhatsApp-rolls-out-TV-campaign-in-India-to-tackle-fake-news.html

Shafi, S., & Ravikumar, M. (2018). Dynamics of Fake News Dissemination: A Case Study in the Indian context. *Media Watch*, 131-140.

Tambini, D. (2017). Fake News: Public Policy Responses. *London: Media Policy Project, London School of Economics and Political Science.*

CHAPTER 24

Factual Criticism in Post-truth India

Shalabha Rachel Abraham

Truth and Post-truth

When alternate facts replace actual truth, valuing feelings and not evidence, it is the beginning of a Post-truth Era. With the rise of fake news, people are compelled to believe in baseless things, without proof or resistance. Humans have always lived in the age of post-truth, as a post-truth species, with the distinctively human ability to create and proliferate fictions, spread them around, and convince millions of people to believe in them. As long as people believe in the same stories, they obey the same legislation and will thereby conjoin effectively. Religion is the perfect example to cite this objective.

Christians believed in the Bible dauntless and never questions its authority, while Muslims put their incontestable faith in the Quran. There is no scientific evidence so far, establishing the presence of the numerous Hindu gods. Still, people continue to believe in these myths from time and ages, proving Homo sapiens never needed solid facts to put their trust in something, which is exactly what the post-truth era offer. The reason why the post-truth phenomena have existed for so long is due to two limpid factors: that they have focused on unity before veracity and have decided to serve power rather than truth. Humans have always preferred truth to power, and that is one impetus why humans have always been powerful.

Post-truth politics, also known as post-factual politics and post-reality politics, is a varied political culture where the fascination towards sentiments, withdrawal from the details of policy, and persistent assertion of ideas, get instilled in the minds of the mass, later turning into established norms and beliefs. Post-truth has been an enduring part of political life which was less noticeable before the onset of the internet and other related social changes.

Even though the term 'Post-truth' was officially adopted into the OED in 2016, India has been living in this post- factual era for years. In India, people value beliefs and opinions more than facts. From politics to religion, food, and fashion, what matters the most here is the 'mass public opinion.' This usually biased opinion is solely dependent on myths and fiction which make India the ideal example of a Post-truth nation.

Criticism in Post-truth India

Criticism is an evaluative technique that involves the expression of opinions, or disfavour of someone or something on the basis of estimated faults or mistakes. Constructive criticism is an effective tool and at the same time a learning process, which enables people to improve their understanding of relevant facts and prevent greater liabilities or failures. Factual criticism along with logical criticism is generally considered pivotal to ensure dependability, invariability, and authenticity in the functioning of any system and institution.

Criticism in pre-post-truth India was no different. Even though there are numerous examples to expound this, one that stands out came from the former minister Ambika Soni, who was infuriated by a piece of criticism by the *Washington Post* about Prime Minister Manmohan Singh. The article stated that the former Prime Minister, who enabled India to be on a path of prosperity, is now "in danger of going down in history as a failure" (Denyer, 2012). The column also stated that he resembled a "dithering, ineffectual bureaucrat presiding over a deeply corrupt government" (Denyer, 2012). The former Prime Minister also had to face some incisive criticism from home and abroad. The *Time* magazine had labelled him 'The Underachiever,' who was immersed in his own "personal and political gloom," (Mahr, 2012) and *The Economist* magazine addressed him as an "embattled prime minister" (F, 2012). These are criticisms of strong words, but not unusual which is just in the spirit of free speech. What was unexpected and irrational was Ms. Soni's reprisal to the criticism. She stated that the article was impermissible, and that "the government had 'apprehensions about a foreign daily publishing something baseless on our prime minister... This is what we call yellow journalism'" (Biswas, 2012).

Criticism, whether positive or negative, is not received well by the Post-truth Indian society. Especially with the governments, criticising their actions is highly offending and unappreciative. A critic in India is considered as an 'enemy', both by the governments and the society. Their opinions do not matter, for the preferences of the autocratic democracy stands above the truth opined by the critic. Regulating criticism is in fact a method adopted by 'bio-politics,' where people are reduced to the state of bodies, and kept in check. To monitor them and force them into submission the governments use biopower, where control and punishment of the 'bodies' ensure the wielding of power. Redacting criticism and punishing or restraining critics can therefore be viewed as a symbol of the post-truth era.

The Great Indian Response to Factual Criticism

Censorship of media and journalism was always the primary step of clamping down on criticism. Internet shutdowns have been an indulging strategy for the governments of post-truth nations, including India, to control criticism. In 2018, a nonprofit group Access Now reported that out of 196 internet shutdowns reported from 25 countries all over the world, "India was responsible for the majority, with 134 incidents-almost 67% of the world's documented shutdowns" (Saaliq, 2019). Since 2014, the internet has been curbed more than 360 times in India, even before the Post-truth era had even officially begun. This drastic rise in internet blackouts all over India is looked upon as a technique for censorship and subduing, in response to the growing opposition to the current government practices.

The Indian governments and concerned authorities had instigated internet shutdowns in various parts of the country to obstruct protests and rallies over the Citizenship Amendment law. Protests led by various groups; including students and politicians had met with communication blockers in and around New Delhi, northern Uttar Pradesh, the eastern states of West Bengal, the northern city of Aligarh and Assam, while the law was passed in Parliament, in December 2019. In Aligarh, where the police charged the students, the internet was shut down for about six days.

Internet and phone services had been suspended for more than four months in Indian-administered Kashmir while its semi-autonomous status was taken away and was demoted into a federal territory in August 2019. "'These shutdowns not only violate the fundamental rights of the people but are a well-crafted response by the state to curb forms of speech,' stated Apar Gupta, executive director of India Freedom Foundation, a digital rights advocacy group" (Saaliq, 2019). The response to these shutdowns from the part of the government was that it is a temporary regulative method to maintain law and order. The government also declared that; "India's action 'proved that the necessary regulation of the internet is a reasonable choice' and an extension of 'internet sovereignty'" (Saaliq, 2019).

Various totalitarian governments across the globe have also used similar strategies. The government of Egypt had banned more than 500 websites in recent years to prevent criticism. The Iranian government also did the same, shutting down the internet, when they faced protests over the rise of the prices of gas laid by the government. Pakistan too had controlled telephone services and had removed Facebook and Twitter accounts for they thought these affected their national laws. The Chinese government, infamous for wielding the most pervasive structure of censorship, has been following this course for eons.

The internet has always been a tool for protestors and demonstrators to assemble masses. It is a medium for their voice of dissent. Like the major regimes of the Post-truth world, India has also warned its citizens against criticising the policies of the nation. "The government is trying to put a lid on our voices by banning communication as it fears the calls for equality and justice are growing louder," opined Akruti Gupta, a student protester (Saaliq, 2019). Akshaya Kumar of Human Rights Watch also added to this by stating that; "Such sweeping measures are more like collective punishment than a tactical response" (Saaliq, 2019).

The Indian government's intimidations to proscribe international social media apps for not yielding with the guidelines are also examples of regulating criticism in the post-truth world. The Indian government had mandated a local regulation for the widely used social media applications in India to furnish traceability of the users' data. WhatsApp, the messaging app, contended that the regulations would demand these services to trace every contact, every chat and every single message. "In doing so, a government that chooses to mandate traceability is effectively mandating a new form of mass surveillance," (WhatsApp Help Center, n.d.) says WhatsApp. The government had also recently prompted Facebook, Twitter, and Instagram to withdraw posts and block accounts defaming the Government of India, regarding the Covid-19 crisis management. The new regulations are a "tool in the government's pocket" (Bhattacharya, 2021) which will be used in future to pressurise such platforms. It is the initial step in the Post-truth era that will lead to a refining system for voicing on the internet, to keep the truth in check so as to ascertain the power to rule.

The Australian newspaper had recently published an article titled, "Modi leads India out of lockdown... and into a viral apocalypse" (The Australian article on India covid cases baseless: Govt, 2021). The report states; "Arrogance, hyper-nationalism and bureaucratic incompetence have combined to create a crisis of epic proportions in India, with its crowd-loving PM basking while citizens suffocate" (The Australian article on India covid cases baseless: Govt, 2021).

In response, the Indian High Commission in Australia exhorted the newspaper to publish a rejoinder and to abstain from publishing such "baseless" (The Australian article on India covid cases baseless: Govt, 2021) articles in the future. The note indicated that the feature had "strangely rushed to blame the... restricted election campaign by the Prime Minister and one religious gathering" (The Australian article on India covid cases baseless: Govt, 2021). The government had also received similar criticism with regard to the management of the pandemic in India, through international media such as *The Guardian*, *The New York Times*, *Haaretz* and *Radio France Internationale*. The boldest of all print media criticisms so far was seen in the latest cover of the English magazine *Outlook*. The cover page of the magazine was designed in plain white background, with one word; 'Missing,' and at the bottom of the page, three-pointers were given in substantiation: Name – Government of India, Age: 7 years. Inform: Citizens of India.

During the 2016 Kashmir uprising, the Jammu and Kashmir state government had banned *Kashmir Reader*, a local newspaper from being 'critical of India' on 30 September 2016. According to the court order, the newspaper was banned because it included "such material and content which tends to incite acts of violence and disturb public peace and tranquillity" (Kashmir newspaper ban criticised, 2016).

These efforts to stifle *Kashmir Reader* had aroused from the government's endeavours to smother upon media and communication in the Kashmir valley. Since July 2016, telecom services had been periodically cut, internet services had been curbed and newspapers had been regularly monitored by the officials. The newspaper resumed publication after the government lifted the ban on 28 December 2016. Newspapers and print media are some of the greatest mediums of protest, criticism, truth and reality. But the post-truth phenomenon with its emphasis on hiding truths, propagating fake news, and controlling people through their emotions pays no heed to non-hyphenated journalism. This era is all the happier in dispersing such mediums or voices.

The current government of India and its prime minister is the first in the history of democratic India to never have held a press conference. It seems as if the government has never felt the need to hold itself liable to the liberty of the press. The government introduced the prime minister to the media, only through strictly strategised interviews, across channels favourable to the government. The interviews depicted the prime minister asking questions, as well as answering them as monologues. The government prefers monologues and does not tolerate questioning or criticism. The ministers have also changed to follow a similar suit.

Where are we Heading to?

In post-truth India briefing, the press with complete transparency has become a far-fetched dream. The gesture of the authorities, as not answerable to the questions and suggestions of its citizens symbolises the advent of the post-truth belief, where truth has lost its significance. Only instilled ideas, false opinions, fake news and emotional profusions matter in such a nation. "In our 'post-factual' era, attempting to expose facts as results of power-laden processes of social construction plays into the hands of anti-scientific obscurantists" (Flatscher and Seitz, 2020).

The government has also made lying an art form. People are made to believe that falsehoods are truths and to observe and disseminate absurd fictions and ideas. The reason why people still chooses to heed these false statements is because of the manipulated media feats, feeble and incompetent opposition, and the peculiar nature of the authorities that make the citizens lay their faith in the governments. With the assertion of power, even blatant lies appear credible.

It has come down to the question that, can't people criticise or protest anymore in India, against the present government, which has not been condoning any denunciation at all lately. The government has been operating as if it is above all formal and institutional inquiry, whether from the press, nor its subjects. The first step in confronting post-truth is to acknowledge it. There is no better time in India than now to address the world with Orwell's excerpt;

> To the future or to the past, to a time when thought is free, when men are different from one another and do not live alone- to a time when truth exists and what is done cannot be undone: From the age of uniformity, from the age of solitude, from the age of Big Brother, from the age of doublethink - greetings!
>
> (Orwell, 2014, p. 32)

References

The Australian Article on India Covid Cases Baseless: Govt. (2021, April 27). *The Indian Express.* https://indianexpress.com/article/india/the-australian-article-on-india-covid-cases-baseless-says-govt-7290945

Bhattacharya, A. (2021, May 28). Modi government's new IT rules raise the question: Is India becoming China? *Scroll.in.* https://scroll.in/article/995919/modi-governments-it-rules-raise-the-question-is-india-becoming-china

Biswas, S. (2012, September 6). Why is India touchy about outside criticism? *BBC News.* http://www.bbc.com/news/world-asia-india-19498675

Denyer, S. (2012, September 4). India's 'silent' prime minister becomes a tragic figure. *The Washington Post.* http://www.washingtonpost.com/world/indias-silent-prime-minister-becomes-a-tragic-figure/2012/09/04/a88662c4-f396-11e1-adc6-87dfa 8eff430_story.html

Escape to Tehran. (2012, August 30). *The Economist.* http://www. economist.com/banyan/2012/08/30/escape-to-tehran.

Flatscher, M., & Seitz, S. (2020). Latour, Foucault, and Post-Truth: The Role and Function of Critique in the Era of the Truth Crisis. *Le foucaldien. 6*(1), 6. http://doi.org/10.16995/lefou.83

Kashmir newspaper ban criticised. (2016, October 5). *BBC News.* http://www.bbc.com/news/ world-asia-india-37559679

Mahr, K. (2012, July 16). A Man in Shadow. *Time.* http://content.time.com/time/subscriber/ article/0,33009,2118776,00.html.

Orwell, G. (2014). *1984.* Spark Publishing.

Saaliq, S. (2019, December 21). India suspends internet and phone services to quell protests. *AP NEWS.* https://apnews.com/article/643423717f6494718e449d ac441c3db9

WhatsApp Help Center. (n.d.). What is traceability and why does WhatsApp oppose it? *WhatsApp. com.* https://faq.whatsapp.com/general/security-and-privacy/ what-is-traceability-and-why-does- whatsapp-oppose-it/?lang=en

CHAPTER 25

Post-truth Era and Marathi Dalit Cinema

Dr. Rajendra Gholap

Cinema as a form of mass media has a great impact on societies in many ways. The glamorous manifestation in cinema appeals to and influences human minds immensely. Being an extension of art and literature, it functions crucially in representing the socio-cultural, political scenarios of the country. Since India's entire social structure is based on castes, the caste system becomes an inexorable entity in the socio-cultural domain. Indian cinema while reflecting the social diversity of the country, serves cultural functions significantly besides entertainment. However, it is apparent that in Indian movies there are certain complications in embodying Dalit life. In view of this, it is an attempt to study the Dalit filmmaker's dilemma in representing factual Dalit life in Marathi Dalit cinema in this post-truth era. He encounters numerous challenges in exhibiting the facts of Dalits due to the dominant caste hegemony which is conspicuously found persisting evermore in India. The power politics of government, film censorship and dominant high caste Hindus have been obstructing the Dalit filmmaker to represent truths of Dalit life in Marathi Dalit cinema.

Literature Review

There are numerous writings relating to Dalit cinema reflecting multi-facets of Dalit life. This review attempts to pinpoint certain crucial works published nationally and internationally. Yengde, in his article 'Dalit Cinema', proficiently writes on the subordinate place of Dalit filmmakers in Indian cinema. He states that the Indian film industry is inherently caste-based and biased in which Dalit inclusion is not a moral concern (Yengde, 2018, p. 1). Borkar, in 'Sairat: A Case Study of Honor

Killing', puts forward the patriarchy and caste-gender relations shown in the movie *Sairat* and the killing of a young female in the name of honour (Borkar, 2019, p. 46). Bharatvaraj and Subramani, in 'Manifestation of Subaltern Narratives in Cinema', argues that the manifestation of subalterns in Hindi Cinema is relatively more in the Gandhian framework rather than excommunicating the Phule-Ambedkarite perspective (Bharatvaraj and Subramani, 2018, p.1). The literature review reveals that researchers have taken ample efforts in writing on Dalit filmmakers, honour killing and the manifestation of Dalit narratives in India. However, no attempt has been made to write on Dalit cinema from a post-truth point of view. Therefore, this paper is an endeavour to study Marathi Dalit cinema in the light of the post-truth era.

Cast-System in India: Facts and Falsifications

As we all know that the post-truth era is characterised by falsification, misrepresentation, distortion, propaganda, lies, fake news, irrational, illogical, prejudices, stereotypes, etc. Marathi Dalit cinema is also not an exception in this milieu. It is intensely observed that Indian Dalit life is hardly represented truthfully whether it is in books, histories, movies or any other form. In order to understand Marathi Dalit Cinema in view of the post-truth era, it is indispensable to know the facts regarding the origin of Dalit life. It is very saddening to realise the way the Dalit has been being treated by the so-called upper caste Hindus by believing illogically and prejudicially in falsely ascribed emergence of Dalits as Shudras, the four-folded *Varna* system and prescription of torturous life for Dalits in Hindu Holy Scriptures.

The origins of Dalit life are found deeply rooted in the *Varna* system, its subsequent caste system and untouchability as an integral part of Dalit life. The creators of the *Varna* system falsely ascribed the emergence of this system to God. It was falsely convinced that God himself created various *Varnas*. It was very craftily stated that God Mahaprajapati brought the four *Varnas* that are, the *Brahmin*, the *Kshatriya*, the *Vaishya*, and the *Shudras* into existence. They said that the *Brahmin* sprang from the mouth of *Brahma*, the *Kshatriya* from the arms, the *Vaishya* from the thighs and the *Shudras* from the feet. Hence, the occupation of the individuals depended upon the caste they belonged to. The *Brahmin* and the *Kshatriya*, being higher in the hierarchy of social order, dominated the other castes for several centuries.

The four-fold classification of *Varna* system did not accept Dalits as human beings. Most of the religious documents like *Manusmriti* and others prescribed an inhuman and torturous life for Dalits. In the tenth chapter of the *Manusmriti* Manu prescribes a horrible kind of life and duties for Shudras. Manu writes that the *Shudras* must not be allowed within the limits of the village. They should be forced to live in isolated, frightening places like burial grounds. In order to be easily identified, they should bear certain marks on their bodies and should live in inferior professions. Their dwelling should generally be outside the main habitations of the upper castes. They should eat the leftover food from broken mud pots. They should wear ornaments of black iron and should wander from place to place. No upper caste person was allowed to have any contact with them and their marriage relations should take place only among themselves. They were allowed to use clothes, beds and ornaments of the executed criminals and were allowed to use refused grains. Such was Manu's horrible prescription for the *Shudras* (Muller, 1886, p. 301-04).

The most shocking part of the entire thing was that Manu's prescriptions were followed, implemented and executed by the upper caste Hindus. Even today in some parts of India, such horrible and heinous treatment is given to the Dalits. The history of the miserable plight of Dalit life in India compels us to condemn Manu thoroughly because his *Manusmriti* is the root cause of the torture meted out to the Dalits. It is for this reason that Dr. B. R. Ambedkar, the emancipator of the downtrodden and the father of the Indian constitution, publically burnt *Manusmriti*. Dr. B. R. Ambedkar, a voice of the Dalits attacked the *Varna* system and the religious texts on which the caste system was based. He asserted that the Hindu society must be reorganised on the basis of the principles of liberty, equality, and fraternity (Moon, 1989, p. 86).

The Dilemma of Marathi Dalit Filmmaker in Post-truth Era

The foregoing discussion on the facts and falsifications regarding the origin of Dalits and the caste system in India is very much relevant to perceive the dilemma of Marathi Dalit Filmmaker in this post-truth era. Nagraj Manjule's Marathi Dalit cinema *Sairat* (2016) has been chosen to study in view of the post-truth era. This filmmaker deserves to be selected for such a significant study for certain valid reasons. Firstly, because he is a born Dalit and therefore has firsthand experiences of caste-discrimination, domination, oppression, humiliation, acute pains, sufferings, caste-based conflicts and its worst effects on the present generation. Secondly, as he is a Dalit, he can project the facts of Dalit life more effectively in Marathi Dalit cinema. However, it is observed that he has had a certain dilemma in projecting truthful Dalit life in cinema.

Nagraj Manjule is a Marathi Dalit poet, actor, director, scriptwriter, producer and more widely known as a Dalit filmmaker. He was born on 24th August 1978 in a small village Jeur in Solapur district of Maharashtra. He belongs to a Waddar community considered as the lowest caste in Maharashtra. Nagraj's Dalit life and Dalit sensibility induce him to expose the plight of Dalits in Indian cinema. He takes it as a movement to resist casteism due to the post-truth ideology which is against social justice. Dr. B. R. Ambedkar is a great source of inspiration for Nagraj. Hence his endeavour in Dalit Marathi film can best be perceived as a resistance of a Dalit against post-truth policies of upper-caste Hindus.

As a Dalit filmmaker, Nagraj Manjule has to undergo certain constraints. Film as a medium of representation has its own limits. The Dalit filmmaker in his attempt to represent Dalit life, has to conform inevitably to the rules and regulations of the Central Board of Film Certification. Despite the intention of manifesting the objective truth of Dalit life in the film, the filmmaker has to acknowledge in the disclaimer that - 'All characters and incidents in this film are fictitious. Resemblance to any person living or dead or any incident is purely coincidental….' The condition of 'disclaimer' is quite evident of negating the facts. It is denied on the grounds that the factual representation may disrupt the peace and may cause anger, antagonism and resultant violence among the people. Although it is true, this truth has another facet that may be perceived in view of the post-truth policy of dominant castes. It is substantial that the CBFC is under the influence of caste-based power politics (Yengde, 2018, p. 1-16). Perhaps the prejudiced upper castes want to sustain the caste system by upholding the four-fold *Varna* system and the prescriptions of *Manusmriti*.

Despite this dreadful power politics, the Dalit filmmaker undertakes to portray Dalit life through a cinematic lens. The Marathi Dalit Cinema *Sairat* is based on the meticulous observation of caste-based conflicts and domination of upper castes in the villages of contemporary Maharashtra. The Dalit filmmaker has very proficiently represented casteism and its worst consequences on the present generation. The scene of a cricket match played by local village teams has very much potential to be perceived through post-truth policies of upper-caste Hindus. The scene reveals that the local leader Tatya Saheb Patil who has been invited as a chief guest for the felicitation programme, uses this stage for his political purpose. Tatya Saheb, in his speech, reminds the gathering of youths of the upcoming elections. In a very boastful manner, he abuses opposition political leaders by using vulgar language. Furthermore, he humiliates low caste leaders of the opposition parties and warns them to take care of their women and children first before entering into politics. These are very degrading and disgracing remarks against lower caste people of the village Bittergaon. The scene exemplifies clearly how these upper-caste Hindus are desperately cunning. On one side they felicitate lower caste winning players but simultaneously they don't lose the opportunity to use the same stage for political purposes. It clearly shows their tenacity to make a show of supremacy and being powerful in the social hierarchy.

The dominance of socio-economic power relations is seen perpetuating in the rural rigid caste hierarchy. The upper-caste Hindus are seen inheriting massive land and thereby becoming empowered rural landowners. On the contrary, the low caste peasants continue to work as labourers under the influence of the upper castes (Gaikwad, 2016, p. 1-6). Superficially it seems that rural life is full of happiness. It is nothing but the post-truth. In fact, these low caste people are not privileged to be self-sufficient even in this twenty-first century. Their persistent traditional caste professions delimit their source of income and resultantly get deprived of living a life of dignity. The control of upper castes over low caste labourers is portrayed in *Sairat* by displaying massive farms, sugar factories, big mansions, political leadership, etc.

The filmmaker doesn't forget to emphasise the problem of the Indian education system in which caste discrimination is ever propagating. He succeeds in manifesting humiliation and exploitation of lower caste teachers. The college in Bittergaon village is governed by the local political leader Tatya Saheb Patil. On one occasion, Prince, the son of Tatya Saheb Patil, behaves very arrogantly with a lower caste teacher. When the teacher was teaching in the classroom, Prince was talking loudly in the classroom. As the teacher gets disturbed in teaching, he informs Prince not to talk on the mobile phone. But this rich politician's son doesn't obey the teacher. Instead, he slaps the teacher in front of all the students. Despite Prince's disobedience of the rules and regulations of the college, he is appreciated by his father. Furthermore, Tatya Saheb Patil orders the Principal of the college to collect money from college teachers to celebrate Prince's birthday. Here, in this context, it is worth mentioning that Hindu culture believes in the reverend place of a teacher in society. Hindu culture regards teachers as next to God. But the fact shows that in the Hindu caste system the upper caste Hindus humiliate, disgrace and exploit low caste teachers on the basis of power politics and caste hierarchy.

The filmmaker very passionately embodies a theme of caste conflict through the romance of budding teenagers representing two different castes. *Sairat* is the epic love story of Parshya and Archie. Parshya, the son of a fisherman, belongs to the low caste whereas Archie, the son of landlord and owner of sugar factory, belongs to a politically influential upper caste. When the love affair is disclosed and noticed by Tatya Saheb Patil, the entire group of upper caste people becomes violent. Parshya, his parents and his friends are abused, thrashed, trampled severely and warned to leave the village. Later on, Parshya and Archie decide to elope. When the upper castes came to know about their elopement, the people of Tatya Saheb keep on searching all places. In this attempt, the upper caste people burn the whole sugar cane farms in the entire vicinity.

Parshya and Archie elope to Hyderabad city where they face series of problems and complexities. On one occasion, Parshya and Archie are rescued from the nuisance of gangsters with the timely help of a woman. The woman takes them to her small house in a slum area. She provides them with food and shelter. With the help of the woman, both of them get good jobs, get settled and do the registered marriage. Their life gets blooming by having a child. Archie keeps her telephonic conversations with her mother. One day, Archie's brother Prince accompanied by her upper-caste relatives visit her house in Hyderabad. There they brutally kill both Archie and Parshya. Thus the ending of both the lovers' life is dreadful and alarming to all the audience. It creates feelings of disappointment and terror in the minds of the spectator. Both Parshya and Archie become the victim of caste conflict. Thus the Dalit filmmaker attempts to manifest caste conflict and its consequences on the present generation. It acutely throws light on the discrimination, oppression, atrocity and honour killing of marginalised people in the Maharashtra state.

Conclusion

The rigid Indian social structure based on the four-folded classification of *Varna* system and the prevalent practices of casteism in India raises certain cross-questions. As there is no rationality behind forming of *Varna* system and the subsequent caste hierarchy, there is no valid reason to discriminate, dominate, oppress and humiliate the Dalits. The facts concerning the origin of the caste system are yet to be validated. The upper-caste Hindus upholding the biased approaches towards Dalits and inflicting inhuman treatment to them intensely needs to substantiate the origin of the caste system. In consequence, it ultimately exposes that the truth of the caste system itself is unconvinced.

The study of Marathi Dalit cinema investigates the correlation between the origin of Dalits and the present scenario of caste-based society in India. It reveals Dalit filmmaker Nagraj Manjule's endeavour to represent the facts of Dalit life despite abundant challenges, constraints and influences in this post-truth era. It is obvious that the influence of dominant social hierarchy and power politics keep on supporting the evil practice of casteism on the basis of prejudices against low caste society. Hence the present study aims at appealing to the entire Indian society to uproot and eradicate the caste system and to be humane by upholding Dr. B. R. Ambedkar's dream to form Indian society based on the principles of liberty, equality and fraternity.

References

Ambedkar, B. R. (1972). *Emancipation of the Untouchables.* Thacker and Co. Ltd.

Bharatvaraj, S. & Subramani, R. (2018). Manifestation of Subaltern Narratives in Cinema. *American International Journal of Research in Humanities, Arts and Social Sciences, 25*(1), 05-08. http://iasir.net/AIJRHASSpapers/AIJRHASS19-102.pdf

Borkar, A. T. (2019). Sairat: A Case Study of Honour Killing. *Universal Review*, 10(2), 46-53.

Dhongade, R. (1992). *Dalit Aatmacharitre, Sahitya Aani Samaj* (Dalit Autobiography, Literature and Society). Dilipraj Prakashan.

Gaikwad, V. (2016). A Conflict of Class Struggle and Oppression of the Marginalized in the Marathi Movie. *Pune Research Discovery*, 1(1), 1-6. http://puneresearch.com/media/data/issues/575c 2691dd9c3.pdf

Gopika, A. K. & Vijayalakshmi, P. P. (2019). Dalit Fiction and Post Truth: Joothan– The Life of a Dalit. *Indian Journal of Applied Research*, 9(7), 6-7. https://www.worldwidejournals.com/indian-journal-of-applied-research-(IJAR)/fileview.php? val=July_2019_1561804549_4516 739.pdf

Hussain, A. (2019). Theorising Post-Truth: A Postmodern Phenomenon. *Journal of Comparative Literature and Aesthetics*, 42(1), 150-162. http://jcla.in/wp-content/uploads/2019/10/AMINA-HUSSAIN.pdf

Kaur, R. & Sinha A. J. (2000). *Bollyworld: Popular Indian Cinema through a Transnational Lens.* Sage Publications.

Kharat, S. (1978). *Dalit Sahitya: Prerana Aani Pravrutti* (Dalit Literature: Nature and Inspiration). Inamdar Bandhu Prakashan.

McIntyre, L. (2018). *Post-Truth*. Cambridge.

Meshram, Y. (1998). *Dalit Sahitya: Udgam Aani Vikas* (Dalit Literature: Origin and Development). Shri Mangesh Prakashan.

Mueller, M. (Ed). (1886). *The Laws of Manu*. G. Buhler (Trans.), Carendon Press.

Moon, V. (Ed). (1989). *Dr. Babasaheb Ambedkar Writings and Speeches Vol.1*. Education Department Government of Maharashtra.

Moon, V. (Ed). (1989). *Dr. Babasaheb Ambedkar Writings and Speeches Vol.3*. Education Department Government of Maharashtra.

Rege, S. (2013). *Against the Madness of Manu: B. R. Ambedkar's Writings on Brahminical Patriarchy*. Navayana.

Srinivas, N. M. (1987). *The Dominant Caste and Other Essays*. Oxford University Press.

Yengde, S. (2018). Dalit Cinema. *South Asia: Journal of South Asian Studies*, 41(3), 1-16. https://doi.org/10.1080/00856401.2018.1471848

Nagraj Manjule. (2021, June 3). In *Wikipedia*. https://en.wikipedia.org/wiki/Nagraj_Manjule

Nagraj M. (Director). (2016). *Sairat* [Film]. Zee Studios. https://www.zee5.com/movies/details/sairat /00movie_1921832123

Sairat (2021, June 6). In *Wikipedia*. https://en.wikipedia.org/wiki/Sairat

CHAPTER 26

Stanislavsky's 'Realism' as a Relevant Mode of Artistic Production in Contemporary Post-Truth Art

Philipp Sulim

Realism as a Mode of Artistic Production

With an increasingly informed and aware audience, there was a demand for higher quality performances and an understanding of what quality acting is. The ease of accessibility to information of the psychological reasons that trigger emotions, why some performances feel artificial and have an absence of 'scenic truth' makes it more challenging for today's actor. Performers can't amaze an intelligent and informed spectator as easily; an audience wants to be surprised and moved. Horror movies that scared people in the 1980s appear almost comedic now. Dramas that evoked a sense of pathos in the past may leave one indifferent now. Art evolves along with human consciousness and perception of the world. Progress in performance has never stopped. While experimentation happens in theatre, creating new styles which can amuse seem to fail to amaze audiences. The feeling of amusement passes fast, but the feeling of amazement stays longer as it is born of experiencing an emotional catharsis, a concept introduced by Aristotle centuries ago.

Realism in performance however has been constantly and consistently amazing the audience for the last hundred years, "This realism is most evident in the classical Hollywood cinema" ("Realism", n.d). If other practices are temporary and manifest particular historical events, like Theatre of Cruelty or Theatre of the Oppressed and quite several other practices, they lose their relevance after a particular problem stops existing or becoming less evident. These modes of theatre are context-specific and context-bound. 'Realism' constantly evolves along with humanity and reflects reality, and therefore has resisted becoming obsolete.

Stanislavsky and the 'System'

Coupled with the evolution of ideas and awareness, the mode of achieving catharsis has evolved as well. Actors who were merely representing their emotions and not living them failed to satisfy the audience's emotional appetite. "Our demands are simple, normal, and therefore they are difficult to satisfy. All we ask is that an actor on the stage lives in accordance with natural laws" (Stanislavsky, 2014). Addressing this failure, Konstantin Stanislavsky developed a completely new approach towards acting, 'the system' which replaced 'the art of representation' with 'the art or experiencing'. Rather than the physicality of an actor more importance was given to the psychology of an actor. Stanislavsky explained acting as a science, an objective method by which any person, even without any talent could become an actor if one follows it. The major components of the 'system' are:

1. Given circumstances – relates to a setting of a script and includes environmental and situational conditions which affect the actions of a character. "The plot, the facts, the incidents, the period, the time and place of the action, the way of life, objective or task" (Stanislavsky, 2017)
2. A through-line and a super-objective or a super-task – A through-line is also called a 'spine' of a play that lines all of the characters' objectives towards a super-objective which is an ultimate goal of a character.

> A super-task and a through-line, the main essence of life, an artery, nerves, the pulse of the play... A super-task (desire), a cross-cutting action (striving) and its implementation (action) is a creative process of experience.
>
> (Stanislavsky, 2017)

3. The subtext is what characters actually mean and want, without saying it but expressing it through intonation, gestures, body language, pauses and different physical actions. "Spectators come to the theatre to hear the subtext. They can read the text at home" (Moore, 1984); The magic if – boosts the creative thinking process by asking one what one would do if one were in the character's shoes thus perpetually discovering something new about a scene.

> When I give a genuine answer to the if, then I do something, I am living my own personal life. At moments like that there is no character. Only me. All that remains of the character and the play are the situation, the life circumstances, all the rest is mine, my own concerns, as a role in all its creative moments depends on a living person, i.e., the actor, and not the dead abstraction of a person, i.e., the role.
>
> (Stanislavsky, 1989)

All of these ideas in 'the system' are pretty much similar to actual human behaviour. The actor isn't acting but experiencing life on the stage, living in a particular reality. Actors experiencing genuine emotions on a stage could transfer them to the audience's hearts and heads thereby making spectators feel and be led to a pure and powerful catharsis. Not surprisingly, other practitioners began following "the system".

Method Acting

Well known "method acting" is an adaptation of Stanislavski's teaching by Lee Strasberg after he watched a show of Moscow Art Theatre (MAT), headed by Konstantin Stanislavski, when MAT was touring the U.S. in 1923 and had a huge success "the much-vaunted Moscow Art Theatre has come, seen and conquered" (Towse, 1923). With Lee Strasberg's "method acting" was taught in Actor's studio. 'The Actors Studio, prestigious professional actors' workshop in New York City whose members have been among the most influential performers in American theatre and film since World War II. It is one of the leading centres for the Stanislavsky method of dramatic training (Britannica, 2019). "The system" of theatrical realism was transferred to the screen in Hollywood and the world cinematography and till now stays the most required acting style.

One of the first staged productions which incorporated the ideas of "the system" was "The Seagull", a play written by Anton Chekhov. Initially "The Seagull" was staged in Alexandrinsky Theatre, St. Petersburg and it was a disaster. The actors were booed causing Chekhov to decide he would never write plays again. But Vladimir Nemirovich-Danchenko, a co-founder of Moscow Art Theatre appreciated the play immensely and insisted that it has to be staged again in MAT on 17 December 1898. The audience was ecstatic. Standing ovations were not enough to appreciate the play; spectators were climbing up on chairs and couldn't stop applauding The reason the "The Seagull" failed in Alexandrinsky theatre was that the old approach to stage plays was used, where an event was foregrounded, rather than characters. Stanislavski's "system" focuses on characterisation and bringing the scenic truth which is essential to realism in playwriting. "Realism" in script writing cannot exist without "realism" in acting. But "realism" in acting can exist without "realism" in scriptwriting.

By implying "the system", the audience could experience that desirable catharsis watching Chekhov's play. His plays aren't about royalty, not about fighting for a nation and the valorous task of saving a country, but about the quotidian life of common people which one can relate to with ease. It is comical and tragic-sad at the same time, the drama of the demotic. The spectators could see something pure, free of politics or opinions which are so needed in the current post-truth society. The truths that are engaged with are the ones that drive our existence the audience is privy to the tragedy of ordinary life.

Realism in Times of Post-Truth Art

Ushering in the era of Modern Art, Realism manifested some significant moments in art history. Coinciding with industrialisation and mass media, the artist became himself part of the narrative of his art. The other significant shift is the gravitation towards everyday life in all its lack of glory, its non-eventfulness as the topic of artistic production. The banality of evil lamented by Hannah Arendt comes to mind or as one would like to rephrase that, the evil of banality! Where sequential plot narratives once fulfilled the viewer/reader, the enchanting incoherence and lack of cohesion of the mundane was irresistible.

If Aristotelian catharsis was evoked by fear and pity, the modern-day reader is moved to this sense of fear and pity not by events of spectacular magnitude but by the sheer ennui that shrouds one in modern living without one even making a conscious choice to embrace it. It rejects nineteenth-century Romanticism with its emotional outpourings. This mode of suffering naturally undid the grand narrative of sacrifice and heroism and redemption. The sense of dread and menace that permeates the stage, the page and our collective imagination is that of the mundane and meaningless. In that sense, the banal acquires and evokes a sense of the sinister and evil. By definition, the banal is that which is so lacking in originality that it is obvious and commonplace and unworthy of attention. That is an apt summation of modern existence in times of automation. It also is dreadful in that it requires enormous amounts of energy and vigour that is emotional, physical and intellectual to fight off this inescapable dystrophy.

With photography and film filling the need for accuracy and documentation, art was liberated from this burden and could occupy itself with deeper modes of representation, that of the causal and casual comedy that is life. Realism resonates with that sense of the comedy of the banality that induces pain by being far too real. There is no suspension of disbelief here, willing or otherwise because one is constantly disturbed by the 'reality' not of the situation alone but the human condition as well. Plots unfold in a tragedy of the non-event, the non-romance, the non-heroic. This steady onslaught of the non-dramatic makes it non-tragic and that in itself is a tragedy.

Realism paved the way for the post-truth condition we find ourselves in now. From objective truths and grand absolutes, the scrutiny shifted to the struggles or lack of romance in everyday ordinary lives. The true horror of the demotic lies in its lack of purpose or causality. Thus, empowered quotidian lives and struggles demand logic of reception and acceptance, where one is guided by emotion over compassion and purpose over meaning. In such times realism becomes an appropriate artistic mode to create dissonance within the world of the magical and mythical.

Fictional Reality

Yuval Noah Harari mentions a fictional reality that overlays an objective reality. He refers to religion, money and corporations as these fictions that subsume the objective reality of Nature. He refers to the difference between man and animals as the mysterious glue that enables human to cooperate effectively.

Post Truth is an era of opinion over fact. Absolute truths that crumbled as centres collapsed in the 1980s gave rise to the individual 'I' as a narrator preferred over the 'we' or 'them'. This demotic dissonance is best processed and portrayed through Realism as it captures a sense of mystery in the sheer incoherence of daily life.

Henri Lefebvre in his treatise on the notions of Spatiality defines two kinds of space, Absolute and Abstract. While Nature is an Absolute Space, unmediated by human intervention, the abstract space is that inhabited by Man. This is the space that is overlaid by various kinds of truth, facts and fictions that shift and collide with the protean currents of socio-political and economic events. It is abstract in that is a fictional reality sculpted by the vagaries of power play. Through the prism of Post Truth, art seems to have become the handmaid of power, reinforcing prejudices and altering perceptions of objective reality.

Realism in Post-Truth Art: A Significant Mode of Telling

In a world where every utterance is received differently and with varying levels of credibility depending on the subjectivity of the audience, Realism as a mode of artistic production remains as the calm, reassuring voice of reason. Whether it is Chekhov, Arundhati Roy, Rohinton Mistry or the plethora of Indian writers in English who successfully employ this mode, the reader audience seeks solace and intellectual mooring in a narrative mode which is neither gimmicky nor startling but depends on a quotidian blandness, even a mundane tone that captures the struggle of the person on the street. It is fascinating that as our external worlds explode with multiplicity and fragmented reality, our inner world demands order and discipline that captures the sheer ordinary truth of the human condition across the world.

While the world erects political barriers and boundaries fueled by race, religion and language and the politics thereof, it is reassuring that artistic processes can offer a space where the truth, while mediated for the medium, can still be accessed in a space where the politics of abstraction can be portrayed in a recognisable form.

References

Britannica, T. (2019, December 12). The Actors Studio. *Encyclopedia Britannica.* https://www.britannica.com/topic/The-Actors-Studio

Harari, Y. N. (2015). *Sapiens – A Brief History of Humankind.* HarperCollins.

Johnson A., (2016, November 17). Post-Truth Is Oxford Dictionaries' Word of the Year for 2016. *NBC News,* https://www.nbcnews.com/news/us-news/post-truth-oxford-dictionaries-word-year-2016-n685081

Lefebvre, H. (1991). *The Production of Space.* Blackwell.

Moore, S. (1984). *The Stanislavski System.* Penguin.

Post-truth Politics: Art of the lie. (2016, September 10). *The Economist.* https://www.economist.com/leaders/2016/09/10/art-of-the-lie?fsrc=scn%2Ftw%2Fte%2Fpe%2Fed%2Fartofthelie

Realism. (n.d.). *Film Reference.* http://www.filmreference.com/encyclopedia/Independent-Film-Road-Movies/Realism.html

Stanislavsky, K. (1989). *An Actor Prepares.* Routledge.

.... (2014). *Building a character.* Bloomsbury.

Benedetti, J., & Eyre, R. (2017). *An actor's work.* Routledge.

Towse, J. R. (1923, January 9). The Plays. *The New York Tribune.*

What About Art in the Post-Truth Era? (2017, January 17). *Widewalls.* https://www.widewalls.ch /magazine/post-truth

CHAPTER 27

The Trending Dynamics of Hegemonic Reverberations: A Post-Truth Authoritarian Rhetorical Analysis of Kamila Shamsie's *Home Fire*

Anusree A. Wilson

Authoritarianism often puts at stake the individual freedom of speech and expression thereby, exercising personal whims over rational thoughts. This concentration of power leads to the point where leaders and elites become anchors of the democratic nation. It puts a veil over the free will of the common people to bring out alternative agendas and proposals with which they could fight against the ruling class and make their own opinions. Post-truth politics of the authority is sufficient enough to instigate fluctuations in the prevailing laws and regulations of the nation.

Authoritarian rhetoric conceals self-motives of the despots who brings about moral failure to the whole system of governance. Such rhetoric is solely based on their priorities set right and brings benefits to only a smaller group of people. Kamila Shamsie's *Home Fire* which is published in 2017 is such a novel that throws light upon the post-truth politics played out by the government authorities to camouflage the truth. Shamsie's brilliant capturing of reality along with heart striking representation has made the novel win the Women's Prize for Fiction 2018 and getting included in the longlist of the Man Booker Prize 2017 and shortlist of the DSC Prize for South Asian Literature 2018. *Home Fire* is a vibrant remaking of Sophocles's *Antigone* in the contemporary world. The plot narrates the lives of two British Muslim families who become enemies against each other as they fight for their own personal truths and agendas to get fulfilled. This research is an exploration into the aspects of post-truth rhetoric in the novel *Home Fire* and illustrates how authoritarian rhetoric and propaganda enables Karamat Lone, the antagonist to stigmatise people for rejecting Islamic ethical codes. The study also brings forward the power of post-truth rhetoric capability in changing the citizenship of the people and other various issues that arise due to these rhetorical powers.

Post-truth Atmosphere in *Home Fire*

In *Home Fire,* the state is depicted as the perpetrator of injustice and xenophobia which is established through post-truth politics inflicted by the authorities to exercise their self-interests. Xenophobic practices often end up deliberately inflicting severe physical as well as mental torture on the less privileged groups so that authorities can carry out their desired policies and agendas. The state's xenophobic practices can be witnessed at the outset of the novel which is Isma's treatment at the airport while going to America.

> 'I've lived here all my life.' She meant there was no other country of which she could feel herself a part, but the words came out sounding evasive. The interrogation continued for nearly two hours. He wanted to know her thoughts on Shias, homosexuals, the Queen, democracy, the Great British Bake Off, the invasion of Iraq, Israel, suicide bombers, dating websites.
>
> (Shamsie, 2017, p.5)

The interrogation officer stands as an epitome of Britishness. The officer acts as a law exercising agency of government through which British laws are put into practice. Post-truth rhetoric carried out by the interrogation officer who is part of the British authority who wishes to alienate the Muslims. All these acts bring out the protection of Muslims in Britain on the brink of jeopardy as this develops troubles to the Muslims in the struggle to maintain their cultural identity.

British Home Secretary, Karamat Lone is the string-puller behind alienating Muslims through unfair rhetorical means to influence others to get things accomplished. Lone being raised from a humble background fights against all odds to reach the position of British Home Secretary. His fate turned out fortunate through the post-truth political tactics that he employs later in his political career.

Even though Lone is from a Muslim background, he shows more affinity towards the British culture rather than the Muslim culture. He is portrayed as a despot who betrays his own faith. He shows neglect and hatred towards his faith as it does not bring any benefit to his schemes and stands only as a harbinger of chaos throughout his life. Thereby, Lone is interested only in political gain's which he could accomplish through the conversion of British Muslims that aid him in winning future elections.

> Everyone always went on about the racism his father had had to face when a section of the press tried to brand him an extremist – but it was London's Muslim population who had turned their backs on Karamat Lone and voted him out, despite all the good he'd done for his constituents. All because he expressed a completely enlightened preference for the conventions of a church over those of a mosque, and spoke of the need for British Muslims to lift themselves out of the Dark Ages if they wanted the rest of the nation to treat them with respect.
>
> (Shamsie, 2017, p.59)

British Home Secretary's position is used as a powerful tool through which Lone uses in his post-truth rhetoric to showcase the codes of behaviour and ideologies of Muslims as outdated. His rejection of Islamic ethical codes has got personal underpinnings. The experiences and challenges that he encountered in his life made him show religious hostility. His affection towards British values arises from his favourable upbringing and opportunities that he only received from the British nation. Shamsie (2017) describes him in the novel as:

> a child of migrants who understands how much his Parents gave up – family, context, language, familiarity – because the nation to which they first belonged had proven itself inadequate to the task of allowing them to live with dignity.
>
> (p. 215)

Lone also believes that his community is still living under dark ages and it is out of this fear of getting neglected that makes him give up his cultural identity. His disregard and fear are concealed through post-truth rhetoric that he employs when he is interviewed about whether he hates Muslims, he gives out a witty reply, "I hate the Muslims who make people hate Muslims" (Shamsie, 2017, p. 231).

This shows out how post-truth politics is employed by Lone to, cover up his dislike towards Muslims from the media. Western ideals struck Lone too deeply that he narrates stories to make others adhere to his path towards glory. This can be witnessed in Karamat Lone's blind and obsessive integration of Western culture into the lives of British Muslims through persuasive post-truth rhetoric.

Penetrating Power of Post-truth Rhetoric in Revoking Citizenship

Post-truth rhetoric has the capability of instilling fear in the minds of people when it is accompanied by authoritative power. Such rhetoric brings forth changes to the prevailing laws without formulating suspicions. In the post-truth age, authorities employ terms like development and expansion to cover up the corruption that happens behind it.

Authoritative rhetoric influences reshaping the laws to get conditioned as per their needs. It is through these means that the authorities make lives of Muslims filled with torture, trials and tribulation. Moreover, it gives them a magic wand to change the citizenship of people from British to un-British. Altogether, post-truth politics places power over reason and wisdom which paves the way for attaining unilateral laws and regulations getting implemented without bringing out any questioning from anywhere.

In the novel, the laws made by the state are obeyed blindly. The State is looked upon with fear. From the words of Isma, the community's viewpoint of the state is very clear. These people have no strength even to defy the false accusations against them. The protagonist of the novel, Aneeka is stern in her responsibility to give a proper burial to her brother to whom the state has denied it. Aneeka abides by Muslim beliefs, to fight against unjust post-truth politics. The faith she follows advocates to give funeral rights for every human being after death. Her conscience urges her to do what is right and not to follow what others declare as right. She is courageous in showcasing her outrage against merciless acts.

> In the stories of wicked tyrants, men and women are punished with exile, bodies are kept from their families – their heads impaled on spikes, their corpses thrown into unmarked graves. All these things happen according to the law, but not according to justice.
>
> (Shamsie, 2017, p. 224-225)

Power and authority come to the prima facie in maintaining law and order which is, in turn, cover up the hidden self-motive of authorities to control the weaker sections of the societies according to their requirements. Former laws are often twisted by the governing body to formulate them according to their needs and make them the new practising law. It is through the skilful articulation that the British Home Secretary using his authoritarian power makes the people act according to his desires. He uses this power to prevent the burial of Parvaiz in London. Moreover, the Home Secretary using his authoritative rhetoric strip even British citizens of their rights of citizenship in cases if they move against the vital desires of the governing body. Earlier laws in Britain only allowed revoking citizenship from dual nationals or naturalized citizens who have a claim to another nationality. The Home Secretary affirms that "citizenship is a privilege not a right" (Shamsie, 2017, p. 198).

Through the authoritative power, it is clear that despots like Lone become successful in revoking the citizenship of even British-born single passport holders. Even repatriation gets affected when citizenship no longer exists. Lone brings out the justification for this by dovetailing it with patriotism. Stripping British nationals from citizenship can be only achieved through effective rhetorical handling.

Post-truth Authoritarian Rhetoric in *Home Fire*

In the post-truth era, government and media hold the apex when dealing with power. These bodies often hold the authoritative status to even decide a person's fate. It is the marginalised and often the weaker communities whose lives become more vulnerable in the post-truth era. On the gender level, it is the women who are more susceptible to post-truth politics. The society around them is assuming the authoritative figure. They get suffered in the post-truth age where they were expected to follow all norms and values of society. They were punished if they violated the codes of behaviour. "She is being left to suffer because she removed her face veil" (Shamsie, 2017, p. 173).

All these set rules and regulations are created only out of a desire to get power over the underprivileged sections of society. These laws of the State which are crafted according to the needs of the ruling party acts as a powerful tool for them to achieve their gains. Post-truth oratory puts a veil over the ruling class evil intentions to cover it from the public and to justify their deeds of unjust practices.

Identity crisis is another major issue of post-truth authoritarian rhetoric. Media is also corrupt in a systemic sense as it fails to portray reality and makes one question its credibility. The news media and the government join hands for mutual manipulation and mythmaking. The media needs sensational news to increase rating, and government officials have to participate in these cooked-up stories for advancing in elections. This news makes tainted truths that mislead the public and also lead to the degradation in the effective functioning of the governing agency. In the post-truth era, news propagates the culture of lying. It puts forward the self-aggrandising tactics to control the public through fabricated truths. They manipulate the public to see the truth through their eyes and turn away from reality.

Parvaiz is classified as a terrorist but the truth is only partially portrayed by the media and government. He loses his citizenship even if he did not commit any serious crimes against Britain. Parvaiz considered only England as his homeland but he hasn't granted forgiveness even after trying to get away from ISIS. Besides, Lone's agenda confirms that Britain is hostile to Islamic fundamentalism, to the extent that those who attempt to escape from ISIS will never be considered as its citizen again. He emphasises the withdrawing of all benefits of a welfare state from the families whose member's joins with the enemies of the state. This is authoritative rhetoric employed by Lone to prevent people from engaging in any deeds that are against the government.

The individuality of a person gets distorted under the post-truth rhetorical narration. Parvaiz's death is reported by the British media in a fictional manner, he is directly classified as a terrorist without proper analysing of the actuality behind it. Media thus brings out feeds according to its own profitable way. It is through the practical assumption that they create the news while keeping the reality out of the scene. Faith gets compromised is another solid picture that the novel brings forth in the backdrop of post-truth rhetoric. Lone in a persuasive way demonstrates the necessity of rejecting Islamic ethics for better living conditions. Through the use of post-truth authoritative rhetoric, Lone persuades Muslim students to choose to be British over Muslim. This is clearly evident in his speech which he gives in his former school.

> Don't set yourself apart in the way you dress, the way you think, the outdated codes of behaviour you cling to, the ideologies to which you attach your loyalties. Because if you do, you will be treated differently.
>
> (Shamsie, 2017, p. 87-88)

Lone wants to change the Muslim students away from their ideologies and make their tastes towards the British to gain more political power. Post-truth rhetoric cultivates preferable ways to make its politics happen. It fails to rectify the corruption in the system as it prevents self-growth. It is this disillusionment that leads to the destruction of trust in any governing system.

Conclusion

The Post-truth era has propagated the culture of lying to the extent that self-motives get sheltered under the roof of authoritative rhetoric. Post-truth authoritative rhetoric bridges the gap between illusion and reality. Power mongers become quite successful in carving out stories that uplift their gains. Post-truth rhetoric often seems beneficial at the surface level, but in the long run, these end up triggering the core of our society. It will lead to the subjugation of weaker sections to the extreme level where their violation of basic rights can occur. The elimination of expression rights will eventually lead to the annihilation of the community in every nook and corner. This will affect them both physically and mentally while struggling to keep pace with the authoritarian classes.

It is portrayed in the novel that post-truth rhetoric is only serving a few while the majority is on the verge of exploitation. People hailing from minor communities like Parvaiz will face life-threatening experiences as their voices meant nothing, before the authoritarian rhetoric. Even if Lone becomes able to get his intentions done through post-truth rhetoric, this will make the credibility of the governing agency questionable. This ineffective functioning of the governing body will only lead the country to peril as it becomes difficult to accept the actual truth. Truth, therefore, must be embraced for the effective functioning of any government body.

References

Chambers, C. (2017, August 5). The ones we love are enemies of the state. *The Hindu.* https://www.thehindu.com/books/the-ones-we-love-are-enemies-of-the-state/article19426329.ece.

Emanuel, L. (2020, March 29). Home Fire Themes. *LitCharts.* https://www.litcharts.com/lit/home-fire/themes.

Felsenthal, J. (2017, August 16). Kamila Shamsie's Brilliant Novel Homefire Is a Newsy Take on an Ancient Myth. *Vogue.* https://www.vogue.com/article/ kamila-shamsie-home-fire.

Green, T. H. (2015). *The Fear of Islam: An Introduction to Islamophobia in the West.* Fortress Press.

Haynes, N. (2017, August 10). Home Fire by Kamila Shamsie review – a contemporary reworking of Sophocles. *The Guardian.* https://www.theguardian.com/books/2017/aug/10/home-fire-kamila-shamsie-review.

Javed, A. (2017, September 7). Book Review: Home Fire by Kamila Shamsie. *Youlin Magazine*. https://www.youlinmagazine.com/article/book-review-home-fire-by-kamila-shamsie/OTMw.

Majeed, Y. A. (2018, July 12). Family and the State in Kamila Shamsie's Home Fire. *The Ploughshares Blog*. https://blog.pshares.org/family-and-the-state-in-kamila-shamsies-home-fire.

Shamsie, K. (2017). *Kamila Shamsie: Home Fire: Adapting Antigone and Googling While Muslim*. YouTube. https://youtu.be/T7aNnaY8Ddg.

Shamsie, K. (2019). *Kamila Shamsie: Home Fire*. YouTube. https://youtu.be/ilRKfXn_ZFU.

Shamsie, K. (2017). *Home Fire*. Bloomsbury Publishing.

Vanderwicken, P. (2014, August 1). Why the News Is Not the Truth. *Harvard Business Review*. https://hbr.org/1995/05/why-the-news-is-not-the-truth.

Home Fire (novel). (2021, April 8). In *Wikipedia*. https://en.wikipedia.org/wiki/Home_Fire_ (novel).

Contributors

1. **Denis Newiak** studied Media Studies at the University of Potsdam, Germany, and Film Studies at the Freie Universität of Berlin. He also studied abroad at the University of Copenhagen and conducted research at the Library of Congress in Washington, D.C. His research focuses in the following areas: aesthetics and narratives of loneliness in television series, social functions of serial television entertainment, disruptive events in science fiction movies. Current publication: *It's All Been There Before: What We Can Learn About the Coronavirus Crisis from Pandemic Movies* (2021).

   Email: mail@denis-newiak.de

2. **Dr. Minu Susan Koshy** currently works as Assistant Professor in the Department of English, Mar Thoma College for Women, affiliated to Mahatma Gandhi University, Kerala. She has published extensively in national and international journals and has served as the resource person at several conferences. Her areas of interest include cultural studies, postcolonial studies and comparative and world literatures. Her books include *Narrating Childhood Trauma: The Quest for Catharsis* (DC Books-Expressions, 2015), a translation of the Malayalam anthology *Tattoo* (Authorspress, 2015), an edited collection of poems titled *Gossamer Reveries* (Authorspress, 2019) and *Mapping the Postcolonial Domestic in the Works of Vargas Llosa and Mukundan: Tales of the Threshold* (Cambridge Scholars Publishing, 2020). She is also a reviewer for the *Journal of Global South Studies* (University of Plattsburgh, New York), *Education, Society and Human Studies*, Los Angeles, and *Studies in English Language Teaching*, Los Angeles.

   Email: minususankoshy@gmail.com

3. **Patrick Agbedejobi** is an independent research specialised in interdisciplinary research. He studied political science at the undergraduate level in Nigeria and a master's degree in European

studies from Germany where he resides. His quest for knowledge led him further to study for a postgraduate of Law in the United Kingdom. His research thus far covers terrorism and media research, African politics and discourse studies, European politics, gender studies and intersectionality to mention but a few.

Email: patreader82@hotmail.co.uk

4. **Cerin Babu** was formerly working as a guest faculty in the Department of English, Vimala College (Autonomous), Thrissur. Currently, she is pursuing research in English Language and Literature from the Department of English, St. Thomas' College (Autonomous), Thrissur under the guidance of Dr. Martin K A. *Email: cerinbabu26@gmail.com*

5. **Manodip Chakraborty** has passed his M.A. in English Literature from Cooch Behar Panchanan Barma University. He is at present a research scholar at the Department of English, Raiganj University. He has been contributing in various national/ international webinars/ seminars. His research interests include Cultural Studies, Chaos Theory, Video Game Studies, Memory Studies, psychoanalysis.

Email id: manodipchakrabortys@gmail.com

6. **Indu Peter** is an Assistant Professor in the Department of English, Kuriakose Elias College, Mannanam, Kottayam in Kerala. She is a Member of the Under Graduate Board of Studies (English) of Mahatma Gandhi University. She secured First Rank with Distinction in B. A. Communicative English (Triple Main) Degree Examination and M.A. English Language and Literature Examination from Mahatma Gandhi University. It has been seven years since she hightailed into the arena of collegiate education as an Assistant Professor. A voracious reader and an ardent lover of art and literature all rolled into one, her research currently focuses on Digital Humanities, Post Truth, Post-humanism, Postmodernism, Media and Culture Studies, etc.

Email: indupeter@kecollege.ac.in

7. **Roshima Uday** is a Research scholar in Govt. Victoria College, Palakkad, Kerala. Her research work centres on Post-Truth and its analysis as a discourse. She has worked as a Guest faculty in M.P.M.M.S.N. Trust College, Shoranur. Her area of interest is Cultural Studies. She has presented research papers in several International and National Conferences and has contributed to an International publication titled, "Dilemmas of Contemporaneity in

the Twenty-First Century Literature: Voices of Dissent and Reparation".

Email: roshima.uday@gmail.com

8. **Dr. Abubakkar K.K.** is working as Assistant Professor in Govt. Victoria College, Palakkad. He has more than 20 years of teaching experience. His area of interest is Cultural studies. He has numerous publications in esteemed journals to his credit.

Email: pathamkulam@gmail.com

9. **Pranjal Bhatt's** prodigious love for language and passion towards educating blooming minds has gained her more than 4 years of total experience in teaching Language & Literature to young learners. Her zeal towards lifelong learning makes her a compelling Research Scholar whose core area of Ph.D. thesis is studying the representation of Identity & Violence in Indian English Graphic novels. Few broader topics that interest her are Indian Literature _ Partition and its Trauma, Gender Studies, Comparative and Feminist Literature, Cultural Studies & Linguistics.

Email: pranjalbhatt32@gmail.com

10. **Shemin K** is currently pursuing her PhD at the Centre for Advanced Studies and Research in English Language and Literature, Farook College (Autonomous), Calicut, Kerala. She has completed her Masters Degree from the School of Letters, M G University, Kottayam, Kerala.

Email: sheminkanniyan@gmail.com

11. **Nipan Nath**, Presently working as an Assistant Professor in Gauhati Commerce College, Guwahati, Nath is also a research scholar of Post-truth hullabaloo seeking to re-visit Borgesian 'library' along with Plato unto Baudrillard and beyond under the supervisor Dr Merry Baruah Bora in the Department of English, Cotton University, Assam. A postmodernist criticism on Adiga's *The White Tiger*, another on Jyotish Sikider's short stories and a deconstructionist analysis on Nilim Kumar's poetry are credited to his profile.

Email id: nipanknath@gmail.com

12. **Dr. Mallika A Nair** is an Assistant Professor & Research Guide reading at the PG & Research Dept. of English,Vimala College (Autonomous), Thrissur, Kerala. Dr. Mallika is a member of the Board of Translators, at Kerala Sahitya Akademi, Thrissur and her areas of interest include Feminine Spirituality, Folklore Studies, Post-

humanism, Post colonialism, Ecological humanities and Narratives of displacement. She is an ardent nature enthusiast and enjoys meditation, long walks and travelling. Dr. Mallika currently stays in Thrissur with her family.

Email: drmallikanair@vimalacollege.edu.in

13. **Josephine Mercy** is an Assistant Professor of the Department of English at Women's Christian College (An Autonomous Institution affiliated to the University of Madras), Chennai, India. Her areas of interest and research are Holocaust Studies, Theological Studies, Cult Literature and American Literature. Her teaching areas are British Literature, American Poetry, Literary Criticism and Theory and Readings in Literature at both under and postgraduate levels. She has presented papers at both national and international conferences and has published research papers in various journals.

E-mail: jomercy.j@gmail.com

14. **Harry C Joseph** is a post graduate in English Literature and a rank holder from Mahatma Gandhi University, Kottayam. He has qualified the UGC NET in 2017. He is an enthusiastic learner and a voracious reader. He is taking online English classes for students from America, Canada, Spain, Japan and Gulf Countries. He is also a resource person delivering talks on literary and non-literary subjects for college students and teachers.

E-mail: harrycheeramkunnel@gmail.com

15. **Dr. Kavitha Gopalakrishnan** is an Assistant Professor at the Department of English, Baselius College, Kottayam. She has to her credit publications in several national and international journals and edited books. She has been the review editor of the international refereed journals WEC and IJML. Her research interests are cultural studies, popular fiction, literary theory and criticism.

Email: kavithagopalakrishnan@baselius.ac.in

16. **Bornali Nath Dowerah** (M.A., NET, M.Phil.) is an Assistant Professor at Department of English, Manohari Devi Kanoi Girls' College, Dibrugarh, Assam, India. She is pursuing PhD from Dibrugarh University, Assam. She has authored six books – *Literature Reader*, *Critical Perspectives*, *Kobitaar Xoraai*, *Crossroads*, *Rāmdhenu* and *Tiny Tales*. She is EAP (English for Academic Purposes) trained teacher from University of Leicester, U.K. in 2018. Besides, she is the founder of student organisation "The Labonya Project" (thelabonyaproject.com) and provides free education to

underprivileged students. She specialises in: English Language Teaching (ELT), EAP, queer young adult literature and psychoanalysis.

Email: bornali.nd9@gmail.com

17. **Irene Ann George** is an Assistant Professor at the Indian Institute of Psychology and Research with specific interests in the realm of Media and Communication. Armed with a Masters in Media and Communication, she looks to delve into the world of advertising to unearth the unknown in the field. Her research expertise lies in the field of Health Communication, Psychoanalysis, Political Communication and Gender Studies.

    Email: irreneann@gmail.com

18. **Abhishek Manikandan** is an Independent Researcher whose interests lie in the field of Journalism and Politics. Owning a bachelors in Journalism, Psychology and English Literature from Christ (Deemed to be University), he has prior experience in Business Journalism from a two-year stint at the Reuters News Agency. His research interests span the fields of Politics, Social Media, Print Journalism.

    Email: abhitwenty20@gmail.com

19. **Sinoj Antony** has been working as an Assistant Professor at Divine Institute of Media Science Muringoor, Kerala under the University of Calicut for the past seven years. He has secured his master's in English Literature and PG Diploma in Journalism and Mass Communication; he was awarded B. Ed Degree from Bangalore University. He is a motivational speaker and resource person of various Faculty Development Programmes across India. He has presented research papers in national and International Conferences and has published half a dozen of journal articles in Scopus indexed as well as UGC care listed Journals. Currently, he is pursuing his Ph.D. from Lovely Professional University Phagwara, Punjab.

    Email: uppoottil@gmail.com

20. **Dr. Ishfaq Ahmad Tramboo**, a motivating and trained English Professor obsessed to inspire the students and research scholars to acquire personal and academic excellence. Consistently striving to develop an engaging and learning environment in which students and research scholars become long-run learners. exceptional track record of research success with numerous published research articles. More than two years of teaching experience, currently

working at Lovely Professional University as an Assistant Professor of English. He is skilled in integrating relevant technologies in order to create a learning environment, fluent in the English language and highly developed in creating an optimistic teaching-learning environment for students and research scholars.

Email: ishfaq.25645@lpu.co.in

21. **Namitha Nandan** is a Research Scholar working in the field of Phenomenology, Post-Truth and Film Studies. She acquired her Bachelor's and Master's Degree in English literature from MG University, Kottayam. She hails from Idukki district of Kerala and is the daughter of Mr. T.K. Nandanan and Mrs. Resmi Nandan. She is also an aspiring poet and storyteller.

Email: namithanandan7@gmail.com

22. **Greenu Ans Thomas** is an ardent teacher and passionate learner of English Language and Literature. She has experience of five years of teaching at college. She has qualified NET, SET and KTET. Her areas of interest include Literary Criticism, Language and Linguistics, Gender Studies and Psychology. She completed her post graduation from St. Thomas College, Palai and graduation from Assumption College, Changanacherry.

E-mail: greenuans@gmail.com

23. **Jaya Singh** is an independent researcher. She was previously associated with the Human Rights Law Network, Delhi. She graduated from the Tata Institute of Social Sciences with a master's in Peace and Conflict studies. Her primary research interests include performative violence, ethno-nationalism, and memory.

Email: jayasinghkakran@gmail.com

24. **Dr. M. Samadhanam Emimal** M. Phil., Ph.D., NET.,SET is an assistant professor in the department of English, Avinashilingam Institute of Home Science and Higher Education for Women, Coimbatore. Her areas of interest and research are in gender studies, children's literature and postmodern literature. She has published many research articles in National and International Journals.

Email: itsmepeace@gmail.com

25. **Ann Mary** is an International teacher of English Language and Literature with 2 years of experience in teaching. She is a TEFL certified, Microsoft Certified Educator (MCE) who has proven excellence in writing, by winning the 'Best Position Paper Award' in IMUN Conference 54.0, under the UNICEF committee. She has

presented and published papers in the domain of film criticism with prime focus on gender studies and Visual Culture. Having cleared the National Eligibility Test (NET), TCBE (Tesol Canada Board Exam), and the Teaching Knowledge Test (TKT) from Cambridge Assessment English makes her a qualified teacher with validated skills to teach and write in accordance with the 21st century learning design.

Email: annmaryann777@gmail.com

26. **Rahul Joshi** is an assistant professor of Journalism and mass communication at Faculty of Mass Media & Humanities, MRIIRS (Deemed to be University), Faridabad, Haryana. He has done her Masters in Journalism & Mass Communication from GGSIP University. He was a Gold Medallist in MA (MC) in GGSIP University. Currently he is also pursuing a PhD in Mass Media from MRIIRS (Deemed to be University), Faridabad. He has Nine years of academic and industry experience. His specialisations are in Radio Journalism & Television Production. He has published over 14 research papers in different reputed International & National Journals.

    Email: rahuljoshi.785@gmail.com

27. **Shalabha Rachel Abraham** is an ardent literarian working as Assistant Professor, in the Department of English at Girideepam Institute of Advanced Learning, Vadavathoor, Kottayam. She has completed her Post Graduation from CMS College (Autonomous) in MA English Language and Literature, and has devoted herself to academic writing. Having published research papers and articles in various journals, she has also contributed to an anthology *PenInk*, and three books; *Ecriture Feminine: Musings on Select Women Narratives*, *Narratives of the Now Past: Onlooking the Contemporary in Literature and Art* and *Arts and Humanities: Mapping the Multitudes*. Her areas of interest include Literary Theory, Literary Criticism and Cultural Studies.

    Email id: shalabhaabraham@gmail.com

28. **Dr. Rajendra Gholap** is the Head, Dept. of English, KRT Arts and Commerce College, Vani, Dist. Nashik, 422215, Maharashtra, India. He has teaching experience of over 23 years. He is a Ph.D. research guide at Savitribai Phule Pune University. He is a member, Board of Studies in English, in Sandip University, Nashik. He has completed UGC research projects and published 37 research papers in national and international reputed and UGC listed journals. He holds various

academic and administrative positions in Universities and affiliated colleges. He specialises in Dalit Literature, African-American Literature, Comparative Literature, Ecocritical and Ecofeminist Study. He has been working as a soft skill trainer and resource person for State and National level Seminars/Conferences/ Workshops.

Email: rd.gholap.nsk@gmail.com

29. **Prof. Philipp Sulim** is a faculty and coordinator of the Theatre Studies Department in Christ (Deemed To Be University, Bangalore). He specialises in 'Stanislavsky's system and realism in theatre. He is a professionally trained actor and practising director who has an interest in the concept of performance as research (PAR).

    E-mail: philipp.sulim@christuniersity.in

30. **Anusree A. Wilson** is a postgraduate scholar in English Language and Literature from St Joseph's College, Moolamattom, Kerala. Her areas of interest are Digital Literature, Cultural Studies, Feminist Criticism, Postcolonial Studies, Film Studies, Environmental Rhetoric, Transnational and Immigrant Literature, Non-fiction Prose Studies and Critical Media Studies. She has done research and presented papers on Digital Feminist Activism and Cultural Studies in various National Seminars.

    Email: anusreewilson@gmail.com

Index